International Peacekeeping

PERSPECTIVES ON SECURITY

RICHARD NED LEBOW, CONSULTING EDITOR

International Peacekeeping

Paul F. Diehl

The Johns Hopkins University Press

BALTIMORE AND LONDON

© 1993, 1994 The Johns Hopkins University Press
All rights reserved
Printed in the United States of
America on acid-free paper

Johns Hopkins Paperbacks edition, 1994
03 02 01 00 99 98 97 96 95 94   5 4 3 2 1

The Johns Hopkins University Press
2715 North Charles Street
Baltimore, Maryland 21218-4319
The Johns Hopkins Press Ltd., London

Library of Congress
Cataloging-in Publication Data

Diehl, Paul F. (Paul Francis)
    International peacekeeping / Paul F. Diehl.
        p.   cm. —(Perspectives on security)
    Includes bibliographical references and
    index.
    ISBN 0-8018-4585-8 (acid-free paper)
    ISBN 0-8018-5032-0 (pbk.:acid-free paper)
    1. United Nations—Armed Forces.
    2. Security, International.   I. Title.
    II. Series.
JX1981.P7D46   1993
341.5'8—dc20   92-21170

A catalog record for this book is
available from the British Library.

To Martha and Robert

Contents

Acknowledgments

MY FIRST INTEREST in international peacekeeping stemmed from the need to formulate a paper assignment for my graduate course on international organizations at the University of Georgia in the fall of 1984. I decided that the class project would concern the conditions for success in peacekeeping operations. At that time, at the height of renewed Cold War tensions, peacekeeping was considered largely ineffective and unlikely to be a major international approach to peace. Eight years later, international peacekeeping is at the top of the agenda of the United Nations and other international decision makers, with the end of the Soviet-U.S. rivalry apparently ushering in a "new world order." Nevertheless, many of the ideas and insights I gained from that initial course assignment have guided this investigation and have found their way into various chapters. For that reason, I am most grateful to my former students in that graduate seminar: Tuan Cheng, Steven Elliott-Gower, Stephen McKelvey, William Richey, Roald Hazelhoff, and Masaki Sato. I am also appreciative of early support from the Department of Political Science at the University of Georgia.

As the book began to take shape, my research assistants, Paul Hensel, Sonia Jurado, and Frank Perri, were helpful in locating various documents and offering advice on composition and argumentation. Financial support for those research assistants came from the University of Illinois Research Board, the Summer Research Opportunities Program of the Committee on Institutional Cooperation, and the MacArthur Foundation through the Program in Arms Control, Disarmament, and International Security at the University of Illinois.

I am grateful to various friends and colleagues who graciously read and commented on different portions of this book: Stephen Cohen, Edward Kolodziej, Jeremiah Sullivan, and Chetan Kumar, of the University of Illinois; Jurgen Dedring, of the United Nations; and Alan James, of the

University of Keele. I am also thankful for the encouragement and good suggestions that I received from Henry Tom, of the Johns Hopkins University Press, and from the initial reviewer of the manuscript, Gene Lyons, of Dartmouth College.

Chapter **I**

Concepts and Development of International Peacekeeping

"Peacekeeping is an uncertain, unpredictable, and
unregulated international operation."

THE TERMINATION of war has always provided a fertile environment for the growth and development of international organizations.[1] The League of Nations, the first universal membership and general purpose international organization, developed from the ashes of World War I; the desire to prevent another war and insure international collaboration was the primary motivation for the creation of that organization. The failure of the League of Nations, culminating in World War II, did not diminish the enthusiasm of the world community for seeking institutional safeguards against threats to international peace and security. The United Nations (U.N.) shared many characteristics with its predecessor, but it has come to encompass a broader range of economic and social functions.

There is considerable evidence to suggest that the end of another war—the Cold War—is ushering in a new era for international organizations. The decline of East-West tensions led to greater cooperation between the superpowers, often in the context of international organizations. The Iraqi invasion of Kuwait led to an unprecedented, unified response by the United Nations. In large part, this was possible because tensions between the superpowers neither escalated hostilities nor paralyzed concerted action by the Security Council. This was in marked contrast to earlier decades in which the effectiveness of international organizations in security matters actually declined.[2]

The end of the Cold War is also being marked by major power retrenchment in various areas of the world. This means that no major power state— and most dramatically so with Russia—is as willing, or as able, to intervene unilaterally with arms or military forces in proxy wars or conflicts far from home (the Kuwait crisis may be a dramatic exception and such actions were

1

taken only following U.N. approval). Into that vacuum, the United Nations may encourage the peaceful settlement of disputes and retard or prevent the process of escalation in those conflicts. Proposals for U.N. peacekeeping troops to supervise democratic elections in Western Sahara are consistent with this expectation. New security apparatus for the United Nations (or regional organizations), as well as the renewal of dormant approaches or the use of traditional approaches to peace in new contexts, are likely to emerge.

Just prior to the collapse of Cold War tensions (if one can indeed pinpoint 1989 as the critical date), the United Nations experienced a number of successes in the peace and security area that foreshadowed its important role in the Kuwait crisis. First, the United Nations achieved the longstanding goal of Soviet troop withdrawal from Afghanistan, accomplished through the mediation efforts of that organization. Second, the 1988 Nobel Peace Prize recognized the continuing contribution of U.N. peacekeeping troops to international peace and security. Finally, the United Nations was able to forge an agreement for the independence of Namibia that included the supervision of democratic elections by U.N. troops. In sum, and perhaps not coincidentally, as the Cold War ended, the United Nations was re-emerging as a force for international peace just a short time after its influence appeared to be on the wane.

Into the next century, international organizations, and the United Nations in particular, will likely rely on their most prominent operational approach to international peace and security: peacekeeping operations. The absence of an international army and the general unwillingness (not to mention the stifled development of appropriate mechanisms) of states to submit disputes to international adjudicatory tribunals has led the United Nations and some regional organizations to adopt the less controversial mechanism of peacekeeping. Furthermore, it is unlikely, at least in the immediate future, that such conditions will change so as to present a broader range of options to decision makers. More probably the existing mechanism of peacekeeping will be called upon to perform new functions as international organizations fill the gap left by the absence of the Cold War; some of these functions may include election supervision (already achieved in Namibia), humanitarian assistance, and arms control verification.

Yet, despite the prominence of the peacekeeping option and the increasing resort to it, there is little systematic understanding of its appropriate application. The aborted Multinational Force (MNF) of British, French, Italian, and U.S. troops in Beirut beginning in 1982, and the resulting loss of U.S. and French lives in terrorist bombings, reveals that decision makers do not always have a clear sense of which situations are suitable for peacekeeping operations and how those operations might be conducted to maximize the prospects for success. Even the United Nations, with extensive experience in such operations, has had difficulties. Continuing violent incidents in southern Lebanon, despite the presence of a peacekeeping force, reveal that even the best-laid plans do not always meet with success. Furthermore, when U.N. peacekeeping operations have been successful in limiting violent conflict in areas such as Cyprus, the organization has not always been able to resolve the underlying sources of dispute, an outcome that would ensure lasting peace and permit the final withdrawal of those peacekeeping troops.

This book is designed to fill some of the theoretical and policy gaps that exist in our understanding of international peacekeeping operations. Its first contribution is theoretical. This book represents one of the few analyses that provides theoretical explanations across a variety of peacekeeping operations for why and how those operations are successful (or not).[3] Most previous studies of peacekeeping have looked only at one operation,[4] and although insightful, they provide few lessons that can be generalized across different contexts. Other studies that cover a broader set of peacekeeping operations are primarily historical or descriptive or, on a few rare occasions, operations manuals.[5] Still others are out of date, as they do not include more recent peacekeeping operations and cannot reflect the dramatic changes in the world over the past few years.[6]

The central portion of this book is concerned with the following question: What are the conditions under which peacekeeping operations are successful in maintaining cease-fire arrangements and promoting resolution of the underlying conflict between the protagonists? In many ways, these goals represent separate processes. The ability to prevent a renewal of hostilities is primarily an operational problem, concerned with how a peacekeeping operation is organized and where it is deployed; the U.N. Interim Force in Lebanon (UNIFIL) experienced serious difficulties with this task, as the 1982 Israeli invasion illustrates. The second goal of conflict resolution is a function of diplomatic initiatives carried out by a different set of personnel in the organization or by interested third parties; for example, although major conflict was averted from 1956 to 1967 through the use of peacekeeping forces (the U.N. Emergency Force–I—UNEF I), the United Nations was unable to secure a peace agreement between Israel and its neighbors. In another sense, however, these two processes intersect. The kind of failure to achieve a resolution of the issues underlying the dispute that we have seen in the Middle East creates incentives for a dissatisfied protagonist to violate the cease-fire and use military force to achieve its goals (e.g., the 1967 Arab-Israeli war). Conversely, significant progress in decreasing tension and working out an agreement lessens the willingness of either side to renew military hostilities.

Although a primary contribution of the book is theoretical, the analysis and conclusions also address policy concerns. I hope to be able to provide guidelines that indicate which scenarios are most appropriate for peacekeeping, and which might be better addressed by other diplomatic means. Furthermore, rather than an operations manual for field commanders, I will offer some strategies for enhancing the likelihood that the peacekeeping force will deter renewed fighting and promote long-term resolution of the conflict.

An analysis of peacekeeping operations would not be complete or fully relevant unless it explored their applicability to other contexts. Accordingly, this book also focuses on alternatives to, and variations upon, traditional peacekeeping operations. These alternatives fall into two categories: institutional and functional. Institutional alternatives refer to proposed changes in the ad hoc arrangements for operations directed by the United Nations. I particularly consider the idea of a permanent U.N. peacekeeping force, although I also give attention to peacekeeping operations carried out by regional intergovernmental organizations as well as to multilateral efforts not under international or regional auspices.

Functional alternatives refer to the role expansion of peacekeeping forces beyond mere monitoring of cease-fires. Such expanded roles may include verifying arms control, interdicting drugs, combatting terrorism, and monitoring elections.[7] I also devote attention to the deployment of troops in a manner more consistent with traditional military missions, such as collective security.

The Concept of Peacekeeping

The term *peacekeeping* has been popularly used to designate a wide range of phenomena. The U.S. troops that participated in the invasion of Grenada were called the Caribbean Peace Keeping Forces. President Ronald Reagan even labeled the MX missile the "Peacekeeper." Most commonly, *peacekeeping* is used to refer to any international effort involving an operational component to promote the termination of armed conflict or the resolution of longstanding disputes. Such a definition encompasses military action to punish an aggressor, such as the Korean "police action," as well as multilateral efforts at negotiation. In many cases, the use of the term seems to contradict the whole notion of peace, much less the idea that such a condition should be preserved or kept.

The conceptual muddle in the use of the term *peacekeeping* is not confined to the popular press or diplomatic enclaves. Those working with or studying peacekeeping operations employ several definitions, albeit relatively narrow ones, of peacekeeping. Several compilations lump together and designate as peacekeeping all international efforts, particularly those of the United Nations and the League of Nations, that involved the deployment of forces to a conflict-ridden area.[8] The United Nations itself has no established definition of peacekeeping. Even the International Peace Academy, devoted to the study of ways to improve peacekeeping, offers a relatively broad definition: "The prevention, containment, moderation, and termination of hostilities, through the medium of a peaceful third party intervention, organized and directed internationally, using multinational forces of soldiers, police, and civilians to restore and maintain peace."[9]

Peacekeeping, which evolved out of the failure of collective security and the inadequacy of peace observation, differs from both. This distinction does not imply that peacekeeping and other forms of conflict intervention do not share certain functions and characteristics; as peacekeeping was developed from the roots of collective security and peace observation, it is not surprising that there is some significant overlap. Nevertheless, peacekeeping does possess some unique attributes that provide the basis for distinguishing it from those other approaches to peace.[10]

Nonenforcement

One distinguishing attribute of peacekeeping is the performance of a noncoercive mission. Troops trained in traditional military maneuvers work to restore order, defend a given piece of territory, or seize and hold that piece of territory. The general goal of a traditional military operation is to deter an opponent or defeat that opponent in battle should deterrence fail; these are missions that include enforcement and coercion with military force.[11]

Peacekeeping operations are significantly different in several ways. First, peacekeeping troops are not designed to restore order or stop the fighting between rival enemies. Peacekeeping troops are usually only deployed *following* a cease-fire agreement by the protagonists. They are not constituted so as to be placed on a battlefield with the mission of stopping the bloodshed. Thus, unlike a collective security operation, peacekeeping troops are deployed after fighting is halted rather than before or during military conflict. The deployment of UNEF I after the Suez Crisis is in marked contrast to operations carried out by India and Syria that have been labeled "peacekeeping" by those countries. UNEF I was put in place following a cease-fire and supervised the withdrawal of forces by all sides. In contrast, Syrian troops have been deployed in Lebanon *during* the height of military conflict between rival Christian and Muslim factions. The Syrian troops had the mission of restoring some level of order in Lebanon and minimizing the bloodshed; this sometimes involved fierce fighting between the Syrian troops and local militias. The Indian intervention into northern Sri Lanka had a similar mission—suppress the Tamil rebel group and restore order. Neither of these national efforts fits the conception of peacekeeping developed in this book.[12]

Second, whereas a traditional military mission involves the defense or attempted seizure of territory, the territorial role of a peacekeeping force is considerably different. Peacekeeping troops occupy a given area but act as an interposition force between the protagonists. This means that they have no offensive role (and no such capability) in the conflict. They do not seek to acquire additional territory, nor do they use military force except under very limited conditions. Indeed, the peacekeeping force does not try to hold a given piece a territory and has no legal or professed sovereignty over the territory it occupies. Its goal is to provide a buffer between hostile forces and prevent dangerous shooting incidents that might escalate hostilities and permanently jeopardize the cease-fire agreement. Peacekeeping forces achieve this goal as much by serving as a confidence-building mechanism as they do by their military capabilities. Thus, a large part of a peacekeeping force's activities involves patrolling the deployment area, searching for violations of the cease-fire agreement, and attempting to resolve conflicts related to the agreement by acting as a conciliator between the hostile parties. These are not functions regularly carried out by a military force.

These two aspects also differentiate traditional military operations from international observer forces. Observer forces are also not designed to restore order or defend territory, although they may be placed in an area prior to the cessation of armed hostilities. Furthermore, they may also patrol areas and help resolve cease-fire disputes. The major difference between peacekeeping and observer forces is that observer forces are not designed to act as interposition forces, although they may be placed in a neutral zone between the protagonists. Observer forces are often fewer in number (indeed, a single individual may constitute such a force) and do not act as a buffer between the hostile parties. They may be stationed on either side of the conflict and do not perform such activities as checking local vehicles for weapons and guarding border areas, as do peacekeeping troops. The difference between observer forces and peacekeeping troops is also more evident in their respective military equipment and instructions on the use of military force, components that also further distinguish peacekeeping from traditional military operations.

Limited Military Capability

Peacekeeping forces also have the distinguishing feature of being only lightly armed. A typical peacekeeping soldier is equipped only with a rifle, and peacekeeping units have access only to vehicles for transportation purposes (e.g., helicopters and personnel carriers) and not to those that might be used for attack (e.g., tanks and fighter planes). Although the military personnel of some poorer countries in the world might also have no more than a rifle on their backs, peacekeeping troops are restricted by their guiding philosophy rather than by economic or technological under-development.

Peacekeeping troops are only lightly armed because their mission is not a traditional one, and they are designed only to use those arms in self-defense; peacekeeping troops have neither an offensive military mission nor the capability to carry one out. Peacekeeping troops are not designed to alter the prevailing distribution of power in the area of deployment, nor do they wish to appear threatening to the disputants or the local population.

This characteristic contrasts with collective security forces, whose only equipment restrictions are dictated by weapons availability and strategy. Furthermore, this differs from purely observation forces, who usually carry no weapons at all. Unlike observers, peacekeeping troops must protect themselves and retain the means to exercise their right of self-defense, a general principle embedded in the U.N. Charter and international law. Peacekeeping forces must also provide a visible deterrent, with the threat of defensive military actions, in patrolling buffer and other demilitarized zones; small, unarmed observer forces are generally considered inadequate for this task.[13]

Neutrality

A third distinguishing conceptual component of peacekeeping is its neutrality. Collective security presupposes an identifiable aggressor who then becomes the target of enforcement action; in this sense, there is a determination of victim and international criminal by the United Nations or some other international agency.[14] Peacekeeping forces do not brand one side or the other responsible for the military conflict. This is not to say that the authorizing body of the peacekeeping forces does not pass any judgment on the conflict or that the organization may not condemn one side or the other.[15] The imposition of peacekeeping forces after the Suez Crisis was preceded by several U.N. actions that constituted disapproval of French and British actions. The use of peacekeeping troops in Namibia reflected the United Nations' longstanding efforts to achieve independence for that nation; repeated denunciations and suspension of South Africa from the organization were part of that effort. Furthermore, the deployment of peacekeeping troops in a conflict may constitute an implicit advantage or endorsement of one side's political position. The deployment of the U.N. Operation in the Congo (ONUC) initially supported the forces led by the prime minister, Patrice Lumumba, and opposed the interests of the Katangan president, Moise Tshombe. Yet peacekeeping forces do not usually overtly favor one side or the other in a conflict. At the very least, they are not designed to provide a military advantage, as is collective security, to either side.

The concept of neutrality goes beyond the purpose of the force to the composition and activities of the troops. Most U.N. peacekeeping forces are composed of military personnel from nonaligned states; typically Canada, Fiji, and Sweden have been among the most generous contributors of troops. Soldiers from the major powers, or those from other states with a vested interest in the conflict at hand (such as Saudi Arabia in Middle East operations), are explicitly not used. One could hardly imagine an effective collective security operation without the active contributions of the major military powers, yet a similar contribution to peacekeeping jeopardizes its neutral character and perhaps its likelihood of success. For example, Arab states would perceive the deployment of U.S. troops on the Lebanese border as supportive of Israel. Similarly, the use of Soviet troops to monitor elections in Nicaragua in 1989 might have increased preelection violence and precipitated complaints that the election was rigged by the Sandinistas.

Neutral behavior (both perceived and objective) of peacekeeping troops must reinforce their neutral composition. Neutrality means that the actions of the peacekeeping troops are not intended to favor one side or the other in the dispute. Thus cease-fire violations committed by Turkish Cypriots are identified and reported with the same accuracy as those committed by Greek Cypriots. Allowing Palestinians to smuggle weapons into the UNIFIL zone in southern Lebanon would be an example of a breach of impartiality.

Permission of the Host Countries

Another distinguishing feature of peacekeeping operations is that they must have the permission of the state or states on whose territory the troops will be stationed. A parallel requirement in collective security (needing the permission of the aggressor to undertake enforcement actions against it) would be absurd. Yet peacekeeping operations recognize and respect the sovereignty of states and assign a role for the implementing agency commensurate with the authority granted by the states involved. The absence of such permission could jeopardize the mission of the peacekeeping operation. It is likely that any attempts to station troops without the consent of the host country would precipitate military attacks on those forces by the host country. Not only would this defeat the purpose of limiting hostilities in the area, but it would be suicidal for the troops in that they have neither the military equipment nor the training to resist actions from a well-armed and determined enemy. Intervention without consent, under most scenarios, would also seem to violate international legal standards.[16] It might be noted that while permission may be easily granted as a part of the deployment of peacekeeping troops, that permission does not constitute an indefinite legal right for the operation; it may be withdrawn at any time by the host state. Such was the case with UNEF I, which Egypt's president, Gamal Abdel Nasser, asked to vacate Egyptian territory just before the 1967 war.

Functions of Peacekeeping Forces

Peacekeeping forces generally perform a range of functions that, all or in part, distinguish them from collective security and peace observation. Peacekeeping troops, however, do carry out observation tasks. These include detecting violations of cease-fires and supervising troop withdrawals.[17] As neutral observers, peacekeepers can ensure that none of the protagonists perform actions that violate the agreement that established the peacekeeping operation and the cessation of military hostilities. Observation tasks might also include the creation of mechanisms to deal with alleged violations and disputes over the interpretation of agreements spelling out rights and obligations of the disputants; for example, there may be some question about the stationing of military personnel in a demilitarized zone if they are only performing construction work. Although a peace observation team may perform most or all of these functions, a collective security operation rarely does, and then only after a victory has been achieved; following the Persian Gulf war, military personnel looked for violations of the cease-fire agreement by Iraq, although a peace observation team and arms control inspectors replaced them shortly thereafter.

Beyond such observation tasks, a second set of functions for peacekeeping troops relates to their roles as buffer or interposition forces. Interposing themselves between the protagonists accomplishes two things. First, it may prevent isolated hostile incidents or accidents that could escalate to full-scale war; each side is restricted from direct contact with the enemy. Second, it provides a moral barrier to hostile action. A state may be reluctant to use military force if it knows that military offensives must go through U.N. forces, risking loss of life and international condemnation in the process. This is part of what James refers to as the "prophylactic" function of preventing a tense situation from deteriorating into open warfare.[18] Peace observation does not include this interposition component, which also runs contrary to collective security strategies of directly engaging the aggressor in a conflict.

A third set of functions concerns the maintenance of law and order, especially common for peacekeeping operations deployed in *intra*national conflicts. Peacekeeping forces perform such police tasks as patrolling the streets and countryside to report incidents and deter criminal and other hostile activity. Peacekeeping forces may also be responsible for administrative duties in a quasi-governmental fashion, although only as a temporary measure and without the grant of sovereignty. These functions may take place only in a narrow region where the peacekeeping force is deployed (a demilitarized zone or disputed territory with an indigenous population), or they may be expanded to include a wide area in the absence of established or competent government authority—the latter was most evident in the U.N. peacekeeping operation in the Congo. Neither observation missions nor traditional military operations are concerned with such activities.

A final function of peacekeeping operations is the performance of humanitarian activities. These include such services as allowing the indigenous population to take advantage of facilities set up to serve the peacekeeping troops, such as medical clinics, assisting with electricity and water problems in the area, and providing transportation or help to local farmers. These activities are not formally part of the operations' mandates, but they are consistent with it and may actually promote the underlying purposes. Aiding the local population helps bring acceptance for the peacekeeping force and lessens the danger that the forces will be the victim of unprovoked attack by local elements who might resent their presence. Humanitarian activities are also generally noncontroversial, lending greater credibility to the claim that the peacekeeping forces are neutral parties not seeking to affect the military situation in the area. Neither observer forces nor collective security operations generally perform these types of activities.

Characteristics of Typical Peacekeeping Operations

It is probably a cliché to repeat that each peacekeeping operation is unique and that in some sense any generalization distorts the details of the events in that operation. Furthermore, any description of a typical peacekeeping operation may give a false idea of what uses that strategy might be put to in the future. Nevertheless, traditional peacekeeping operations have shared a number of operational characteristics.[19]

First, peacekeeping operations inherently have been reactive to international conflict. The term *preventive diplomacy* is sometimes used interchangeably with *peacekeeping*, but this is misleading.[20] Peacekeeping operations are not placed between hostile parties before the onset of military conflict. The United Nations, like many organizations, is crisis driven; peacekeeping operations are not often suggested, much less authorized, until lives have been lost and the prospects for war expansion are great.

Before a peacekeeping operation can be placed during a crisis, there must be some opportunity for U.N. intervention. Most often this is a cease-fire agreed to by the protagonists, as was the case in the UNEF II operation, which was sent to the Middle East as a part of the cease-fire agreement in the 1973 Yom Kippur War. On occasion, the peacekeeping operation may be deployed in an attempt to stabilize the situation amid sporadic, but still significant, violence of noncrisis proportions; the 1989 operation in Namibia fits this profile. Thus, typical peacekeeping operations are not deployed in low-level disputes, and must await the opportunity for intervention that is provided by the consent of the parties.

A second set of characteristics surrounds the authorization of the typical peacekeeping mission. At the height of the Cold War, some peacekeeping operations relied on the political support of a majority of members in the General Assembly, bypassing the Security Council because of the political stalemate there. More recently, the Security Council has reassumed the mantle of leadership on peace and security issues. Although the Security Council is the authorizing body, consent of the host state (and usually of the other protagonists) is necessary before the process can begin.

The authorization of the mission is far from open-ended. The mandate of the operation is spelled out by the Security Council, although vagaries in the language and traditional bureaucratic discretion in implementation may provide considerable leeway for the actual conduct of the operation. Peacekeeping operations are usually authorized for limited periods of time, subject to periodic reauthorization as needed; a typical term of authorization is six months. There are several possible explanations for this brief time limit. The most optimistic is that Security Council members recognize that peacekeeping deployments are temporary Band-Aids in a crisis and that the six-month period permits quasi-permanent solutions to be instituted in their place. More credible is that the political interests of the council members, especially of the permanent ones, explain the short authorization terms. Many times, the consensus of the members does not extend beyond a desire to avoid war. A peacekeeping operation may facilitate this outcome, at least in the short run, but a long-term authorization period will favor the status quo, which is unlikely to be supported by all parties. Beyond the lack of political consensus, it could also be argued that states deliberately limit the term of deployment to maximize their leverage vis-à-vis the reauthorization of the operation at each renewal deadline. By forcing a renewal every six months, Security Council members can reopen the bargaining about an operation's purpose and conduct. A six-month renewal also allows the members to reevaluate those terms in light of changed circumstances since the last authorization.

A third aspect of a typical peacekeeping operation is its formation mechanisms. Peacekeeping operations remain distinctly ad hoc. Once an operation is authorized, the secretary-general begins to acquire commitments from member states to provide troops and material for the peacekeeping force. Troops usually came from neutral countries that have little or no stake in the outcome of the conflict. Several U.N. members maintain national training programs that earmark troops for peacekeeping duty. Other countries devote some portion of regular military training to peacekeeping methods so that troops will be available if needed. States that do not provide troops, for political or other reasons, may volunteer helicopters, vehicles, or other equipment to the peacekeeping force. Some costs of the operation are borne directly by those contributing men and material. The U.N. budget or voluntary monetary contributions by member states cover other costs. It may appear that a mad, last-minute scramble is hardly the most efficient way to organize a peacekeeping operation, but most operations nevertheless are deployed and functioning within several days or weeks of authorization.

Although the previous three characteristics resemble the modes of operation for peace observation missions or proposed collective security operations, considerable differences arise with respect to the fourth characteristic—size. The size of peacekeeping operations generally ranges from one or two thousand to twenty thousand depending on the willingness of states to contribute troops, the mission assigned the operation, and the breadth of the area of deployment. In contrast, peace observation teams have usually numbered less than one thousand and quite often less than one hundred. On the other hand, an effective collective security operation could never hope to be effective with the limited manpower of peacekeeping or observation missions. Traditional military operations must be much larger to defeat an aggressor state's army; in the Persian Gulf war, several hundred thousand troops were deployed against a comparable Iraqi force.

There is considerably more variation in the fifth characteristic—command and control. The exact structures and procedures may still be evolving, even after more than thirty years' experience with peacekeeping operations. Nevertheless, peacekeeping operations are under U.N. command, not solely under the direction of national commanders. The peacekeeping units are designed to be better integrated than units in traditional military operations, such as those deployed in Korea and Kuwait. The commander of the operation is often from a neutral state. It has become more common for the United Nations to fill leadership posts in peacekeeping operations with individuals who have experience in prior operations. In all cases, the peacekeeping operations receive extensive staff support from the secretariat.

Peacekeeping is therefore the imposition of neutral and lightly armed interposition forces following a cessation of armed hostilities, and with the permission of the state on whose territory these forces are deployed, in order to discourage a renewal of military conflict and promote an environment under which the underlying dispute can be resolved. Peacekeeping functions including observation, interposition, maintaining law and order, and humanitarian activity. These functions are not mutually exclusive; depending on the type of conflict, some or all may be part of the peacekeeping mission. In any case, peacekeeping operations are conceptually and operationally distinct from collective security and peace observation missions, although they may share some commonalities and have similar historical roots.

It may be that the term *peacekeeping* is used in so many different ways because it is not mentioned in the U.N. Charter (as are collective security and other approaches to peace) and because the strategy has evolved out of ad hoc responses to various crises. Yet some of the roots of peacekeeping can be traced back to the League of Nations experience. As we trace the historical development of peacekeeping, it should become clear how peacekeeping came to share some common points with peace observation and why it is significantly different from collective security.

The Origin and Development of Peacekeeping Operations

The origin and development of peacekeeping operations largely parallel those of international organizations in general. Yet, the peacekeeping strategy specifically evolved out of experience with peace observation missions and the failure of collective security under the League of Nations and the United Nations.

Before the advancement of intercontinental transportation and the birth of the modern nation-state, there were no extensive international interactions of any kind beyond some trading relationships and imperial connections, much less collective efforts at global or regional security. The earliest incidence of collective military action at the international level might be the Crusades.[21] In that instance, several states banded together, with the encouragement of the Vatican, to save the Holy Land from the scourges of those who were regarded as pagans. Yet these actions were hardly designed to restore peace and security, as were their modern-day successors, and one also could argue that the operations were not coordinated under provisions set up by a global or regional intergovernmental organization.

The Crusades proved not to set a precedent. In the fourteenth century came a proposal, never actualized, for a world government that included arrangements for an international army.[22] After the Napoleonic Wars in the nineteenth century, the major powers acted in concert to preserve the status quo, and this included collective (broadly construed) military action that, again, only faintly resembled the organized and internationally sanctioned operations that would occur in the next century.

The closest analogue to peacekeeping operations before the establishment of the League of Nations occurred in China at the time of the Boxer Rebellion in 1900. An allied force of several nations was constituted to rescue the foreign legations in Beijing during the height of the violence, but it did not operate under a unified command.[23]

Early international efforts at collective military action shared a number of characteristics. First, they operated on an ad hoc basis, organizing and disbanding as the need arose and according to the crisis at hand. This attribute persists in international observation and peacekeeping operations to this day. Second, beyond the ad hoc arrangements, these early actions had little precedent to follow. Thus, they operated without specific guidelines, often with little coordination between national units. This circumstance would change in the twentieth century, when peacekeeping operations relied heavily on guidelines established by previous operations in terms of personnel, deployment, and conduct. Finally, early efforts went forward largely without the approval or the direction of an international body, in most cases, because international organizations as we know them today did not exist. The protection of international peace and security was largely indistinguishable from the interests of the major powers in the world, a condition that would change, at least organizationally, with the creation of an appropriate international mechanism for authorizing and coordinating global security actions—the League of Nations.

The League of Nations Experience: Collective Security

The end of World War I and the desire by the global community to make that truly "the war to end all wars" led to the formation of the first general-purpose, universal membership organization—the League of Nations. Although that organization had economic and social functions as well, its primary purpose was to ensure international peace and security through collective consultation and action. In the course of drafting the League of Nations Covenant, France proposed that military sanctions be executed by an international force. The British and U.S. delegations objected to this provision, and accordingly it is absent from articles 10 and 16 of that document. Nevertheless, those articles do outline, in broad form, collective security procedures. Article 10 states: "The Members of the League undertake to respect and preserve as against external aggression the territorial integrity and existing political independence of all Members of the League. In case of any such aggression, the Council shall advise upon the means by which this obligation shall be fulfilled."

The provisions of that article are a far cry from installing discretionary power in an international police force to meet threats to international security. Yet article 16 is less equivocal in outlining the possible international military response to aggression: "Should any Member resort to war . . . it shall, *ipso factor*, be deemed to have committed an act of war against all Members. . . . It shall be the duty of the Council in such case to recommend to the several Governments concerned what effective military, naval, or air force the Members of the League shall severally contribute to the armed forces used to protect the covenants of the League."

These provisions supplied the legal authority for the League to take collective military action, only one option at the disposal of the Council.

Furthermore, the operations were to be organized on an ad hoc basis, much as were their historical predecessors. Finally, military operations would probably not be under the control of the League or be truly international forces. There is enough ambiguity in the language of the articles and sufficient political reasons to believe that the military actions would be loosely coordinated national efforts undertaken by the major powers with the approval of the League.

The collective security procedures of the League of Nations were not tested until more than a decade after the inception of the organization. In 1931, Japan attacked Manchuria and occupied the capital city; China appealed to the Council of the League for assistance. Over the objections of Japan, the Council recommended withdrawal of the Japanese troops, yet stronger actions under article 11 of the League Covenant would necessitate a unanimous vote, a result unlikely because of the potential Japanese veto. This state of affairs all but precluded forceful action against any of the members, a problem that foreshadowed similar difficulties with the superpowers in the United Nations.

Rather than stiff economic sanctions or an international military action against Japan, the League was able to authorize only a fact-finding mission to the area. During the long process of inquiry, Japan set up the puppet state of Manchukuo and directed its aggressive eye toward the rest of China. By the time the fact-finding report was presented to the League, Japanese aggression had borne its full fruits, and it was impossible to undo the harvest.[24] Japan added insult to this ineffectiveness by withdrawing from the organization.

The next major test of the League's collective action mechanisms would yield only slightly better results. Italy attacked Ethiopia in 1935 and ultimately conquered that country, for which the League instituted economic sanctions against Italy. Yet, many of the League members as well as the United States either failed to institute those sanctions fully or blatantly ignored them. The major downfall of the League's actions against Italy was the British and French willingness to recognize Italian domination over parts of North Africa. Britain and France mistakenly thought that appeasing Italy would lead that country to recognize British and French interests on the African continent and perhaps would secure them an ally against rising Nazi power in Germany.[25] The willingness of major powers to place their own interests ahead of those of the international community again foreshadowed Cold War tensions and the paralysis of the United Nations in coming decades.

After failing to meet these challenges, the League was not up to dealing with the specter of war in Europe in the late 1930s and was largely an anachronism until the outbreak of World War II. Primary among the many reasons for the failure of the League was the inability and unwillingness of the major powers to act against their own interests; the unanimity rule in the League that stifled serious action magnified this problem.[26] The absence of established mechanisms and available troops either complicated these efforts or mirrored the inherent unwillingness of states to grant supranational authority to the League. Several of these problems would appear again in the United Nations, albeit in different forms, and set the stage for the formation of the peacekeeping strategy.

The League of Nations Experience: Peace Observation and Inquiry

Despite the failure of its collective security arrangements, the League of Nations was active in several disputes and crisis. During these disputes the League began to perform some peace observation functions that were to evolve into the peacekeeping strategy in later years.[27] The League Covenant makes no mention of peace observation, yet article 11, authorizing the League to "take any action that may be deemed wise and effectual to safeguard the peace of nations," opened the door to actions not specifically mentioned in the Covenant or envisioned by its authors. Furthermore, article 15 provided for the Council to report on the facts of disputes and make recommendations on how those disputes might be settled peacefully. These two articles would form the basis for League actions that combined the missions of fact-finding and observation.

The first League action came very early in the life of the organization. A dispute over the Aaland Islands between Sweden and Finland led the League to create a commission of inquiry to investigate the situation and recommend solutions to the controversy.[28] At first glance, a fact-finding mission would seem to offer few precedents for future peace observation. Indeed, this dispute was not so severe as to suggest that military conflict was imminent or even likely. Yet this simple case established a precedent that the League could successfully intervene in a dispute and act in a neutral fashion in pursuit of a peaceful solution. The acceptance, albeit without enthusiasm, of the fact-finding report by the protagonists also helped establish the League's reputation as a fair arbiter.

Throughout the 1920s, the League involved itself in a number of disputes. The usual method was to create fact-finding commissions that would report back to the Council, following the strategy outlined in the Covenant and the precedent established in the Aaland Islands case. In the dispute between

Poland and Germany over Upper Silesia, troops were sent to supervise the plebiscite in the area.[29] Yet these were hardly international troops, as France, Italy, and later Britain sent and retained control over their own forces. Furthermore, these could not be considered neutral forces, in that the sponsoring countries each had interests and supported a particular outcome of the dispute. Although such action did not resemble later peace observation missions, it did represent a key instance of the use of internationally sanctioned forces in a supervisory role.

The Greek-Bulgarian crisis of 1925 provided another opportunity for League involvement and the establishment of another precedent that would later form the basis of peace observation and peacekeeping missions.[30] Before the Council authorized a fact-finding mission, it insisted that there be a cease-fire, which was subsequently achieved. This is now a virtual requirement for authorizing peacekeeping operations. The recommendations of the commission of inquiry included the pullback of forces and their separation at a safe distance, supervised by neutral observers. A committee composed of representatives from both disputants and some neutral parties, including a League chair, was to discuss problems with the cease-fire and limit the escalation potential of hostile incidents. The construction of a buffer zone and the establishment of such a committee are now standard operating procedures for peacekeeping operations.

Shortly after the Aaland Islands dispute, a more serious conflict arose between Poland and Lithuania over the province of Vilna.[31] More than just deploying a fact-finding mission this time, the League was successful in negotiating a provisional line of demarcation and a neutral, demilitarized zone between the disputants, thus setting the physical and political conditions for the introduction of an international force.

An international force of 1,500 from states that had no seat on the Council (in marked contrast to the Upper Silesia force) was designed to replace irregular Polish troops that occupied the disputed territory and to supervise a plebiscite in the area. Unfortunately, such a force never assumed those roles. First, both disputants, and Lithuania in particular, placed roadblocks in the way of League efforts, illustrating the difficulty (or perhaps impossibility) of neutral international intervention without the cooperation of the disputants. Furthermore, major power interests, as exercised by France and the Soviet Union, made Council action both within and out of the League rather difficult. Although this case was successful in that war was ultimately avoided, the problems encountered bear some similarity to contemporary problems in the United Nations. Peace observation was thwarted by the noncooperation of the parties involved and major power disagreements, problems not that different from those noted earlier in the failure of collective security. Nevertheless, this failure would prove to be a stepping stone in the successful deployment of an international force in the Saar, which may be the League model closest to present-day observation or peacekeeping forces.

The League of Nations action in the Saar may be the first true example of an international peace observation force.[32] Yet the conditions under which the operation functioned were extraordinary and indeed helped contribute to the success of the mission. The Saar, lying between France and Germany, was to be an internationally administered territory for a period of years following World War I, at which time a plebiscite would decide the final disposition of the area, with options including unification with France or Germany. Thus the usual problem of obtaining permission of the host country for the stationing of an international force was not an issue in this case: the League was the equivalent of the host state. This became particularly important when Germany made several hostile gestures toward the establishment of the force. The French were also less than fully cooperative, perhaps believing (correctly) that the territory would ultimately be returned to Germany.

The Saar force was made up of troops from Britain, Italy, and other European countries, not exactly a neutral force in its composition, but the way it was commanded represented a significant advance. Unlike previous missions in which nations maintained control of units, this force was under the direction of the League through its appointed commander, General J. E. S. Brind.[33] Although the troops were to maintain order prior to and during the plebiscite, they did not function as an international police force. They patrolled the territory but would only take action in emergency situations and then only in response to a request by the local authorities. The level of military force was to be kept at a minimum, reflecting what would become the standard for limitations on the use of military force in peacekeeping missions. Despite some threats from local officials and the massing of German troops near the border of the disputed territory, the operation was a success, with little or no violence.

The Saar expedition is important not only because it represented the first truly international force, but also because the report of General Brind contained several recommendations that would become centerpieces of observation and peacekeeping strategy in the future.[34] Among his recommendations was that troops in future operations be drawn from countries that had no direct interest in the dispute, all but guaranteeing that major power forces would not be involved. Brind also noted that only a small number of troops were necessary to complete the mission, and that it was the moral influence of the Saar force rather than any direct action that was responsible for successfully deterring trouble in the disputed area. These two elements underline the absence of an enforcement capability and identify the prevailing strategy in preserving peace, in contrast to collective security actions. This legacy would manifest in peacekeeping operations two decades later.[35]

The League of Nations Legacy

Most historians regard the League of Nations as a failure because it did not restrain Japanese, Italian, and finally German aggression. Yet from those failures, and also from some successes in peace observation and inquiry, the League established procedures and precedents about the proper timing and form of international intervention. First, it became evident that intervention was most successful when the major powers were not directly involved. With the exception of the Saar plebiscite, an unusual and prearranged set of circumstances, the League was most successful when Britain, France, and others were not the main protagonists. Secondly, the League was more successful in intervention when hostilities had not reached full-scale war; collective security proved ineffective, and it was much easier to arrange a cease-fire at a lower level of military conflict. Third, the support of the disputants was critical to any League action and to the deployment of an observation force in particular; such support was also essential to a final disposition of the conflict and acceptance of League recommendations. Fourth, the League found it useful to separate the combatants physically, often establishing a neutral zone or line of demarcation. The idea that neutral, lightly armed troops should be placed in that area (i.e., peacekeeping troops) had not yet been advanced, although it is a logical extension of that action.

Beyond these lessons, several other experiences influenced future operations. League actions in observation and inquiry gradually evolved to include neutral personnel. What started out as national contingents from the major powers became neutral observers from non-Council members under the direction of an international commander. The League had finally wrested some autonomy from its members in the conduct of its operations. This autonomy would be expanded, albeit with significant limits, in the U.N. experience. Another legacy, perhaps one less fortunate, was that operations were largely ad hoc and reactive to situations. The League was unable to put together a permanent force or even set guidelines for the conduct of its actions. Furthermore, it often was able to take action only after violence was widespread in a dispute, thereby limiting the courses of effective action.

It was also clear from the League experience that the reliance on observers to perform fact-finding missions was impractical, at least as a modus operandi for all circumstances and without some supplemental measures. First, inquiry proved cumbersome and time consuming, especially in rapidly escalating crises. Unless both sides agreed to a cease-fire and awaited the recommendations of the Council, an aggressor could gobble up territory, much as Japan did in Manchuria, while the fact-finding mission did its work. By the time a report could be submitted, the conflict might be over, the aggressor enjoying the fruits of its actions and hundreds of thousands of lives lost. It became clear that inquiry alone was not a sufficient mechanism to stop the fighting. This is not to say that fact-finding was fatally flawed as an approach to peace, but rather that it was not appropriate to all situations.

Beyond the time delay, intimately tying the mechanism for stopping the conflict to the resolution of the dispute (i.e., charging the observation team both with supervising the situation and with recommending how to resolve the conflict) carries with it some inherent risks. There is the problem that the successful maintenance of peace depends in large part on the acceptance of the recommendations by the dispute parties. If there are mediation or conciliation initiatives, their progress affects the willingness of each side to refrain from the use of force. That is, a breakdown in negotiations might lead to a breakdown in the cease-fire facilitated by the observer team. Furthermore, the neutrality of the observation team might be questioned if its recommendations seem to favor strongly one side or the other. The League of Nations strategy did not separate various functions in international intervention. The United Nations' continuing tenure, however, brought a recognition of distinct phases of conflict (e.g., the conflict escalation phase and the post-cease-fire phase) and of the need for varying the approaches to peace according to those phases. Yet before the United Nations would make this adjustment, it would have to relearn some of the lessons of the League of nations experience.

The United Nations Experience: Collective Security Redux

There has been a view (especially common at the end of the Second World War and to some extent still held today) that the United Nations represented a fundamentally different organization than the League of

Nations.[36] Those who put together the United Nations at Dumbarton Oaks and San Francisco formally ignored the League. At the initial session of the United Nations, neither speakers nor diplomats mentioned its name, perhaps for fear of placing a curse on the new organization born from the League's ashes. The transfer of land and assets from the League to the United Nations drew little attention and was regarded more as a symbolic act than a substantive one.

Despite their alleged differences, the League and the United Nations shared a number of fundamental similarities and, not surprisingly, passed through several of the same learning phases (albeit more quickly in the case of the United Nations) in their strategies for dealing with threats to international peace and security. Philosophically, they sprang from the same roots. Those who founded each organization placed their faith in the continued cooperation of the victorious coalition from a world war. Furthermore, both sets of founders designed the organizations so that their main *operational* action in matters of peace and security would be some form of collective security. This may not seem surprising in the case of the League, which was influenced by an idealistic era that included the Kellogg-Briand Pact outlawing war. Nevertheless, one might have expected something different from the United Nations, in that it had the bitter League experience with collective security to learn from, as well as some previous successes with peace observation.

The U.N. provisions for conflict intervention resemble those of the League but are laid out more explicitly and rely on an increasingly coercive sequence of actions. According to chapter 6 (articles 33–38) of the U.N. Charter, protagonists are given a number of dispute resolution alternatives to the use of military force. Beyond such options as mediation and judicial settlement, the United Nations, through the Security Council, is empowered to investigate the dispute (article 34) and recommend means (article 36) or terms (articles 37 and 38) of settlement. This was largely the mode of operation for the League of Nations—inquiry and conciliation. Yet when it came to the use of force, the United Nations had both the rationale and the mechanisms to take collective action.

Chapter 7 of the U.N. Charter lists some courses of action for U.N. members to take should peaceful methods of settlement outlined in chapter 6 fail. Reliance on sanctions, the tack taken against Iraq following its invasion of Kuwait, might fail, and the Security Council might need to authorize the use of military force. Article 42 directly identifies the collective security option: "[the Security Council] may take such action by air, sea, or land forces as may be necessary to maintain or restore international peace and security."

In one sense, the U.N. strategy and mechanisms for dealing with threats to international peace and security were similar to those that had achieved little success under the League. Many of the initial options centered around the Security Council's making suggestions for resolution of the dispute after some deliberation and inquiry. The collective security option was also a last resort, although again the autonomy of the organization was limited to specific authorizations by its members. Surprisingly, the charter did not mention the notion of peace observation, and peacekeeping operations were yet to be created. International organizations still lacked formal options between enforcement measures and mediation.

In many ways the United Nations was like the proverbial old dog, but it nevertheless did apparently learn a few new tricks from the League of Nations experience. The first major change in its security apparatus was an alteration of the voting system. Under the League, the Council required unanimity before authorizing certain actions under article 11, which effectively limited the range of actions directed against one of the Council members. The U.N. Security Council voting system requires only nine of fifteen votes to take action, provided none of the five permanent members of the council (United States, Soviet Union—now Russia—China, United Kingdom, and France) oppose the resolution.[37] Thus the United Nations replaced unanimity among all members under the League with the requirement for acquiescence among the most important subset of its members—the major powers. This was designed to ensure that the major powers would be united (thought to be a necessity for concerted global action) and to make decisions for action somewhat easier than in the League.

Beyond a change in the voting system to authorize peace and security action, the U.N. Charter included the infrastructure to carry out that action. First, it provided for a Military Staff Committee (article 47) that was "responsible . . . for the strategic direction of any armed forces placed at the disposal of the Security Council." Although actual command of such forces was deferred until a later time, establishing the Military Staff Committee was the United Nations' effort to have a direct say in the conduct of forces on an international mission. It also assumed continuity of action and establishment of procedures for the use and conduct of those forces. The committee was designed to be a significant step forward from the purely ad hoc national efforts thought to characterize League of Nations actions.

Yet the provisions for supply of troops remained distinctly ad hoc. Article

43 provides: "All Members of the United Nations . . . undertake to make available to the Security Council, on its call and in accordance with a special agreement or agreements, armed forces, assistance, and facilities, including rights of passage, necessary for the purpose of maintaining international peace and security." Similar to the League, the United Nations would not have its own military forces but would have to rely on the contributions of its members, although the command of those forces would now be under the control of the international organization. Nevertheless, that some national troops were at least earmarked for duty in the U.N. collective security actions was something of an advancement over League practice.

Even though the United Nations made adjustments based on the League of Nations experience, the net results did not differ dramatically with respect to collective security.[38] Changing the voting system from one of unanimity to one based on a major power veto only perpetuated the stalemate of the League's Council; the veto provision prevented the Security Council from taking meaningful action against any of the major powers.[39] By confining the Security Council to operations against or involving states other than the major powers, and given that major powers have global interests and that their disputes provide the greatest threat to international security, this limitation is substantial.

Yet even in the set of minor power disputes, the veto proved a strong impediment to action. The rapid escalation of the Cold War after World War II increasingly polarized the international system. Few states could be said not to belong to one superpower's camp or the other. Thus, when faced with a crisis in Iran or Turkey, for example, the Security Council was stifled by the veto of one of the superpowers. The development of proxy wars in the Middle East and elsewhere made it virtually impossible for the United Nations to take any strong action. Even though unanimity was not required, the presence of the veto had the same effect, and the United Nations took little strong action in the area of peace and security.

For many of the same reasons as in the League of Nations, the U.N. attempt to develop a better mechanism for carrying out collective security operations was also a failure. Earmarking troops for U.N. service may have been a good idea, but it depended on successfully negotiating the initial agreements to provide those forces. Unfortunately, Cold War disagreements prevented states from ever coming to resolution on that matter, destroying what little advantage might have been achieved. Furthermore, the Military Staff Committee never lived up to expectations. With no operations to supervise, and no troops readily available in any case, it quickly became moribund, and the United Nations found itself squarely back where the League of Nations had ended, with neither the will nor the mechanisms to launch enforcement actions.[40] Before the United Nations turned to peace-keeping, however, it performed its first collective security operation in Korea.

When the North Korean army invaded South Korea in 1950, U.N. action was swift and largely consistent with the tenets of collective security. Nevertheless, the Korean situation represented an anomaly of circumstances that was not to be repeated until perhaps the operation to liberate Kuwait. First, the North Korean attack left little doubt about the identity of the aggressor and the threat to international peace; it might thus be regarded as an unambiguous case. Second, the Security Council's resolution endorsing a call for states to provide aid to South Korea passed quickly because the Soviet Union was at the time boycotting the Security Council over the China-Taiwan membership issue. Had the Soviets been present, it is unlikely the measure would have passed. Nevertheless, the United States had already agreed to provide assistance to South Korea.

It might seem at first glance that the Korean situation would establish an important precedent for collective security actions. Were this the case, the strategy of peacekeeping might never have emerged. Instead, the Korean intervention was almost a one-shot wonder. In subsequent conflicts, the aggressor was not so clearly evident, as in the 1967 Middle East war. Israel took the first military actions, but only in response to the mobilization of Arab forces. Should Israel be considered the aggressor because it fired first, or should the Arabs states be held responsible because they were preparing an imminent attack?[41] The problem becomes even more complex when dealing with internal conflicts in which the United Nations might be forced to defend a rather obnoxious status quo, such as South Africa. In addition, the Soviet absence from the Council, which facilitated the passage of the initial resolutions, has not been repeated; all the major powers have been careful to leave at least one representative even during a symbolic walkout.

Two other characteristics of the Korean operation also revealed the weakness of the U.N. collective security effort. First, much of the operation was authorized under a "Uniting for Peace" resolution in the General Assembly.[42] The Soviets' return to the Security Council blocked further action. Going through the General Assembly was an end run to permit the United Nations to take action. Yet the expansion of the General Assembly membership and the reluctance to repeat this exercise prevented that organ from ever again authorizing enforcement action as a solution to Security Council stalemate.[43] Nevertheless, the technique of going to the General Assembly to avoid a Security Council veto would later be resurrected to create the first true peacekeeping operation.

The second aspect of the U.N. operation in Korea that revealed U.N. weakness was that the action can be better understood as a U.S. operation approved by the United Nations. Only one-third of U.N. members contributed forces to the Korean effort. The United States provided more than half of the ground troops and almost all of the air and naval support. The commander was an American who took orders from Washington rather than from the U.N. secretary-general or any U.N. organs. In that sense, and much like many League of Nations actions, Korea was not a truly international operation.

The Iraqi invasion of Kuwait again provided an unambiguous case of aggression, and the United Nations, relatively unencumbered by Cold War animosities, authorized member states to use all means necessary to liberate Kuwait.[44] Despite the analogies commonly made at the time to the Vietnam War and the Munich appeasement, the closest parallel is with the Korean War. Beyond easily identifying the aggressor and the absence (here political rather than physical) of the Soviet Union as a significant player, the most obvious commonality was the U.S. leadership in the military operation. Sanctions and the use of military force were authorized at the behest of the United States, and primarily U.S. personnel, under the direction of the U.S. president, carried out the internationally approved mission.

After little more than a decade of existence, the United Nations found itself stalled by many of the same forces that had crippled the League of Nations. Disagreements among the major powers and the lack of appropriate mechanisms once again made collective security an unrealized dream. Nevertheless, peacekeeping operations developed quickly out of the precedents set by the failure of collective security and the success of early U.N. peace observation missions.

U.N. Peace Observation

The United Nations continued the tradition of peace observation that had begun under the League of Nations.[45] As collective security proved unworkable, these missions provided the new organization with experience in conflict intervention and, in a few instances, offered guidelines that would be adopted under peacekeeping.

Civil instability in Greece after World War II provided the first opportunity for peace observation.[46] In line with League experience, a U.N. fact-

finding mission was dispatched. Yet because Greek Communists were involved in the civil unrest, the conflict became part of the emerging Cold
War at the international level. Because of the Soviet veto in the Security
Council, the General Assembly had to take the lead and set up an observation force, with posts at the Greek borders with Albania, Yugoslavia,
and Bulgaria. The force did not maintain continuous supervision of the
border areas, as would a peacekeeping force, but did make frequent inspections to discourage the supply of rebel troops from abroad. The mission
was largely a success in that Greece was stabilized, but there were various
complaints, especially concerning the Albanian border and the covert supply of guerrilla forces. Nevertheless, this mission demonstrated that peace
observation could function (1) in a Cold War dispute and (2) when stationed
only on one side of the border.

The first U.N. attempt at truce supervision was in assisting Indonesian
independence from the Netherlands.[47] Observers were placed at the disposal of the "good offices" commission that was trying to negotiate a
peaceful withdrawal of Dutch forces from Indonesia. That peace observation
operation's main purpose was to provide a calm atmosphere under which
mediation efforts might succeed, one of the primary goals of U.N. peacekeeping operations today. Having secured an agreement for the independence of Indonesia, the observers later monitored the demobilization
and withdrawal of Dutch forces, another function peacekeeping operations
would later acquire.

Despite the precedent-setting value of the operation, there were several
problems. First, the members were not from neutral countries, raising
partisan suspicions about the force. In fairness, however, few countries in
the world in the late 1940s were nonaligned and disinterested. This would
have to wait until decolonization expanded membership in the international
system and the Non-Aligned Movement altered its political direction. Second, the status of the observers was not clearly defined. Even the observers
were unsure whether they acted as private individuals, as representatives
of their native states, or as international servants. Third, the force had no
independent logistical support but had to rely on the disputing parties for
transportation. Although observation missions always rely on the cooperation of the protagonists, this kind of reliance could have jeopardized
the ability of the observers to perform their basic duties, a mistake that
future U.N. actions would not repeat. Fourth, the observers had no direct
means to prevent hostilities—they were unarmed and did not act as an
interposition force. Ill-defined demarcation lines and military actions by

the Dutch made this inadequacy glaringly apparent. Overall, perhaps be-cause of a lack of experience in these matters, the United Nations had many difficulties with this operation.

Following the 1948 war in the Middle East, the U.N. Truce Supervision Organization (UNTSO) was charged with observing the truce and its lim-itations on the movement of troops and material.[48] Although this type of activity seems to resemble later peacekeeping operations in the region, this initial impression is misleading. The observation mission had only a small number of personnel (less than six hundred) and dealt mostly with re-sponding to complaints from the parties. Various hostile incidents followed its initial deployment in 1948 and later the breakdown of order in the region during the Suez Crisis. UNTSO also had difficulties because of its vague mandate, the ill-defined boundaries between Jordan and Israel, and the large number of refugees moving through the region.[49]

The United Nations also sent an observer mission a few years after World War II to another trouble spot, one that would endure as long as has the Middle East. In conjunction with a fact-finding and mediation mission that achieved a cease-fire in 1949, a U.N. team was dispatched to Kashmir in the center of the Indo-Pakistani conflict and stationed with regular Indian and Pakistani troops.[50] The observer force has investigated complaints, provided information on troop movements and actions, and helped local authorities to maintain order. This mission remains in place today, although India has scaled back its cooperation with the force and has tried to ignore its presence; the observer force no longer serves as an important conduit for resolving differences over Kashmir.

The failure of collective security demonstrated the limitations of the United Nations in dealing with threats to international peace and security. The early U.N. peace observation missions were an attempt to fill the void left by collective security. The mixed record of peace observation and the new challenge of the Suez Crisis led the organization to seek a new strategy. It was in that 1956 crisis that peacekeeping as we know it today was born.

UNEF I and the Birth of the Peacekeeping Strategy

The first true peacekeeping operation came about because peace obser-vation, in the form of UNTSO, could not meet the challenges of the Suez Crisis, and there was not sufficient political consensus for a collective se-curity action. Because of the failure of diplomatic efforts, the Arab-Israeli conflict continued, as did the presence of UNTSO. Order began to break down as tensions built in the early 1950s, with numerous clashes between

Israel and the Arab states. In August 1955, there was a serious engagement of Israeli and Egyptian troops in the Gaza Strip. Three months later, Israel attacked Syrian positions near the border of the two countries. With the risk of full-scale war apparent, the Security Council authorized the U.N. secretary-general, Dag Hammarskjöld, to investigate the situation; the hope was that his efforts would lead to tension reduction and perhaps would generate some new ideas on how the international community might defuse the escalating violence. In particular, Hammarskjöld sought to find some way of supplementing the efforts of UNTSO. His mission was a temporary success, as a cease-fire was arranged between Israel and Egypt.

When the situation began to deteriorate rapidly, the UNTSO had neither the mandate nor the means to stop or even diminish the military conflict. One problem is that the United Nations largely conceived of itself as having a limited role in the conflict. Hammarskjöld compared the United Nations to a good nurse (instead of a surgeon) working with a sick patient.[51] A good nurse is most useful in monitoring a patient, implementing the treatment prescribed by a doctor, and handling minor emergencies in the health of the patient. A nurse is not always trained to deal with major emergencies or with situations that require delicate medical operations. Carrying the analogy to U.N. activities, that organization saw itself as useful only to supervise cease-fires or implement policies agreed upon by the disputants; U.N. initiative, innovation, and autonomy were limited. Peace observation, largely consistent with this nurselike role, was ineffective in promoting the resolution of the Arab-Israeli conflict and certainly proved inadequate to deal with the Suez Crisis in the latter half of 1956. That crisis prompted a fundamental change in thinking about the U.N. role in and mechanisms for dealing with active threats to international peace and security.

In June 1956, the British handed over control of the Suez Canal to Egypt. A little more than a month later, on July 26, President Nasser nationalized the canal, setting off the Suez Crisis.[52] U.N. and other diplomatic efforts failed to resolve differences between Israel, Egypt, Britain, and France. The Security Council was paralyzed as the Soviet Union vetoed what some might regard as a compromise resolution and others as pro-Western.[53] Israel invaded Egypt on October 29, setting off the second Arab-Israeli war in a decade. One day later, Britain and France issued an ultimatum to Egypt and Israel demanding that forces be moved away from the canal and that British and French troops fill the void to ensure free passage. Egypt rejected this ultimatum. On the last day of October Britain and France vetoed a Security Council resolution that asked all parties to refrain from the use of military force, again demonstrating the weakness of the Security Council and collective action.[54] British and French air strikes against Cairo and the area surrounding the Suez Canal followed shortly.

The United Nations was up against dilemmas that made a business-as-usual approach impossible. First, any meaningful action had to occur outside the confines of the Security Council. Britain and France would veto any action they deemed inimical to their interests. On the other hand, the Soviet Union would cast a negative vote when presented with a proposal that threatened the interests of Egypt. The United States, caught in the middle, might align itself with either side depending on the proposed action. Second, a peace observation force was not a viable option. UNTSO was already in the region and had failed to deter the calamity. Furthermore, a small number of unarmed personnel would be unable to act as a buffer once the various military forces were separated.

The first thought under these conditions was to invoke a precedent allegedly established by the Korean operation, an example still fresh in the mind of many U.N. members. In this conception, the General Assembly would authorize Britain and France to lead an operation in pursuit of keeping the canal open. Yet this was unrealistic, as some states condemned British and French actions in the region. Many U.N. members saw the two fading colonial powers as the aggressors rather than as the guardians of international peace and security. Thus, there was unlikely to be any collective security operation, even one approved outside the Security Council.

The General Assembly faced the circumstances that peace observation was inadequate to the task, but collective enforcement was politically impossible. Furthermore, Britain and France insisted on some sort of international police force before they withdrew their troops. Addressing this problem, the General Assembly passed Resolution 997, which called for a cease-fire, withdrawal of forces, and reopening of the Suez Canal.[55] How to facilitate these goals was still unresolved in the minds of U.N. diplomats and Secretary-General Hammarskjöld. On November 4, 1956, the General Assembly passed the seminal Resolution 998, which authorized the secretary-general to set up a U.N. force to be dispatched to the region.[56] Although some heralded this resolution as the beginning of peacekeeping, the peacekeeping strategy evolved as a consequence of it rather than being elucidated by it. First, the resolution did not make clear what kind of force was envisioned, spelling out neither a fully articulated strategy nor guidelines for its operation. Second, support for the force was fragile. Although none of the member states opposed the resolution, nineteen of the seventy-six voting members abstained. The support of those countries was contingent upon the force's makeup and its mission.

Because of the wide latitude given the secretary-general, it was largely he who defined what this new strategy called peacekeeping would involve. Yet one should not underestimate the contribution of the Canadian foreign minister, Lester Pearson, who developed many of the ideas behind U.N. peacekeeping and designed the framework adopted for the peacekeeping force. What made the UNEF I deployed on November 15, 1956, different was not so much that all its components were new, but that the combination of the components was unprecedented.[57] First, UNEF I was under the direction of the secretary-general and under the field command of a neutral officer appointed by the U.N. executive head. This was a significant step forward from any previous peace observation missions in which units were directed by their own national commanders. In this sense, the troops were truly international servants, even enjoying a form of diplomatic immunity from local law. Second, UNEF I troops did not include any force contributions from the major powers, a strategy used in a few observation missions in the past that now became a guiding principle for peacekeeping operations.

Third, UNEF I was designed to be a strictly neutral force in action and purpose, in addition to troop composition. The force was not designed to affect the military balance in the area or to favor one side or the other in its activities. Finally, and perhaps most importantly, UNEF I acted as an interposition force between the protagonists. This represented a qualitative difference from any peace observation forces before, which had neither the personnel nor the mission to serve as a physical barrier between hostile parties. Various aspects of prior observation missions combined with new principles to form a new strategy of peacekeeping.

Specifically, UNEF I was charged with monitoring the cease-fire between forces and supervising the withdrawal of these forces from the area. It later acted as a buffer (an insurance policy) against the future engagement of Arab and Israeli forces. Importantly, its mission was limited to these functions. It played no role in reopening the canal or in the delicate negotiations that followed concerning the management of the canal, in contrast to the fact-finding and conciliation functions often tied to peace observation.

UNEF I, which remained in the Middle East for almost eleven years, is important not only because it was the first peacekeeping operation, but because its mode of operation became the model for almost all future efforts at peacekeeping.

Plan of the Book

Having provided the conceptual and historical background to peace-keeping operations, in the remainder of the book I am concerned with assessing their utility and evaluating alternatives to their traditional modes of operation. In chapter 2 I identify the criteria under which the success of peacekeeping operations are evaluated. I also include the criteria for the selection of cases that form the basis for discussion in the rest of the book. Chapter 2 concludes with a historical description of the cases studied.

I devote chapter 3 to determining the conditions under which peace-keeping operations are most successful. I draw from previous works about peacekeeping the relevant factors thought to influence success or failure, then assess the impact of those factors on the cases under study; I conclude the chapter by drawing generalizations about the circumstances most con-ducive to successful application of the peacekeeping strategy. In chapter 4 I look primarily at the role of peacekeeping operations in resolving the underlying sources of conflict in a dispute. In particular, I identify draw-backs of peacekeeping and suggest the interrelationship between peace-keeping operations and mediation efforts.

In the next two chapters I propose alternatives to the traditional form and mission of peacekeeping operations. Institutional alternatives in chap-ter 5 include a permanent U.N. peacekeeping force as well as peacekeeping operations undertaken by multinational forces or regional organizations. In chapter 6, functional alternatives to peacekeeping missions include elec-tion supervision, drug interdiction, and arms control verification. In chapter 7 I summarize the book's findings and discuss the role of peacekeeping operations in meeting future challenges to international peace and security.

Chapter **II**

Cases of International Peacekeeping

Before considering peacekeeping cases in detail, criteria by which to evaluate their success or failure need to be identified. This foundation helps clarify the logic behind the sample of peacekeeping cases selected for further study. A description of the history of each case is followed by an evaluation of its success or failure, based on the criteria established.

Success in Peacekeeping Operations

The volumes written on peacekeeping operations devote little systematic attention to what constitutes a successful mission. This is not to say that practitioners and analysts are unconcerned with the success of the mission. Rather, they generally define success in terms of the fulfillment of the operation's mandate. There are at least two problems with this approach. First, the mandates given operations are frequently vague, and there is much room for debate on the scope and detail of the operation's mission; this alone makes it difficult to assess whether the designs of the mandate have been achieved. Second, such an approach also ignores the common purposes peacekeeping operations share regardless of mandate.[1] With little basis for comparison across operations, the capacity for generalization is limited.

Analysts most often assume that successful operations are obvious, even though specific criteria for success go unstated. It is thus clear to many that the U.N. Interim Force in Lebanon (UNIFIL) has had serious problems and that the recent U.N. Transition Assistance Group (UNTAG) operation in Namibia was a success. This reliance on face validity runs into difficulties when the alleged success is less than obvious or subject to considerable disagreement, as in the operation in the Congo, ONUC. In seeking generalizations from systematic and replicable criteria, two primary standards with several operational indicators of success are limitation of armed conflict and conflict resolution.

Limitation of Armed Conflict

It seems logical that a strategy labeled "peacekeeping" should be judged on its ability to keep the peace. Regardless of other missions outlined in their mandates, all peacekeeping operations are charged with limiting hostile actions by the protagonists. Thus the first criterion for judging the success of peacekeeping operations is their ability to deter or prevent violent conflict in the area of deployment.[2]

A general problem of causality arises in assessing the success of peacekeeping operations. Can one really attribute violent incidents in an area to the failure of a peacekeeping operation? Might not the kind of the dispute itself and the particular configuration of actors present make the likelihood of violence high under any conditions? The best-designed and best-implemented peacekeeping operation is going to run into problems under those circumstances. We expect that peacekeeping operations are inappropriate mechanisms for some types of conflicts. Violence during the operation's deployment may result not from some flaw in the operation but from a misapplication of the peacekeeping strategy.

For the purpose of this analysis, I do not distinguish violence directly attributable to the shortcomings of the peacekeeping operation itself from that resulting from other causes. In this sense, I am measuring peacekeeping operations on the achievement of the intended outcome. There are several reasons for this approach. First, it would be nearly impossible to assign or parcel out responsibility for armed conflict to different factors in a comparative case study with limited observations and variation. Second, it is assumed that outcomes are the only relevant concern for international decision makers. A smoothly operating peacekeeping operation is little better than a poorly organized one if the respective protagonists renew warfare. Finally, one of the purposes of this book is to identify the conditions under which peacekeeping is successful, only some of which relate to the organization of the operation itself; others relate to the type of conflict and the actors involved. In this way, the outcome is the most important barometer for success, as the causes of success and failure will be many. Decision makers do not look at peacekeeping operations in a vacuum. They look at the context of the operation as well as the operation itself in making the decision to employ the peacekeeping strategy. Thus, in order to enhance the theoretical and policy-relevant conclusions, I evaluate peacekeeping operations on their ability to deter or prevent violence and become concerned with specific responsibility for that success or failure only when we look more closely at the factors of mission characteristics, authorization, and context outlined in chapter 3.

Given that the limitation of armed conflict is one criterion of the success of peacekeeping operations, the next question is how an operation achieves this outcome. The conceptual characteristics of peacekeeping operations (see chapter 1) indicate that they do not stop violence as a police force or army might; peacekeeping forces have neither the equipment nor the mission to do so. Rather, peacekeeping forces rely on several different means to inhibit armed conflict. The first is their moral or symbolic value as an international force representing the world community's desire for peace. Any protagonist choosing to renew hostilities will bear the costs of international disapproval and perhaps sanctions. Second, as an interposition force the troops do more than force a hostile party to go through the peacekeeping force in an attack. By separating all sides in a dispute, the peacekeeping force is able to prevent accidental engagements near border areas or minor disputes that stem from physical proximity, which could escalate to full-scale war. Incidents at the Chinese-Vietnamese border in the late 1970s might not have occurred, much less escalated, had a peacekeeping force been deployed at the border. The component of the operation that involves the reconciliation of claims and complaints adds to this function. Third, through patrols in the area of deployment, the peacekeeping force can detain violators of the cease-fire (e.g., those who might be running weapons into the area), assuming the violation is small, and prevent incidents that could escalate to war. Furthermore, patrols are part of confidence building on each side, suggesting by their presence that the protagonists have less to fear from a surprise attack; they therefore are less driven by the preemptive urge themselves.

Having identified a specific conceptual criterion for success, the next step is to be equally systematic in identifying replicable indicators for that criterion. As noted earlier, there has been a tendency to rely on vague notions of face validity for assessing the success of peacekeeping operations. There are several degrees of military conflict, some more serious and bloody than others, and therefore one might conceive of several levels of success for peacekeeping operations. First, one would hope that a peacekeeping deployment would inhibit full-scale war. The Correlates of War Project defines war as an armed engagement between opposing sides that results in 1,000 or more battle-related deaths.[3] Such a definition yields a list of conflicts consistent with most historians' conceptions of war. Thus, one looks to see if civil, interstate, or internalized civil war begins or resumes during the deployment of the peacekeeping force. If war does occur, one also looks to the time involved between the deployment of peacekeeping forces and the outbreak of war. Even if peacekeeping operations ultimately fail, they may at least claim some credit for delaying the bloodshed; this may be a modest achievement when they are placed between states that have a recurring pattern of warfare.

People die and the peace process is jeopardized even if the carnage does not meet the threshold for war. Peacekeeping forces should also be able to deter or prevent crises and other incidents that have a strong likelihood of escalating to war. Thus one also looks to acts of violence that are short of war. Here the focus is on the occurrence of "militarized disputes" between the protagonists in the conflict. Militarized disputes are actions in which a state has threatened, displayed, or used military force short of war. These actions must be explicit, overt, nonaccidental, and government sanctioned. The occurrence of a militarized dispute between the protagonists would indicate that peacekeeping operations had failed to prevent the states involved from nearing the brink of war.[4]

Because militarized disputes are government-approved state actions, armed conflicts such as terrorist attacks, unsanctioned military actions, and military activity in a civil war do not fall in the category of militarized disputes. Two other indicators detect those relevant incidents. U.N. peacekeeping operations sometimes report "shooting incidents" and other hostile activity that occurs during their deployment. The frequency of these incidents may suggest how successful the peacekeeping operation is in limiting armed conflict. Similarly, the number of fatalities experienced by the peacekeeping troops might indicate how much of that conflict was directed at or through the operation. As some peacekeeping troops die on routine patrol from accidents and other causes unrelated to military action, peacekeeping force fatalities must be accepted as an indicator with some reservation.

In summary, one may judge the success of peacekeeping troops by their ability to prevent the onset or renewal of warfare, as well as to limit the death and destruction of violent incidents short of war in their area of deployment. They accomplish this by acting as a buffer between protagonists, which lessens the likelihood of direct engagement and builds confidence among the opposing sides that a preemptive attack is not imminent.

Conflict Resolution

Although the limitation of armed conflict is certainly peacekeeping's most important function, the strategy's intention is broader. Peace is more than the negative denotation "the absence of war." At one extreme, peace signifies the elimination of all conflict between the parties. Given the level of conflict that exists when a peacekeeping operation is deployed, some means of dispute resolution following a halt to armed conflict must be found. Peacekeeping is designed to assist in this process of reconciliation. Thus a second criterion on which to judge the success of peacekeeping is its ability to facilitate the resolution of the disagreements underlying the conflict.[5]

Peacekeeping is designed to provide a fruitful environment for negotiations between warring parties. Parties engaged in military conflict are thought to be less likely to talk with their enemy, much less offer meaningful concessions at the bargaining table. An exception may be a "victor's peace" imposed on the losing side; yet these often provide no lasting end to the conflict. Peacekeeping relies on the hope that the absence of military combat will allow enmities to dissipate enough for negotiations to take place. Indeed, peacekeeping is an important first step in cooperation; generally, both sides must agree to accept peacekeeping and, in the case of the host states, accept troops on their soil as a means of limiting the conflict.

Once there is acceptance of the peacekeeping option, each side may be open to conciliation or mediation efforts because of the spillover of cooperation from that initial agreement. The hope is that the initial agreement will lead to an echo effect of mutually reinforcing, reciprocal, and conciliatory actions, cooperation at one point in time will increase the likelihood of cooperation in subsequent interactions between the same parties; of course, the echo effect could just as easily reinforce noncooperative behavior, should that pattern emerge between the parties.[6] A valuable cooling-off period might also follow the introduction of peacekeeping troops and the beginning of conciliatory efforts.[7]

By providing some assurance that the cease-fire will continue, peacekeeping operations also allow negotiators to concentrate on the matters at hand without immediate cause to worry that an opponent is acquiring a tactical advantage during the talks. The atmosphere for negotiation is not further poisoned by the renewal of fighting. This ideal stands in contrast to peace talks between the United States and North Vietnam during the late 1960s and early 1970s; the ongoing Vietnam War fouled the negotiating environment, and the cease-fires were short-lived. A stable peace proved illusory, despite the parties finally achieving some agreement.

This second criterion is not wholly separate from the first standard of assessing success. One might think of the limitation of armed conflict as a necessary but not sufficient condition for conflict resolution. If there is continuous violence, the parties will be unlikely to negotiate with an opponent whom they believe is acting in bad faith. Negotiations may break off over controversies occurring on the field of battle. Thus one may anticipate that a peacekeeping operation that fails in its mission of limiting armed conflict will be doomed in its efforts at conflict resolution. The achievement of conflict limitation, however, is no assurance that the conflict will be resolved. The protagonists may be content with the status quo or deterred from resuming armed hostilities and remain unwilling to make significant concessions or even to enter into negotiations. In those cases a protracted stalemate occurs, and the peacekeeping operation can be judged only partly successful.

The same difficulty of attributing success or failure to peacekeeping operations solely with respect to limiting armed conflict arises here, but the inferential leap is considerably longer. Although peacekeeping forces have a direct role in lessening the likelihood of renewed violence, they only provide the context for reconciliation and may not be involved in the actual peace process. Ensuring the proper environment may be important, but other efforts at mediation, negotiations, and conciliation seem to have more to do with the ultimate success than a stable context. Furthermore, reconciling the competing preferences of the disputants may be impossible, no matter how well intended or executed the peace efforts. Yet for the moment we look to the outcome of the conflict—resolution, stalemate, or renewed conflict—to evaluate the effectiveness of peacekeeping operations.

Many of the peace observation missions reviewed in chapter 1 included efforts to resolve the conflict in addition to their observation functions. Most commonly, the observers were part of a fact-finding mission that would make recommendations to the parties and the League of Nations Council on how to resolve the conflict. Peacekeeping operations under the United Nations generally have not adopted this mode of operation. The deployment of peacekeeping forces has often remained separate from any efforts at resolving the dispute. Yet the same institution, the United Nations, has frequently made parallel efforts to find a permanent solution to the conflict. Nevertheless, one must note when evaluating peacekeeping operations according to their ability to resolve disputes that most do not include conflict resolution strategies.

The identification of conflict resolution indicators would seem to be easy at first glance. The most obvious indicator that the disputants have made peace with each other is a formal agreement. One would hope that under the context created by the peacekeeping forces, the protagonists would be able to compromise; the end product might be a treaty that reflects that agreement. Still, there are several dangers with relying exclusively on the presence of formal agreements as an indicator of conflict resolution. One is the risk of missing other evidences of reconciliation. Conflicts not resolved through detailed legal instruments may be resolved by an informal understanding between the parties or may dissipate slowly over time as the bases of dispute wither away. One looking only for a formal peace agreement will miss these processes. On the other hand, treaties are not necessarily a guarantee of long-term conflict resolution. "Victor's peace" agreements, for example, do not represent the willingness of the losing state to accept the conditions of settlement, other than the cessation of hostilities that it is losing. Some evidence suggests that even agreements made with the free will of the participants do not guarantee long-term peace: Goertz and Diehl found that treaties involving the exchange of territory were significant predictors of future conflict between the signatories.[8] It may be that if parties have to resort to legalism, there is not the underlying reservoir of trust that is essential to peace and stability in the long run.

Apart from formal agreements, two other indicators of conflict resolution relate to the withdrawal of peacekeeping forces. The first indicator concerns the timing of peacekeeping withdrawal. If peacekeeping forces contribute to conflict resolution, their presence in the area should ideally be brief. Peacekeeping operations are designed to be temporary measures. One reason for the short deployment authorization of peacekeeping forces (see chapter 1) is the expectation that the conflict can be resolved quickly. Thus, a successful peacekeeping operation is one that has a short duration (*ceteris paribus*). Conversely, peacekeeping operations that linger for years without prospects for withdrawal do not achieve the desired result of resolving the conflict. Their continued presence alone signifies that it is not safe to remove them; that is, that the likelihood of military conflict is still high.

Although the timing of peacekeeping withdrawal is a useful indicator, neither peacekeeping operations nor the authorizing body (e.g., the Security Council) can completely dictate when peacekeeping forces are withdrawn. Peacekeeping forces are deployed with the consent of the host state, which can be withdrawn at any time. If the host state asks peacekeeping forces to leave within a year of deployment and without a resolution of the conflict, they can hardly be considered successful, especially if the reason for the withdrawal request is to allow the host state to initiate military actions without inhibition.

Therefore, beyond the timing of the withdrawal of peacekeeping forces, one must also consider the conditions surrounding that withdrawal. At this stage, the assessment is more subjective. For peacekeeping operations to be judged successful, there must be a low chance of conflict escalation at the time of their withdrawal. An attack by the host state immediately following the peacekeeping withdrawal would be an example of a colossal failure. On the other hand, if the peacekeeping forces were withdrawn by the Security Council for financial or political reasons, the judgment is less clear. At the extreme, if the peacekeeping forces are removed because there is no longer a perceived need for them, then one might make a positive assessment of the mission.

In summary, the first criterion for the success of a given peacekeeping operation is its ability to limit armed conflict between the protagonists. The second is the peacekeeping operation's role in the resolution of the underlying dispute between those protagonists. The ideal peacekeeping operation is one that is able to prevent or deter fighting during its brief deployment, in the course of which the disputants reach an agreement and no longer need an interposition force.

Case Selection

One of my goals in this book is to identify empirical generalizations about peacekeeping operations and thereby draw policy-relevant guidelines for their future use. The conventional way to achieve this in the social sciences is to study previous operations and look for common patterns across cases. I have already noted the difficulty of attributing success or failure directly to a peacekeeping operation. A more serious problem for the research design is the sparse number of cases from which to draw generalizations and the relatively large number of variables to analyze.

Following the creation of UNEF I in 1956, there have been only ten peacekeeping operations according to the United Nations and the conceptual definition noted in the first chapter (see table 2.1), hardly a broad base from which to derive generalizations. (In contrast, those who study international conflict have all too many wars and uses of military force to study and compare.) The inherent risk in a small-N study with many variables is that conclusions may depend largely one or two deviant cases according to a particular variable. One can hardly be confident that the key factor in question will be repeated in the future, or more importantly, that the effect of that factor will be the same.

The problem of a small N/V ratio (number of cases/number of variables)

Table 2.1 U.N. Peacekeeping Operations, 1945–1992

Operation	Dates
United Nations Emergency Force–I (UNEF I)	1956–67
United Nations Operation in the Congo (ONUC)	1960–64
United Nations Security Force in West New Guinea (UNSF)	1962–63
United Nations Peacekeeping Force in Cyprus (UNFICYP)	1964–present
United Nations Emergency Force–II (UNEF II)	1973–79
United Nations Disengagement Observer Force (UNDOF)	1974–present
United Nations Interim Force in Lebanon (UNIFIL)	1978–present
United Nations Transition Assistance Group (UNTAG)	1989–90
United Nations Transnational Authority in Cambodia (UNTAC)	1992–present
United Nations Protection Force (UNPROFOR)	1992–present

is a common one in the field of comparative politics.[9] There, scholars often must compare a handful of states across a variety of dimensions. Several strategies exist for trying to alleviate the difficulties of studying only a few cases.[10] One strategy is to increase the number of cases in the study. This approach is more successful in studies that are able to draw a sample from a reasonably large population; in those instances, one can increase the sample size, look at more years of a state's experience, or interview more respondents, as the circumstances permit. In studying peacekeeping operations, the size of the population is only ten, and one cannot widen the time frame or identify more cases.

There are several other possibilities, however, for increasing the number of cases studied. One might change the unit of analysis from peacekeeping operations as a whole to peacekeeping years, looking at incidences of violence in a given year of a peacekeeping operation rather than over its whole life. The net result would be to increase the number of observations almost tenfold. Several problems, however, make this approach untenable. First, it becomes very difficult, if not impossible, to evaluate peacekeeping operations according to the second criterion — conflict resolution. The ability to achieve conflict resolution is something that must be considered for the mission as a whole and not on a year-by-year basis. One could not credibly say that failure to achieve conflict resolution in a given year makes the peacekeeping force unsuccessful during that time while it is successful in another year. It may be that the success in the given year was largely the product of negotiations under a conducive environment (facilitated by the peacekeeping operation) in the alleged year of failure.

Second, there is little variation in the characteristics of the operation and the conditions of its deployment year to year (i.e., the area of deployment, the mandate, etc.). Thus one could not attribute any variations in violence from year to year to those factors. It is clear that peacekeeping operations must be evaluated as whole and not according to an artificial means of increasing the number of cases for analysis.

One might also suggest increasing the number of cases by including peace observation missions in the domain for study. Yet the benefits here are small, and the costs are great. The United Nations has conducted only eleven observation missions through 1991, offering precious few additional cases for study.[11] On the negative side, observation missions differ considerably from peacekeeping operations. Peace observation missions assume different roles and are constituted differently (see chapter 1). The net effect is that they cannot properly be compared on the same dimensions as peacekeeping operations, and they are likely to be influenced by some different factors. Adding observation missions to the study thus seems to be counterproductive in the search for generalizations about peacekeeping.[12]

Unable to increase the number of cases, one is left with a comparative case study strategy, focusing on a small number of cases. Nevertheless, within these confines one may take two other steps to address the problem.[13] One is to limit the number of variables thought to be important, perhaps by combining them in some common configuration; I limit them to those identified by scholars and practitioners as relevant to the success of peacekeeping. I further aggregated them into three categories to facilitate more broadly drawn generalizations, rather than relying on slight variations on a single factor or single case deviations on that factor. More importantly, one may select cases to ensure both that the cases are comparable and that they vary according to the factors of interest. This strengthens the ability to draw generalizations because of the comparability and makes clear conclusions more likely because of the variability. It also has the effect, however, of reducing the number of cases slightly.

My evaluation of peacekeeping success and failure focuses on six operations: the U.N. Emergency Force, with operations after the Suez Crisis (UNEF I) and following the Yom Kippur War (UNEF II), the U.N. Operation in the Congo (ONUC), the U.N. Peacekeeping Force in Cyprus (UNFICYP), the U.N. Interim Force in Lebanon (UNIFIL), and the Multinational Force of U.S., British, French, and Italian troops stationed in Beirut (MNF).

A number of principles guided the selection of these six cases. On one level, they share similarities that facilitate meaningful comparisons. All can be considered traditional peacekeeping operations that involve the deployment of neutral interposition forces on the territory of the consenting state. They have also usually followed the agreement of an opponent to a cease-fire. Thus, we look only at those operations that meet the conceptual requirements of a peacekeeping force.

In addition, we look only at operations deployed prior to the resolution of the disputes between the parties. This is in line with the traditional application of the peacekeeping strategy (i.e., most peacekeeping operations have followed this model) and of course is suitable for evaluating those operations according to the second criterion of success noted earlier. Therefore, the U.N. Transition Assistance Group (UNTAG) that supervised elections in Namibia is temporarily excluded. That peacekeeping operation was deployed to facilitate the implementation of a peace agreement, rather than to provide the proper environment to negotiate that agreement. Also excluded is the U.N. Security Force in West New Guinea (UNSF). The role of the peacekeeping troops in this operation was to facilitate the transfer of administration of the territory from the Dutch to the Indonesians; this is another instance in which an agreement was already largely in place. The U.N. Disengagement Observer Force (UNDOF) patrolling the Golan Heights between Israel and Syria is also excluded so as not to overwhelm the analysis with the Arab-Israeli conflict. (The most recent peacekeeping operations in Cambodia and Yugoslavia have just begun at this writing and therefore cannot yet be evaluated.)

The sample has a number of features that make it suitable for drawing generalizations about peacekeeping operations. First, the six cases vary according to the factors thought to influence the success or failure of the peacekeeping strategy. Second, the sample permits a comparison of international intervention in two different contexts: civil and interstate conflict. The sample includes operations sent into areas wrecked by internal instability, as well as those concerned mainly with the separation of warring states; a few cases share some characteristics of both types. Some conclusions are then possible about whether peacekeeping is more appropriate to one type of conflict than the other. Third, the sample includes different operations within the same geographic area, the Middle East, involving many of the same protagonists. The environmental context is held constant to some extent, allowing the assessment of the effect of the differences in the operations. Two segments of the same operation (UNEF I and II) make for an almost perfect analysis of this kind. The diversity of the other cases allows us to see if the generalizations hold in other geographic areas.

Finally, to draw conclusions about peacekeeping operations that apply to the peacekeeping strategy in general meant including a non-U.N. operation in the sample, yet many of the regional efforts resembled occupying forces more than they did peacekeeping operations as defined here. Operations such as the Inter-American Peace Force (IAPF) in the Dominican Republic and the Syrian interventions in Lebanon seemed designed for preserving regional hegemony rather than from more altruistic motivations—the same might be said of India's intervention in Sri Lanka. Even neutral forces, such as the Economic Community of West African States (ECOWAS) operation sent to war-torn Liberia, performed largely enforcement actions.

The Multinational Force and Observers (MFO) deployed in the Sinai following the Israeli-Egyptian peace agreement was, of course, sent *after* some significant resolution of conflict, not before. The MNF, which in the second phase of its mission was dispatched as an interposition force between Israeli and various Lebanese factions prior to conflict resolution, is a suitable case for study. Thus we are able to judge in a preliminary fashion whether peacekeeping operations should be the exclusive domain of international organizations, in particular the United Nations, or whether multinational groupings might be just as effective.

With only six cases, there may be some question as to the generalizability of any conclusions. There is no guarantee that future instances of peacekeeping will necessarily resemble past operations; yet there is a tendency by the United Nations and other organizations to rely on past procedures and precedents in conducting activities. The small number of cases is an unavoidable limitation, given the infrequence of peacekeeping in world politics.

These caveats aside, one might still question generalizations drawn from a sample that has four of six cases associated with the Arab-Israeli conflict, a longstanding dispute that most people would regard as among the most intractable in the world. Yet I regard this argument as misguided for several reasons. First, even though all cases pitted Israel against its Arab neighbors, they are not identical conflicts. The UNEF operations involved Israel and Egypt in what was primarily an interstate and dyadic conflict; even though Syria and Jordan were relevant actors, the UNEF operations were confined to the Sinai area. In contrast, UNIFIL and MNF were enmeshed in internationalized civil wars with multiple actors. Even though in some sense all four cases involved the Arab-Israeli disputes, the conflicts thus revolved around different issues and actors and can be said to be part of different contexts. In addition, the four cases vary according to the relevant factors thought to influence the success or failure of peacekeeping operations. Although the Arab-Israeli conflict might seem intractable—peacekeeping operations may actually be deployed to only the most difficult circumstances—Israel and Egypt were able to sign a peace treaty after the deployment of UNEF II. Intractability is also not unique to these four cases, as evidenced by the problems in conflict resolution UNFICYP encountered. Finally, none of the conclusions drawn in this study come exclusively from the experience of the four Middle East cases; therefore, the cases do not in themselves overwhelm the conclusions. The results generally apply to the other cases of international peacekeeping, whether in the Middle East (e.g., UNDOF) or not (e.g., UNSF). In these ways, the sample of six cases yields generalizable results, subject to the caveats noted above.

U.N. Emergency Force–I

UNEF I, the first U.N. peacekeeping operation, was designed to defuse the Suez Crisis of 1956 (see chapter 1). UNEF I achieved its first two goals relatively quickly; the withdrawal of Israeli, British, and French forces from the region and the separation of forces took place without serious incident. Peacekeeping troops then faced what proved to be the long-range mission of monitoring the cease-fire between Egyptian and Israeli forces in the Sinai and the Gaza Strip.

The period from 1957 to the withdrawal of the force in 1967 was relatively quiet.[14] No major incidents, as there would be with ONUC and UNFICYP, threatened the operation of the force. There were many technical violations of the cease-fire agreement, however, especially by incursions of the Israeli air force into prohibited air space, yet these violations were minor and did not prompt any dramatic responses from the parties. Despite the relative calm during most of its deployment, UNEF I received serious warning signs outside the area of deployment beginning in 1964. The Palestine Liberation Organization (PLO) was created that year, and guerrilla raids against Israel from Jordan, Syria, and Lebanon began. The most serious led to Israeli air attacks in retaliation, culminating in the downing of six Syrian fighter planes in April 1967.

Despite the heightened tension, quiet reigned on the Egyptian-Israeli border. Yet, fearing war with Israel, Syria invoked its defense pact with Egypt and called for that state's assistance in the event of war. President Nasser of Egypt responded to this request and involved Egypt in the escalating dispute, hoping to reassert his country's leadership in the Arab world. He asked that the UNEF troops be withdrawn in May 1967. As the peacekeeping forces were stationed only on Egyptian soil and, in accordance with peacekeeping philosophy, remained only with the permission of the host government, the secretary-general of the United Nations, U Thant, complied with the request, ending the UNEF I operation. Shortly after that, of course, came the Six-Day War in which Israel launched a preemptive attack against united Arab forces near its borders.[15]

The Six-Day War provides fairly strong evidence that UNEF I was unable to stop serious armed conflict. Nevertheless, such a one-sided conclusion is probably misleading. First, the war occurred only after UNEF I was asked to withdraw, suggesting that the presence of the peacekeeping force exercised some restraint on President Nasser. Why else would he want it withdrawn, when he could have easily overrun UNEF I positions and gained the advantage of surprise? Second, the period of over ten years without war during UNEF I's occupation is the longest sustained period of peace in the Arab-Israeli conflict since 1945. UNEF I had the effect, for an extended period, of removing some of the pressure on Egypt from its allies to take action against Israel.[16] No other mechanism or proposal before 1956 or after 1967 has provided such stability. Thus, while the ultimate failure to deter war was evident (and that war has had dramatic consequences in the region), the peacekeeping operation did achieve some success for an extended period.

That conclusion is reflected in several indicators. There were few violent incidents in the deployment area, and the loss of life by UNEF I personnel was minimal. In contrast, many instances of PLO infiltration and Israeli retaliation occurred along the borders of other Arab states not supervised by U.N. peacekeeping forces. Similarly, there were two militarized disputes between Israel and Egypt during the pre-1967 term of deployment (1958 and 1960). This is a lower frequency than in earlier periods, and there were no fatalities. In contrast, there was almost one militarized dispute per year between Israel and her other neighbors during this time, and fatalities did occur. The record of UNEF I in limiting armed conflict is thus a good one, albeit marred by one significant exception.

The record of UNEF I on the second criterion is much less ambiguous. That the Six-Day War occurred, followed by another war in 1973 (not to mention continuing animosities between Israel and her neighbors), demonstrates that the underlying dispute was not solved by the time of the UNEF I departure. There were no significant negotiations and certainly no formal agreements. One might credibly argue that just before (and certainly after) the 1967 war the protagonists were farther from achieving a resolution than they had in 1956; the creation of the PLO, the emergence of Nasser as a Pan-Arab leader, and numerous terrorist incidents seemed to poison the stable environment for reconciliation provided by the peacekeeping force. In summary, UNEF I can be judged a relative success in limiting armed conflict, but a clear failure in resolving the conflict between the Arabs and the Israelis.

U.N. Emergency Force–II

The second segment of the U.N. Emergency Force, UNEF II, logically followed its predecessor in the environment of persisting disputes and intermittent wars in the Middle East. The 1967 Arab-Israeli war only seemed to make the disputes more intractable; Israel now held the West Bank and Gaza Strip, and the Arab states bore a deeper resentment toward their Jewish neighbor.

The six years between 1967 and 1973 were without war, except for a "war of attrition" involving numerous clashes between Israel and Egyptian forces. The period without a peacekeeping force separating the protagonists ended with a surprise attack by Egyptian and Syrian forces against Israeli positions on the Jewish holy day of Yom Kippur in October 1973.[17] The Arab forces made some striking initial gains, yet the resupply of Israeli forces by the United States bolstered Israel and allowed it to beat back the attack and then begin offensive actions, marching toward Egypt. Egypt then turned to its superpower patron, the Soviet Union, with an urgent plea for assistance. It quickly became clear that if the Soviets resupplied the Egyptians by air, a direct engagement of the Soviet and Israeli militaries might follow. The next, almost unthinkable step could have been direct Soviet and U.S. intervention—indeed, both superpowers had their forces on alert, albeit not at the highest stage of readiness.

Initial attempts by the Security Council to achieve a cease-fire had failed, but the prospects of an expansion and escalation of the war finally led all sides to agree to halt the fighting. Observers from the U.N. Truce Supervision Organization (UNTSO), already in the area, were sent to monitor the cease-fire as plans for UNEF II went forward. Drawing on UNTSO personnel and coordinating with that group, UNEF II came into being in late October, less than three weeks from the beginning of the war.[18] The operation had the initial responsibility for observing the cease-fire and ensuring that part of the Egyptian army trapped inside Israeli lines received adequate food. Furthermore, the peacekeeping force was to take over the checkpoints in the area from the Israeli military.

The preliminary, ad hoc arrangements proved successful in stabilizing the situation. In early 1974, regular procedures and force composition for UNEF II became final.[19] The next phase of the mission involved the disengagement of forces, with U.N. troops acting as a temporary buffer between Egyptian and Israeli military units. A further disengagement was negotiated in 1975, and a demilitarized zone patrolled by UNEF II soldiers went into effect. Although the process teetered on the verge of total breakdown several times, desperate diplomatic maneuvering by the U.S. president, Gerald Ford, and the secretary of state, Henry Kissinger, was able to break the deadlock and keep the process moving along incrementally.

UNEF II experienced no major incidents over the next few years, and once again the area endured a hostile peace. Yet unlike its predecessor, UNEF I, this operation would be withdrawn in a relatively short time and under conditions favorable to the resolution of the underlying conflict. The dramatic visit to Israel by the Egyptian president, Anwar Sadat, raised the possibility of lessening the chances for another Arab-Israeli war. This process culminated in the Camp David accords, normalizing relations between Israel and Egypt and returning to Egyptian control land seized during the previous two wars.

The Camp David accords and the peace treaty the following year represented the beginning of the end for UNEF II. That peacekeeping operation or another U.N. operation was supposed to supervise the implementation of the peace agreement, yet political wrangling ultimately led in July 1979 to UNEF II's mandate not being renewed. Sometime afterward, a non-U.N. force, the MFO, was deployed and remains in place.

UNEF II qualifies as a strong success according to both criteria for effectiveness. During the time of deployment, there was no war between Israel and Egypt (or any other Arab neighbor). Furthermore, the two countries experienced only one militarized dispute between them during that time. Even in that instance, the dispute concerned the disengagement of forces before UNEF II was fully operational and only UNTSO personnel were in place. In contrast, Israel and Syria confronted each other several times in the same period, despite the presence of peacekeeping forces on the Golan Heights. The loss of life during deployment was minimal for the protagonists. UNEF II troops experienced forty-seven deaths over the almost six years of deployment, with only five of these attributable to hostile fire. One can thus judge UNEF II a strong success in limiting armed conflict.

With respect to conflict resolution, UNEF II was also successful. Clearly, one cannot give direct credit to the peacekeeping operation for Anwar Sadat's dramatic diplomatic breakthrough or the Camp David process. Nevertheless, one might argue that without the calm environment provided by UNEF II, those initiatives would not have been possible. Virtually all indicators of success on this criterion are present. First, there was a formal agreement between the protagonists and a return of the disputed territory to Egypt. Second, the peacekeeping force was able to withdraw in a reasonable period of time (less than six years), at least relative to all other U.N. peacekeeping operations in the area. Finally, when the force was withdrawn, the chances for war between Israel and Egypt had been significantly reduced. Indeed, there has not been a war between the two states since, and relations are considerably better between Israel and Egypt than between any other Arab-Israeli dyad. Some of this credit must go to the MFO operation, but even without that force, the hostility between the two sides has shrunk so much that a war is unlikely in any event.

Although UNEF II did not resolve all conflict between the disputants, the operation limited armed conflict during its tenure, and that stability facilitated unprecedented progress toward conflict resolution in a difficult dispute.

U.N. Operation in the Congo

The U.N. Operation in the Congo (Opération des Nations Unies au Congo, or ONUC) traces its origins to the problems associated with granting independence to colonial territories before adequate government mechanisms are in place. The Congo received its official independence from Belgium on June 30, 1960, yet the country was split along tribal lines, and the removal of the colonial regime meant the disintegration of administrative order. Less than a week after independence, seemingly the only organization capable of holding the country together, the Congolese army, mutinied. The collapse of law and order led the Belgian government to deploy troops in order to protect Belgian nationals.[20] At the same time, the province of Katanga declared itself independent from the Congo, apparently with some support from Belgium. Perhaps not surprisingly, the Congolese government regarded the Belgian incursion as a violation of sovereignty, and there was genuine fear that the Belgians wished to reoccupy the country.

The Congolese prime minister, Patrice Lumumba, appealed for assistance to the United Nations, and on July 14 the Security Council called upon Belgium to withdraw its forces from the Congo. It also authorized the secretary-general to provide the Congolese government with such assistance as would be necessary to restore order until national troops could take over.[21] The United Nations organized ONUC and dispatched it to the capital city to help ensure the territorial integrity of the Congo, assist in restoring law and order, and supervise the withdrawal of Belgian forces. In the course of these duties, the force would patrol areas threatened by violence and protect Congolese political leaders. The force was to remain strictly neutral in its protection of life and property; it was not supposed to influence the outcome of any civil conflict or internal political struggle.

ONUC encountered some initial difficulties in restoring order in the region, but by July 23 Belgian troops had withdrawn from all areas except Katanga. The crisis then focused on that region. Authorized by the Security Council, ONUC troops were sent into the middle of the secessionist struggle.[22] The force assumed many of the security duties held by Belgian forces, who by now openly supported the rebellion. Although ONUC was charged with restoring law and order and facilitating the withdrawal of Belgian troops, it saw the secessionist movement as essentially a civil matter to be resolved by Katangan rebels and the Congo government. Had they resolved it quickly, U.N. forces might have withdrawn quickly and to the applause of the world community.

Prime Minister Lumumba wanted ONUC to cooperate with the Congolese forces to regain control of the rebel province. The United Nations refused, not wishing to take sides in the conflict. Lumumba, with Soviet aid, launched an ill-fated attack using the Congolese army to put down the rebellion. The president of the Congo, Joseph Kasavubu, opposed this action and dismissed Lumumba. Further events only complicated these actions. Lumumba declared that he dismissed Kasavubu, and the army chief of staff staged a coup against the person appointed to replace Lumumba. The turmoil in the Congo was not confined to Katanga. The whole country plunged into civil war.

The operation of ONUC was tied up in the chaotic politics of the Congo.[23] The Soviet Union backed Lumumba and criticized the way in which Secretary-General Hammarskjöld conducted the operation. The permanent members of the Security Council from the West backed Kasavubu. The stalemate emerging in the Security Council moved most of the deliberations to the General Assembly. Nations battled in the United Nations over which government in the Congo to recognize, how to respond to Lumumba's subsequent arrest, and ultimately what action to take in response to Lumumba's death at the hands of his captors. It began to seem that the United Nations was powerless to stop the escalating violence.

Paradoxically, the death of Lumumba spurred the secretary-general to more aggressive actions. Hammarskjöld received approval from the Security Council in February 1961 to have ONUC intervene directly in the civil affairs of the Congo.[24] This mandate also included trying to reconvene the Congolese parliament. This was far more authority than had previously been granted peacekeeping operations and probably violated some basic principles of peacekeeping, including neutrality and not affecting the balance of power in the area. The move allowed the United Nations to use offensive military force as a last resort in order to prevent an all-out civil war. Hammarskjöld assured the council that the expanded mandate would not be used to impose any political solution or to accomplish any other ends. The United Nations also established a conciliation commission to find a way to make peace between the warring factions. Finally, ONUC succeeded in getting a cease-fire between the parties as well as an agreement on a new unified government for the country, which unfortunately only decreased the instability; Katanga was still in rebellion.

ONUC then made some largely unsuccessful efforts to expel mercenaries from Katanga and restore order. Complicating those efforts was the death of Dag Hammarskjöld in a plane crash on his way to meet President Tshombe of Katanga. The United Nations expanded the mandate of ONUC even further, authorizing ONUC to use all means necessary, including military force, to control Katanga.[25] ONUC launched offensive military actions in Katanga and seized most of the province. Shortly thereafter, Tshombe signed an agreement that, if ratified and implemented, would have ended the secession. It was late 1961, and it seemed that ONUC could return to its purely peacekeeping role and soon withdraw. Such optimism proved unfounded.

U.N. efforts at national reconciliation between Katanga and the central government bogged down in negotiations and the failure to implement various plans. Meanwhile, ONUC forces were under fire from Katangan forces. Rebel forces harassed ONUC by denying them access to certain areas, firing on their positions, and performing other hostile actions.[26] ONUC was forced to take military action again to secure full control of the Katangan capital. More than a year from the date of the agreement that was supposed to end the conflict, Tshombe signed a truce agreement to end the secession, and major conflict ended. ONUC supervised the situation for the next eighteen months, while the central government established its authority throughout the country, and finally withdrew in June 1964.

Unlike other peacekeeping operations, ONUC is something of a paradox of success in its operation. One might consider it largely a failure according to the criterion of limiting armed conflict yet judge it at least a partial success for helping resolve the civil conflict and reestablish the control of the central government.

ONUC largely failed to limit armed conflict in the area. The level of battle was sufficient to label it a full-scale civil war.[27] Rather than a series of crises or disputes, the fighting was virtually continuous for extended periods of time. The ONUC operation also was the bloodiest of the peacekeeping operations studied here. One hundred thousand Congolese died during the civil war, many during several massacres of rival groups.[28] The death toll was far lighter for Belgian forces and ONUC personnel, whose casualties were nonetheless significant. Katangan forces attacked and kidnapped ONUC personnel on several occasions. One might credibly say that things grew considerably worse after ONUC arrived, and a few years passed before there was real progress in stopping the fighting.

I noted earlier that limiting armed conflict might be a prerequisite for achieving final conflict resolution. The paradox in this case is that ONUC failed in the first task but nevertheless was able to make some headway in the second. On the positive side, there were tireless conciliation efforts by the United Nations to end the fighting, and several apparent agreements were reached. The United Nations was first able to facilitate a reconciliation of forces in the Congo, excluding the Katanga province. Negotiations also produced a withdrawal of foreign forces and mercenaries. Achieving peace in Katanga was more difficult, but, despite some false starts, the secessionists did sign an agreement for a cease-fire and reunification with the rest of the country. Furthermore, when ONUC finally withdrew in 1964, the prospects for the renewal of full-scale civil war had diminished considerably. Nevertheless, maintaining law and order was still a significant problem for a period thereafter.[29] ONUC did ultimately succeed in its specific mandates of restoring order in the country and supervising the withdrawal of foreign forces. According to two indicators then, one might judge ONUC as somewhat successful.

Several concerns might temper the determination of success in this instance, however. First, it is questionable whether one can attribute any success to the employment of the peacekeeping strategy. Upon its initial deployment, ONUC generally followed the precepts of the peacekeeping strategy—neutrality, self-defense, and so on. During that time, it experienced its most significant problems. Restoring order and ultimately quelling the rebellion came only after coercive measures involving the offensive use of military force by ONUC, hardly the kind of action envisioned under peacekeeping. Thus, one might say that ONUC as a peacekeeping force was a failure, but ONUC as a traditional military operation was more successful.

ONUC does not rate well by a second indicator of success, length of deployment. The ONUC operation was considerably shorter than several other peacekeeping operations. Nevertheless, its mission was more limited. One might presume that restoring civil order should take less time than negotiating a settlement to the Arab-Israeli conflict. Certainly, the operations dragged on longer than U.N. members and officials anticipated. That the mandate of ONUC had to be changed at several junctures suggests that its approach was inadequate and results were not in accordance (both in speed and substance) with initial expectations.

One is thus left with a mixed bag of conclusions regarding the effectiveness of ONUC. It was not successful in limiting violence, although it had some success in resolving conflict; the latter conclusion must be understood with the caveat that such success may not be the result of the peacekeeping strategy employed.

U.N. Peacekeeping Force in Cyprus

The crisis in Cyprus during the early 1960s in some ways resembled the challenges posed by the situation in the Congo. A newly independent country, here Cyprus, was having difficulties controlling all areas of the country, with the threat of partitioning the country a real one. Furthermore, the intervention of external states threatened to expand the conflict and the bloodshed. Yet the U.N. peacekeeping operation in Cyprus would have much different consequences than the one in the Congo.

The island of Cyprus had long experienced turmoil between the Greek and Turkish communities who shared the island.[30] Colonial rule under the British managed to keep the lid on the worst of that conflict, but tensions persisted nonetheless. Yet the decolonization movement touched Cyprus, and arrangements had to be made for the independence of the island. To head off future problems, Britain, Turkey, and Greece signed the London and Zurich agreements (1959) that laid out the constitution of the soon-to-be independent Cyprus. Provisions included power-sharing arrangements that prevailed between the Greek and Turkish communities, not unlike the arrangements in Lebanon for so many years. The hope was that this would maintain peace on the island for the foreseeable future.

The hope was short-lived. Disagreements between the Greek and Turkish residents over the administration of the island flared quickly. A Greek proposal to institute a majority-rule system of government, which would favor the Greeks who outnumbered the Turks by almost four to one, intensified the enmity. In December 1963, fighting broke out between the communities, and there was a threat that Greece and, in particular, Turkey would intervene.

After several months of political maneuvering, the United Nations finally authorized the creation of UNFICYP in March 1964.[31] The mandate of the operation was to prevent a recurrence of fighting, restore law and order in the area, and promote a return to normality on the island. The specific tasks included insuring freedom of movement between the ethnic communities and facilitating the evacuation and dismantling of fortified positions by Greek and Turkish Cypriots. UNFICYP forces also manned roadblocks for inspections, investigated incidents, and coordinated actions with the Cypriot police.[32]

The operation went well for UNFICYP during the initial deployment period; every aspect seemed to be fully operational and successful. Yet the peace was broken in August 1964 when fighting started in one sector and the Turkish air force was sent to the area. This crisis dissipated as both sides agreed to a cease-fire under the authority of the UNFICYP commander. A major incident occurred in 1967, and armed conflict returned. Again the United Nations not only succeeded in reestablishing a cease-fire but persuaded each side to withdraw its nonindigenous military personnel—soldiers and civilians from Greece and Turkey aiding each side.

Despite these crises, the first ten years of UNFICYP were relatively quiet, and the operation seemed successful in limiting armed conflict until 1974, when UNFICYP entered a new chapter in its existence.[33] The Cyprus government was the victim of a coup d'état in July of that year. Leaders of the coup wanted to join the island to Greece and requested assistance from that state. Meanwhile, Turkey did not intend to stand by and permit this outcome; the Turkish government was also alarmed by reports of human rights violations committed against Turkish Cypriots. Turkish forces invaded the island, occupying the northern portion of Cyprus.

A cease-fire prevented what could have been an internationalized civil war between the Cypriot communities, Greece, and Turkey. UNFICYP became responsible for patrolling the 180-kilometer demilitarized zone established between the Greek and Turkish forces.[34] Since that cease-fire, the situation has been mostly stable, with UNFICYP continuing its observation as well as performing humanitarian functions for the local population. There has been only one major incident in the last two decades, and fortunately this did not prompt a renewal of violence. In 1983, Turkish Cypriots declared their independence and established a separate republic in the northern area controlled by their forces. In 1994, UNFICYP marks its thirtieth year in existence, with little prospect of withdrawing anytime soon.

The record of UNFICYP is mixed. On the first criterion of limiting armed conflict, the peacekeeping operation has been mostly successful, with occasional dramatic failures. The Turkish invasion in 1974 is the only incident that qualifies as an interstate war, resulting in over one thousand fatalities. The only positive aspects of the incident were that Greek intervention was avoided and the warfare was not more extensive. Despite this brief war, Cyprus has avoided this most serious level of conflict at all other times during the deployment of the UNFICYP.

The record of success in limiting conflict short of war is also sporadic. Although there have been several militarized disputes between Turkey, Greece, and Cyprus prior to and after the 1974 invasion, there was little or no loss of life in these incidents. There have also been several conflicts between Greece and Turkey that were not directly over Cyprus, but problems on that island helped stimulate animosity between the two states; had those disputes escalated, the Cyprus question would almost certainly have been part of any war.

Internally, the situation in Cyprus has also ebbed and flowed, but at generally low levels of conflict. Most of the time, shooting incidents were infrequent, occurring at a rate of only a few per month. Since 1974, the situation has improved considerably. Yet at times of high tension, as in 1967, the number of incidents has increased dramatically, numbering over fifty per month. It is important to note that the 1983 declaration of independence by the Turkish community did not prompt any significant violent incidents. Furthermore, the 148 UNFICYP soldiers killed is a relatively small total, given the frequency of incidents and the length of deployment.[35]

Overall, except for the 1974 invasion, UNFICYP has been able to head off the most serious armed conflict, despite several disputes or incidents that might easily have escalated to war. Furthermore, the loss of life on all sides has generally been minimal. Most of the period after deployment, and particularly since 1974, the situation has been relatively calm. In these ways, UNFICYP is at least partly successful. Nevertheless, the peacekeeping operation has experienced a number of serious incidents and disputes, with sporadic and sometimes dramatic failures. One might argue that UNFICYP has not deterred the protagonists from using military force when they considered their interests threatened.

According to the second criterion of promoting conflict resolution, the record is considerably more gloomy. That the operation is still in existence after almost thirty years is, on the one hand, a testament to its perceived usefulness by the protagonists and the world community. It is also an indication that the conflict has not been resolved. Negotiations between the Greek and Turkish communities have seen little progress. The declaration of independence in 1983 is a strong sign that at least one side sees the division of the island as permanent. There have been no agreements resolving issues in dispute, other than those related to establishing cease-fire lines and providing access between different sectors of the island. In terms of conflict resolution, one may label UNFICYP a failure.

U.N. Interim Force in Lebanon

The U.N. Interim Force in Lebanon (UNIFIL) was deployed in response to a longstanding problem and remains in place today because that problem has not been solved. Southern Lebanon continues to be a battleground between Israeli forces, Palestinian units, and various Lebanese militias. A typical year throughout the first part of the 1970s saw persistent factional fighting in the area. In addition, Palestinian terrorists and others attacked Israeli targets, followed by Israeli retaliatory raids in southern Lebanon against Palestinian targets. Although this violence threatened international peace, there was little reaction from the world community apart from the establishment of a few UNTSO observation posts in Southern Lebanon. The United Nations is usually crisis driven and needs some dramatic incident to galvanize it into strong action.

The dramatic events necessary in this case began on March 11, 1978. Palestinian guerrillas operating from a base in southern Lebanon attacked a tourist bus in Israel, killing thirty-seven and wounding twice that many.

Several days later, the Israeli army crossed into Lebanon to "clean out" the terrorist bases. Israel quickly established a "security zone" of control in southern Lebanon. On March 19, the Security Council authorized the creation of UNIFIL.[36] The peacekeeping troops were charged with supervising the withdrawal of Israeli forces, restoring international peace and security, and assisting the Lebanese government in gaining effective control over the area.

UNIFIL ran into difficulties almost from the beginning.[37] The PLO did not support the operation and resisted turning over territory to U.N. control; UNIFIL troops, trying to establish a presence in certain areas, came under attack. Furthermore, it was unclear what the area of UNIFIL deployment was to be. The PLO argued against allowing the peacekeeping troops into zones they believed lay outside the agreement. The United Nations eventually relented on these disputes, preferring not to seize control of territory by military force.

UNIFIL had little better luck with Israel. Although the initial steps of Israel's withdrawal went smoothly, the final phase was to have serious repercussions. Instead of turning over the area closest to the Israel-Lebanon border to UNIFIL troops, Israel relinquished control to Christian forces headed by its ally Major Saad Haddad, a move that prevented UNIFIL from effectively limiting either Palestinian incursions or any future military invasion by Israel in response. The number of attacks against UNIFIL troops was comparable to the Congo experience, in which peacekeeping troops were actively engaged in a civil war.[38]

The presence of UNIFIL troops and a security zone occupied by allied Christian forces appeared to Israel to make little difference in halting attacks from the north. Consequently, in June 1982, Israel invaded Lebanon, slicing through UNIFIL positions and moving all the way to the edge of Beirut. After Israel pulled back, with the deployment of the MNF, UNIFIL resumed its mission of trying to prevent violence in southern Lebanon. Today Israel maintains an occupation force in the UNIFIL zones. There are often clashes between UNIFIL and Israeli troops as the latter try to seek out and punish Palestinian guerrillas. UNIFIL's role has become largely humanitarian, as it has little power to enforce peace.

Israel withdrew from much of the UNIFIL zone in 1985 but retained control of its "security zone" just north of its border. UNIFIL continued to experience attacks, and there were sporadic but serious violent incidents in the area. The situation remains much the same today, with little prospect that the situation will improve or that UNIFIL's mission will soon end.

UNIFIL is almost universally regarded as a failure in limiting armed conflict. The Lebanon war of 1982 was the most vivid failure of the mission. Yet even in the absence of war there have been numerous disputes between Israel and her neighbors over Lebanon. Furthermore, violent incidents involving subnational actors have been common. Sometimes the UNIFIL troops have been the targets of those actions—including kidnappings and direct attacks—with more than 170 peacekeeping soldiers losing their lives in the process.[39] There is perhaps no other peacekeeping mission that has failed so consistently to limit the armed conflict. Perhaps the only positive sign has been that violence in the areas fully controlled by UNIFIL has been less than in areas under partial occupation by one antagonist or another. In addition, UNIFIL has stopped thousands of Palestinian infiltration attempts, although it has been unable to stop perhaps at least as many more. Furthermore, it is apparently the view of many U.N. members and analysts that the situation would be even worse without UNIFIL; thus, despite all the problems, the UNIFIL mandate has been consistently renewed at regular intervals.[40]

UNIFIL's performance in conflict resolution is even more dismal. Israel's unilateral actions clearly indicated that it believed UNIFIL's presence made little difference in limiting armed conflict and promoting long-term stability. During UNIFIL's tenure there have been no significant agreements other than cease-fire and withdrawal agreements following military actions.[41] The length of the force's deployment is now well into its second decade; it is thus clear that conflict resolution has not been achieved. The level of violence in the area also demonstrates the hostility that lingers, and that is perhaps as strong as ever. At best, UNIFIL might decrease the number of violent incidents in the area, but the number that still occur is large. Yet regardless of whether peacekeeping troops are there or not, the southern Lebanon area remains one of the world's hot spots, and settlement of the conflict appears as elusive as ever, despite whatever stability might come from agreements between Lebanese factions and from Syrian intervention.

Multinational Force

The deployment of the Multinational Force (MNF) came about largely as a result of the failure of U.N. peacekeeping; the inability of UNIFIL to keep peace in southern Lebanon and the failure to authorize another U.N. operation led to a search for multinational alternatives. Problems began in the early 1980s when an already unstable Lebanese situation became worse. Syria moved SAM-6 missiles into the Bekaa Valley, prompting Israel to threaten a preventive strike if they were not removed. There were also continuing attacks from southern Lebanon against Israeli targets, despite an increase in the number of UNIFIL soldiers. By 1982 the prospects for another Mideast war between Israelis and Arabs were great, this time with Lebanon as the locus of battle.

The trigger for the war was the attempted assassination of the Israeli ambassador in London on June 3, 1982. One day later Israel retaliated with massive air strikes against Palestinian targets in Lebanon; the PLO responded by shelling Galilee. On June 6 the Israeli army poured across the border with the expressed aim of establishing a twenty-five-mile security zone north of the Israeli-Lebanese border. Israel also sought to limit future threats from Palestinian guerrillas and Syrian missiles. The Israeli army pushed quickly beyond the twenty-five-mile zone to the outskirts of Beirut, overwhelmingly defeating Palestinian and Syrian forces.

Because of U.S. diplomatic pressure and a hesitancy to engage in house-to-house fighting, Israel resisted invading West Beirut, where PLO forces were trapped. An agreement was reached whereby those forces would partially disarm and depart from Beirut under the protection of an international force. This might normally have been a U.N. force, but Israel would not accept that organization as the supervising agency; Israel's bad experience with UNIFIL and general alienation from the United Nations made it distrustful of U.N. guarantees. The MNF was put together with U.S., French, and Italian troops, who served as an interposition force between the Israelis and the PLO fighters and supervised the PLO's departure.[42] The evacuation generally proceeded without serious incident, and the first phase of MNF's mission was a success.

The MNF withdrew from Beirut, leaving the situation in the hands of the Lebanese army, yet on September 14 President Bashir Gemayel was assassinated. The next day the Israeli army moved into West Beirut positions in contravention of the earlier cease-fire agreement. Shortly thereafter, Israeli army officials permitted Christian militiamen to enter two nearby Palestinian refugee camps. A night of killing in those camps left over a thousand dead. The situation in Lebanon appeared to be veering out of control, with none of the local forces capable of maintaining order. The new government of Lebanon requested that the MNF be redeployed to maintain order. The MNF was back for a second tour of duty with the same three countries, now joined by Great Britain, contributing troops; this tour would have more dramatic consequences.

There were serious violent incidents in the area. Several times, the MNF forces came under fire and retaliated with high levels of force, including air strikes and bombardments from offshore ships. Factional fighting also intensified. In October 1983 the U.S. and French compounds of the MNF were victims of terrorist truck bombings. Popular support for the MNF plummeted in Lebanon and outside, and U.S. military action through its peacekeeping troops escalated. By the beginning of 1984, the Lebanese army was on the verge of collapse, and Moslem militiamen were moving to seize key positions in West Beirut. The British were the first to withdraw their peacekeeping contingent, and the Italians and Americans soon followed suit. The last to leave was the French force in March 1984.

The success of the MNF varied according to which phase of the operation one studies. Here we will regard both phases as if they were parts of one operation. The initial deployment, in a period of heightened tension, achieved the desired goal of the PLO's evacuation without major incident or bloodshed. The second deployment had a far different success quotient. Although interstate war was avoided, the civil war intensified during the MNF's second tour. Almost 350 peacekeeping troops were killed by hostile fire, along with countless numbers of the indigenous population, some the victims of bombardment by the MNF forces.[43] Every day, clashes between the multiple factions seemed to dot the Lebanese landscape. The second deployment of the MNF not only failed to limit armed conflict generally, its actions may even have intensified that conflict. Perhaps the only success the MNF could claim was in preventing further massacres, the original catalyst for the redeployment of the multinational force.

Both phases of the MNF deployment were unsuccessful in resolving the underlying conflict. The assassination, massacres, and troop movements following the first withdrawal of the force demonstrated that the MNF had not stabilized the situation. That the MNF had to be called upon for a second phase is tantamount to proof that conflict resolution was not achieved. The withdrawal of the second phase occurred in the context of a deteriorating situation, as much for the protection of the peacekeeping forces as for any other reason. There were no agreements resolving the conflict; the civil war continued, as did the Syrian and Israeli presence in the country. Except for a brief interlude, the MNF was a colossal failure.

Summary

The six peacekeeping operations under study here produced a mixed bag of results. With respect to limiting armed conflict, only UNEF II might be judged a strong success, although, except for the notable failure of 1967, its predecessor, UNEF I, monitored the longest period of peace in the Middle East since World War II. The Congo and Cyprus operations had varying records of performance, working well at some points but experiencing major difficulties at others. MNF and UNIFIL were both trapped in the Lebanese quagmire and failed to abate the violence there.

Peacekeeping operations were much less successful in promoting conflict resolution. UNEF II was the only operation able to stimulate a peaceful agreement between the protagonists. ONUC achieved some measure of long-term peacemaking, but at the cost of using military force rather than adhering to standard peacekeeping principles. The other operations either withdrew in the face of defeat (MNF and UNEF I) or persist today as testaments to the unresolved hostility in the regions (UNFICYP and UNIFIL).

Chapter **III**

Peacekeeping and the
Limitation of Armed Conflict

DECIDING which factors are critical to the success of peacekeeping operations is problematic. There are few signposts for guidance. One is initially drawn to some of the principles of peacekeeping strategy as factors that may make an operation more or less successful; in the case of neutrality, for example, it might be argued that MNF troops were not neutral ones and that this was responsible for the mission's failure. Nevertheless, it is probably a mistake to focus exclusively on the characteristics of the operation itself. Peacekeeeping operations cannot create all the conditions for their own success.[1] We must also pay attention to the context of the peacekeeping mission. A tourniquet properly applied to a severed leg can be very effective; the same treatment for a concussion would be fatal. Correspondingly, the success or failure of peacekeeping operations may depend on the kinds of conflict into which they are introduced.

To ascertain the factors affecting the success or failure of peacekeeping operations, three sets of conditions come into play. First and most obvious are the characteristics of the peacekeeping operation itself. These include the composition of the forces (neutral versus non-neutral) as well as the manner and efficiency of their command and coordination. Geographic concerns such as the locus of deployment are also appropriate subjects for inquiry; the rationale underlying this set of factors is that problems with peacekeeping might be the result of complications in the implementation of the strategy. For example, non-neutral troops patrolling a densely populated area may clash with local groups.

Peacekeeping operations do not, however, function in a vacuum. Thus, a second set of factors relates to the authorization of the mission. The dictated provisions of the mission inherently constrain peacekeeping operations. The scope and clarity of the mandate, defined by the authorizing body, may lead to problems if the scope is limited or the terms vague. Did the operation receive adequate financing or did a lack of funds from the authorizing body constrain it? These are important parameters that may fatally restrict peacekeeping operations.

Finally, the political and military contexts of the peacekeeping operation constitute the third set of factors thought to influence success or failure. One may expect success to vary according to the kind of conflict encountered, and the cooperation or lack thereof of relevant actors. Another concern is the behavior of the superpowers, especially in U.N. operations, in authorizing and implementing the operation. One might suspect, for example, that the superpowers may be able to sabotage a peacekeeping operation through direct or indirect manipulation. It may be that even the best-run peacekeeping operation with the clearest authority may have difficulties if it is applied to an inappropriate situation.

Although here these three sets of factors are presented separately and serially, they are not necessarily independent of one another. For example, the neutrality of the troops may influence the attitudes of the actors (e.g., subnational groups) toward the peacekeeping operation.

To identify the different aspects of these three sets of factors, I initially rely on some principles of peacekeeping strategy, conventional wisdom about what aspects are important, and the limited empirical evidence drawn from single case studies. This is not to say that these factors automatically or clearly affect the success of peacekeeping operations. Rather they provide a starting point for empirically derived generalizations about peacekeeping operations.

Characteristics of the Peacekeeping Operation

The first set of concerns involves the internal characteristics of the peacekeeping operation, ignoring for the moment what the dispute or the mission of the force is. The assumption here is that the success or failure of a peacekeeping operation might result, in part, from the organization, deployment, or direction of the force. Thus the focus is on force composition (with special attention to neutrality), command and control issues, and the locus of deployment, characteristics largely within the purview of the sponsoring organization. Therefore, one might suspect that problems with peacekeeping operations stemming from these characteristics are most amenable to corrective action.

Neutrality

Among the most fundamental tenets of peacekeeping strategy is that troops be neutral.[2] Indeed, this is part of the rationale for using the United Nations as the implementing agency rather than relying on a multinational force. The assumption is that the United Nations is better able than individual states to form a neutral force. Neutrality first means that the troops cannot be drawn from states that have an interest in the conflict at hand. Presumably this includes those states in immediate geographic proximity to the site of the conflict, as well as those aligned with one of the protagonists. In addition, neutrality has come to signify that the peacekeeping force should not rely on personnel from the major power states, especially the superpowers. Finally, neutrality in composition, in concert with the overall philosophy of peacekeeping, is supposed to guarantee neutrality in behavior—that the peacekeeping force will not favor one protagonist over another.

The supposition that neutrality of the troops is an essential ingredient of peacekeeping success rests on several reasons.[3] Neutral troops are more likely to be accepted by the parties involved, thereby giving them greater confidence in the peacekeeping operation. It is hard to imagine a disputant accepting or supporting a peacekeeping operation composed of troops that it viewed as hostile to its interests. Furthermore, neutral troops are less likely to stir up controversy during the course of their deployment; disputants will be less likely to attribute their actions to the interests of the nations that supplied the troops. Even if the troops behave in a neutral fashion, that behavior has to be perceived as such by the disputants for the troops to complete their mission. Neutral composition removes one excuse that disputants can use to justify hostile actions against, or nonsupport of, a peacekeeping force. By virtue of prior agreement with the host states, peacekeeping personnel are generally only subject to their home state's jurisdiction for criminal offenses; this is further reason for peacekeeping troops to have the trust of the host state. Despite what may objectively appear to be a neutral force, almost any peacekeeping operation will, at some time, be accused of bias; neutral troop composition seeks merely to minimize the incidence of such accusations.[4]

U.N. peacekeeping operations have generally held to the stipulation that nonaligned countries supply the troops. UNEF I consisted of troops from a variety of countries including Brazil and two that would subsequently become traditional suppliers, Finland and Sweden. Several other European states also contributed troops. The only state that on the face of it had strong ties with one of the disputants was Canada, with a close historical relationship with Great Britain. Nevertheless, Canada and Lester Pearson, the Canadian foreign minister, were leading advocates of the peacekeeping force. In this instance, and despite its close political ties, Canada played the role of a mediator and had no direct stake in the outcome of the conflict. There was thus little question of neutrality with regard to the force's composition. Furthermore, no serious charges of favoritism arose during the deployment. One might plausibly say that the neutrality of the UNEF I force was a part of the ten-year success of the operation, but it was of course not enough to head off the 1967 war.

UNEF II boasted an even more diverse composition, with troops from all inhabited continents (sample countries are Peru and Nepal). In addition, and perhaps surprisingly, one member each of NATO (Canada) and the Warsaw Pact (Poland) also provided contingents, yet neither was closely aligned with the superpowers in this conflict or had the inclination or ability for any but an evenhanded performance. The neutrality of the troops was never seriously in question. Although a significant flap arose when Israel refused to allow some of the troops on its soil because the home countries of those troops did not recognize the state of Israel, this incident did not prove harmful to the operation in the long run.

The Congo operation is unique in that states in the region of the conflict—Africa—provided some of the troops: Ghana, Liberia, Mali, and Nigeria. (In the conflict's early stages, the Congolese National Army also assisted ONUC.) Although African troops hardly constituted a majority of the force, this is not in line with traditional peacekeeping guidelines. Nevertheless, the inclusion of those troops was designed to give greater credibility to the force, as there was a desire to avoid the appearance of a peacekeeping force made up solely of white men from colonial powers such as Portugal.

Some African states objected to the conduct of the ONUC operation and ultimately withdrew their troops and support. Although this move undermined the political standing of the already battered force, it did not seem decisive in the mission. The problem with ONUC was that regardless of composition it could not play a neutral role. Its mandate and the circumstances it faced inherently favored the extant government of the Congo against all other parties. In this sense, it sacrificed neutrality at the outset, and the troops had little choice but to support one side in the conflict. Perhaps under different conditions, ONUC troops could have played an impartial law-and-order role.

UNIFIL troops appeared to be neutral in composition, except perhaps that many of the contributing states regularly voted against Israel in the

United Nations, yet one can count few countries that either support Israeli interests or abstain on key votes. Only France among the contributors might be said to have any ties to the area. France had a close historical relationship to Lebanon and has played an influential role in that country. Nevertheless, the French contingent was only a small portion of the UNIFIL troops. Thus one might say that the composition of UNIFIL met the standards for neutrality. Yet Israel complained that UNIFIL was biased in favor of the PLO and its allies, that, for example, UNIFIL returned weapons seized in inspections after a period of time had passed. This complaint relates more to the behavior of the peacekeeping force than to its composition. Israel interpreted the failure of UNIFIL to do its job as an indication that it did not *want* to do its job of stopping Palestinian attacks. Whether this failure reflects non-neutral behavior or just incompetence on the part of UNIFIL is at least a debatable question.

The Cyprus operation is another peacekeeping mission that seems to have stretched the intent of the founding fathers of the peacekeeping strategy. UNFICYP included a contingent from Great Britain, the former colonial sovereign on the island, as well as from several Commonwealth states (e.g., New Zealand and Australia), although one might have expected a force insulated from British influence to avoid any conflict of interest. Yet surprisingly little trouble has arisen over the question of neutrality, and one might conclude that the mission has had some success despite not adhering strictly to the neutrality requirement—one can certainly not attribute its problems to the force's composition or behavior.

Troops for the MNF force came exclusively from Western states, some of which had a strong interest in the outcome of the conflict. Perhaps there was little choice in the matter, as Israel would not accept a traditional U.N. force with troops from nonaligned states. Nevertheless, the real and perceived impartiality of the troops helped undermine the mission. The United States and its peacekeeping forces directly supported the Gemayel government, actually helping train the government's soldiers. France also was perceived to favor the Christian elements in Lebanon. It was bad enough that the initial presumption was that the U.S. and French troops were not neutral, but their behavior during the operation only seemed to confirm that suspicion. Britain and Italy, unlikely choices for a U.N. operation, nevertheless were able to stay away from controversy and attacks by playing a neutral role in the conflict, especially by providing humanitarian assistance. The lack of neutrality was a significant reason behind the MNF failure.

Most U.N. peacekeeping missions have troops drawn from neutral countries. Even when contributor states may have some ties to the disputants, those contributors' troops will likely be only a small portion of the overall troop strength. In this light, neutrality is unlikely to be major factor in accounting for the success or failure of U.N. operations. Yet as the MNF operation demonstrated, if a peacekeeping operation is composed primarily of troops from interested states *and* those troops openly favor one side in the conflict, there is bound to be serious trouble. This is not to say that neutral/troop composition is a prerequisite to a successful operation. The UNFICYP experience and the Multinational Force and Observers (MFO) in the Sinai demonstrate that troops from interested states can still be effective if their behavior remains neutral. Indeed, Moskos found that peacekeeping personnel become socialized in peacekeeping ethics and behavior with service in such operations, with experience having a much greater effect than prior training; of course, there is still the critical period at the outset of the operation in which non-neutral behavior is a risk.[5] Yet the best chance of avoiding difficulties seems to combine neutral troops with the philosophy of not favoring one side or the other.

Operational Characteristics

A second set of concerns revolves around the command, control, and coordination of the peacekeeping mission. Emmanuel Erskine, an official with UNIFIL, refers to operational concerns as the single most important factor in the success or failure of a peacekeeping operation; other commentators on the subject also cite their significance.[6] Perhaps this is not surprising in that many such individuals have professional service experience with peacekeeping missions, and the operational characteristics are those factors that were of most immediate concern to them. Nevertheless, several aspects of peacekeeping logistics may affect an operation's success.

One concern is the overall command of the operation and, in the case of U.N. operations, the role of the secretary-general.[7] One might hypothesize that operations more firmly under the control of one commander (in five of the six cases, the secretary-general), as opposed to a more decentralized power sharing arrangement, will be more successful; presumably less political maneuvering is involved and less opportunity for inconsistent policies or inaction in the face of crisis. One might also look to the actions of the field commander of the peacekeeping operation. Traditionally, in U.N. operations the secretary-general asks a member country to provide a qualified individual, and the executive head accepts whomever the home country nominates. This system does not guarantee the most qualified individual for the job. Operations outside U.N. jurisdiction, such as the MNF, are led by senior military officers of the states providing troops.

Other possible sources of difficulty arise from the mechanics of integrating various national units into one. U.N. operations maintain peacekeeping troops as national units coordinated by an overall U.N. command. Multinational forces are distinctly ad hoc in their arrangements. Various other problems may arise from differences in command rules, language, culture, and even food.[8] These problems can drain the efficiency of the operations and perhaps cause mistakes with dire consequences.

Empirically, the concern with operational problems seems overstated, or at the very least not a major factor in the success or failure of peacekeeping operations. Early peacekeeping operations such as UNEF I and ONUC saw active involvement and control by the U.N. secretary-general. There appeared to some advantage in this arrangement, but the costs included a certain measure of controversy resulting from the objections of U.N. members who disagreed with some of the operations' actions. The erosion of support for ONUC might in part have resulted from the controversy over Secretary-General Hammarskjöld's management of the operation. Later operations, including the very successful UNEF II, tended to share power between the secretary-general and the Security Council—for example, the commander of the peacekeeping force had to be approved by the council. Contrary to expectation, the role of the secretary-general does not seem to account for the variation in success across operations.

Command and control issues also did not seem to enhance or diminish the effectiveness of peacekeeping operations in any significant way. Although one might argue that some of the choices for commanders of the force were not the best, it would probably be incorrect to assert that they bear responsibility for the failures of the operations.[9] Four of the U.N. operations had a central command, which yielded some benefits in coordination. ONUC was somewhat disorganized because it lacked a true central command.[10] It did, however, have a coordinating body to ensure that the different forces were not working at cross purposes. ONUC's only serious problem occurred when it was unclear who gave orders for a particular maneuver during the operation. The MNF was linked only through liaison officers. The sharing of intelligence and the mapping of joint strategy correspondingly suffered. Of course, MNF was at a disadvantage in that its field commanders were military officers with limited experience in peacekeeping operations. There were some problems in all operations with language and cultural differences, but these proved to be minor annoyances rather than serious sources of disruption for the forces.

Most peacekeeping operations have run smoothly, with command, control, and coordination problems affecting the efficiency of the missions but not their overall success. Language and other problems can be cumbersome, but an inherent tradeoff lies in making a peacekeeping force representative versus making it efficient. Most command and control problems should dissipate in the future. With the benefit of experience, the United Nations can now send trained personnel into the field and choose from among many experienced individuals to direct the peacekeeping units.[11] Any future multinational effort can learn from the mistakes of the MNF. Barring an unprecedented case of complete incompetence, problems of command, control, and coordination are unlikely to ruin a peacekeeping operation.

Locus of Deployment

The site of peacekeeping operation and the characteristics of that territory are in part contextual variables. That is, peacekeeping operations cannot dictate the location of tension or cease-fire lines. Neither can they move the disputants to another part of the globe that has the ideal geographic conditions for an interposition force. Yet the locus of deployment is not entirely fixed by the situation; the requests of the authorizing agency or the field commander can influence the size of the buffer zone, the area for patrol, the number of observation sites, and other aspects of the operation. It may thus be possible to set up a peacekeeping operation in ways that improve its chances for success. The major concern is to make detection of cease-fire and other violations easy. Being able to detect violations allows the peacekeeping operation to head off problems that could escalate to war. More importantly, good detection is a deterrent to either protagonist's plans for a surprise attack. The fear of getting caught and the loss of a preemptive advantage from surprise may be enough to prevent disputants from taking hostile actions.

Conventional wisdom and experience in several operations suggest some expectations about the effect of the local geography on peacekeeping success. One expectation is that the larger the area of deployment, the more difficult it will be for the peacekeeping force to achieve its mission.[12] Peacekeeping forces usually number only several thousand, and it is impossible to maintain constant vigilance over thousands of miles, offering more opportunity for violations to remain undetected. Other characteristics of the deployment zone, however, partially offset the disadvantage of a large area to patrol.

The terrain of the area can also affect the operation. An open area with little vegetation or few buildings provides an easy line of sight to detect hostile activity. In contrast, natural barriers such as mountains or hills or man-made obstructions, such as factories or houses, decrease the ability of peacekeeping forces to supervise the area of deployment. The world has not yet seen an exclusively naval peacekeeping force, but there have been suggestions to that effect.[13] A naval mission might be even more difficult than a land operation, given the potentially greater breadth of the peace-keeping zone and the problems inherent in patrolling such areas.

Low population density also offsets problems with a large area to some extent.[14] With few people in a desert area, for example, almost any move-ment is a sign of trouble. In contrast, an urban area means that thousands of people are constantly moving about, and it may be next to impossible to stop all of them at checkpoints to detect smuggling of weapons or explosives. Thus peacekeeping forces are unlikely to be most effective when they are the only group in the area, and hostile movements will be most obvious.

Beyond a concern for detecting violations, the peacekeeping troops must be in an adequate position to act as an interposition force. This first means separating the disputants by an adequate distance.[15] If engagement, acci-dental or otherwise, is too easy, violent incidents will tend to occur and escalate. Just as a peacekeeping deployment area can be too large, it can also be too small if it does not properly separate the combatants. One difficulty lies in preventing attacks from the air. Peacekeeping forces usually have only helicopter reconnaissance and cannot prevent disputants from clashing in the airspace over or beyond the deployment zone.

The peacekeeping force must also be deployed so as to protect itself. If the force is in an area where attack or infiltration is easy, then fatalities involving the force are likely. Although a peacekeeping force is not a military one in the traditional sense, it still needs to adopt the defensive positions that are the most invulnerable to attack while providing the locus necessary for achieving its goals.

The UNEF operations were stationed in roughly the same areas. To their benefit, the Sinai is a desert terrain that provided for easy observation. Furthermore, the sparsely populated area presented few problems, and the peacekeeping forces were in little danger of attack from any hostile party. Problems with the large area of deployment were more than offset by these characteristics. The only problems they experienced were minor inconve-niences related to water purification in the desert and the difficulty of modern transportation across sand. Overall, one cannot say that geography was the dominant factor, but it certainly contributed to the positive results of these two operations.

The Congo operation served a very large area; one could argue that most of the country was subject to ONUC concern and action. Even the large force of over twenty thousand troops was not really enough to do the job properly. The peacekeeping force was operating in populated areas at times, and there were few clear lines separating the combatants, of which ONUC became one. Furthermore, the remoteness of the area required shipping supplies via air cargo. The geography of the conflict certainly posed some complications for the mission, yet it would be a mistake to regard this as a crucial factor, in light of the influence of other factors. One geographic advantage in the latter stages was that ONUC was able to confine its concerns primarily to the province of Katanga, narrowing somewhat the geographic problems encountered.

Geography proved something of an advantage for the UNFICYP operation. As an island nation, Cyprus was not vulnerable to supply or invasion by Greece and Turkey as if it were directly contiguous to those two states. The Mediterranean thus provided a natural buffer to hostile activity by third party states. Furthermore, the Greek and Turkish communities occupied separate parts of the island after 1974 with the creation of a separate Turkish republic, making it easy to draw lines of demarcation. UNFICYP troops are stationed in populated areas, and at a few points the buffer zone between the two communities is very narrow. Contrary to expectations, this geographic configuration has been responsible for few incidents.

The locus of UNIFIL deployment has exacerbated that operation's many problems. The UNIFIL zone is a large rural area that is easy to infiltrate, and consequently detecting arms trafficking is difficult. UNIFIL headquarters and troop positions are vulnerable to sniper fire and shelling, and the many checkpoints are not enough to maintain control over the area. The diverse group of people living in the area has made it quite difficult to distinguish friend from foe. In addition, UNIFIL has been unable to stop some of the main forms of cease-fire violations: rocket and air attacks. Combined with frequent population movement in the area, the ill-defined zones of operation make UNIFIL ineffective as an interposition force.

Parts of the MNF actually benefitted from what was overall a disastrous plan of deployment. The Italian contingent was located near refugee camps, which—except for the earlier massacre—were unlikely to be a site for serious military action. The British contingent was mobile, not a tempting target for detailed military or terrorist attacks. As a whole, however, MNF never really created much of a buffer between the opposing sides and was itself quite vulnerable. Indeed, no demilitarized zone was established. Small contingents of MNF soldiers were responsible for all of heavily populated and urban Beirut and the surrounding areas. The French had the worst possible position at the Green Line separating east and west Beirut, without sufficient space to keep the warring factions apart; not surprisingly, sniper and rocket fire across the Green Line was commonplace. The U.S. group, at the airport, could do little to keep rival groups from fighting each other and was vulnerable to attack from positions in the surrounding hillsides. The actual area of operation was very small, while the area of responsibility was very large. MNF seemed ill positioned in a difficult geographic situation, and it suffered accordingly.

In general, geographic considerations were important to the success of peacekeeping missions, although one cannot consider them the most important factor. It appears that to enhance the chances for success, peacekeeping forces should be placed in areas that are relatively invulnerable yet easy to patrol and that separate the combatants at a safe distance. Nevertheless, a favorable location is no guarantee that the mission will turn out well. At best, one might hope that a particular deployment will minimize the opportunity for violent incidents that could escalate the conflict.

Characteristics of Authorization

Mandate

The mandate of a peacekeeping operation defines its mission and often sets out goals to be achieved. On some occasions, the mandate also provides precise plans for deployment and duties to be performed. The key aspects of the mandate are its clarity and specificity.[16] Clarity refers to how precisely the purpose and actions of the force are spelled out—is it clear why the forces are there? Specificity concerns the amount of detail provided as to the how and where of those duties.

The mandate may influence the success of peacekeeping operations in several ways. First, a clear and detailed mandate sets the expectations of the actors involved, presumably reflecting consensus among the protagonists and the authorizing agency on what the peacekeeping force will do in the area. Thus, less room exists for disagreement over varying interpretations of the mandate. This helps ensure continued support for the operation among the protagonists and members of the authorizing body. Withdrawal of support or attacks on the peacekeeping force stemming from disagreements over peacekeeping duties or actions are less likely when the force's mission is clear.

Second, a clear mandate helps ensure public support for the peace-keeping operation, which may be particularly critical for a multinational force. In order to swing the weight of domestic and international public opinion behind a peacekeeping operation, the force must have clearly iden-tifiable goals and duties. Without those, the public may not understand why the troops are there or may question the validity of the peacekeeping strategy in the situation at hand.

Empirically, vague mandates have created several problems for peace-keeping operations. The most obvious case was the mandate of the second deployment of the MNF, "to provide an interposition force at agreed lo-cations and thereby provide the MNF presence requested by the Govern-ment of Lebanon to assist it and Lebanon's armed forces in the Beirut area."[17]

Each of the four states contributing troops to MNF sent separate letters to the Lebanese government, which had requested their presence; although all emphasized assisting the Lebanese government, the ambiguity of MNF's responsibility led each to interpret its mission differently. The United States actually trained the Lebanese armed forces in combat techniques; this served to alienate many factions in Lebanon, who regarded this action as incon-sistent with MNF's purpose. The French also took an active role in the political situation. In contrast, the Italian and British contingents concen-trated on less controversial activities, such as providing humanitarian as-sistance. Perhaps it is not surprising that the French and U.S. units were the ones subjected to terrorist bombing attacks.

The vagueness of the MNF mandate also served to undermine popular support, especially in Britain and the United States. Each government found it difficult to justify the continued deployment of peacekeeping troops when it did not appear to serve national interests and when the troops seemed to be exposed targets for hostile action.

ONUC encountered similar difficulties with its mandate. The title of Ernest Lefever's major book on this operation indicates the importance of this problem: *Uncertain Mandate*. The initial charge of ONUC seemed fairly clear but included few details on how ONUC was to achieve the goals laid out for it. That ONUC was supposed to assist the Congolese government in regaining stability seemed incompatible with the restriction that ONUC was allowed to use military force only in self-defense. Part of ONUC's problems began when the operation later went beyond this restriction in pursuit of the law-and-order objective. Furthermore, different states interpreted the vague mandate differently, with serious political disagreements resulting. African states and the Soviet Union focused on the Belgian threat to stability in the Congo, perhaps seeing the role of the United Nations as removing another vestige of colonialism. In contrast, the United States and other countries saw the key issues as one of internal disorder, as opposed to external intervention.[18]

ONUC received no clear instructions on how to perform such functions as securing the withdrawal of foreign mercenaries. This left considerable discretion in the hands of the secretary-general, who U.N. members and local groups criticized for not always following their interpretations of what needed to be done. Finally, ONUC's mandate changed over time, resulting in some controversy over the force's expanded role and some confusion as to whether it had exceeded its original purposes. In general, problems with the ONUC mandate complicated an already difficult situation for the peacekeeping troops.

The mandate for UNIFIL created difficulties by failing to specify all the areas of deployment and by containing provisions for operation that were unrealistic under the circumstances.[19] There were numerous logistical difficulties as well as considerable disagreement over the demarcation of UNIFIL lines. Nevertheless, it would be unfair to attribute most of UNIFIL's problems to its mandate. Similarly, UNFICYP's mandate was fairly clear, and only some disagreements over command caused any complications to the mission.[20]

Both versions of the UNEF operations benefitted from clear and distinctly limited mandates. In one sense, these limitations prevented the peace-keeping operations from having a major impact in the area. The United Nations also specified their roles and area of deployment, limitations that prevented the kind of open-ended commitment that was either unrealistic or that led the forces to assume controversial roles.[21] Few disputes arose among the protagonists or within the United Nations on the duties of UNEF I and II. Perhaps not coincidentally, the operations were also among the most successful in limiting armed conflict.

Clear and detailed mandates assist in the implementation of a successful peacekeeping operation. A vague mandate creates problems when different actors have varying expectations about its scope and implementation. Furthermore, an open-ended set of functions may lead a peacekeeping operation to exceed some of the basic principles of neutrality or self-defense that are the cornerstones of the peacekeeping strategy.

Although a clear mandate is important, it may only be a function of the political consensus or lack thereof underlying the mission and may generate little support in the deliberative bodies that authorize such operations. This is often why U.N. resolutions in general tend to be vague, a necessity to build the voting majority necessary to pass them. In controversial situations, some operations might never receive authorization except with a vague mandate. In summary, although one cannot question the importance of a clear mandate, one can overestimate its relative significance; a clear mandate may be a surrogate for strong international consensus behind the purposes of the mission.

Financing

Peacekeeping operations can be expensive, in view of the supplies, equipment, salaries, and various administrative costs over a period that might stretch to several decades. Does the funding or do possible shortfalls affect the likelihood that an operation will be successful? Each of the U.N. peacekeeping operations studied here had a slightly different method of covering costs.[22] They do share some similarities, however. None of the operations has been funded out of the regular U.N. budget, as had been true of some previous observation missions. The typical method has been to pay for peacekeeping out of a special account; member states pay an assessment based on a formula similar to the one used for the regular U.N. budget, although this arrangement has varied over time. Voluntary contributions cover other expenses. These may be monetary contributions by states that feel a strong commitment to the operation, or contributions in kind (e.g., helicopters or supplies) by interested states or those providing troops to the operation.

One of the problems in the United Nations is the lack of a mechanism to enforce contribution assessments. Without any adequate means for penalizing those who do not pay, there is little incentive other than self-interest or moral obligation to meet the required assessment. Article 19 of the U.N. Charter does stipulate that members' voting and other privileges can be suspended if they fall behind in their contributions to the organization, and the International Court of Justice has determined that peacekeeping costs constitute such general expenses of the United Nations.[23] That article has become largely irrelevant, however, since the United Nations withdrew an attempt to implement it in 1964.[24]

The lack of a coercive mechanism, not surprisingly, has led some states to ignore their financial obligations to peacekeeping operations. In such a system, there is a natural tendency to "free ride" on the part of the smaller states; the larger states will feel compelled to contribute and continue the operation, as they have a major stake in its continuance.[25] Furthermore, many Third World nations have pressing domestic economic problems that lead them to be in arrears on what they owe the United Nations. Most prominently, some states withhold contributions from peacekeeping operations because they disagree with the mission or believe that the expenses should be borne by those who benefit most by the operation—the protagonists. All these factors contribute to the discrepancy between peacekeeping expenses and the money needed to cover them.

There are several ways a funding shortfall might affect the success of a peacekeeping operation. First, an operation might have to end prematurely, before it has had a chance to stabilize the situation or before conflict resolution has been achieved. Second, its area of operation or its troop strength may have to be limited because there are not enough personnel to patrol the interposition zone properly. Finally, the peacekeeping force may go without some equipment or support essential to detecting violations or ensuring the confidence of the disputants.

Empirically, U.N. operations have all experienced some financial difficulties, much as has the United Nations as a whole. (U.N. peacekeeping operations' debt today totals over $500 million.[26]) Nevertheless, these did not seem to affect adversely any of the six operations in a serious fashion. Both UNEF operations had minimal difficulties from financing. For example, UNEF II was unable to purchase mine sweepers and helicopters; this had little or no impact on the success of the operation, although the equipment might perhaps have made the mission more efficient. UNIFIL also wanted more equipment to patrol the designated area, yet even given that equipment it is unlikely that UNIFIL would have been more successful, as other factors appear to have been more responsible for that operation's failure. Similarly, there was some withholding of funds from UNFICYP with little noticeable impact.

The only U.N. mission in which poor financial grounding played a role was ONUC. Several states, most notably France and the Soviet Union, withheld contributions, causing a serious financial crisis; there seemed to be constant pressure as a result to complete the mission. It is clearly an arguable point, but such pressure may have contributed to the use of military force by the peacekeeping troops to put down the Katangan secession. Financial considerations might also have been important in the decision to withdraw troops in 1964, although this was well after the Katangan secession was put down; nevertheless, the impact on the success of the mission was not dramatic.[27]

The MNF did not have many of the problems inherent in a U.N. operation. Each nation contributing troops paid its own expenses. Accordingly, there were no financial shortfalls for MNF. There was some questioning in the U.S. Congress about the cost of the operation, but this had little influence on the conduct of the operation and was not a primary reason for the withdrawal of U.S. troops. One suspects that financial concerns might not even have been mentioned had the MNF mandate been clearer and the results more favorable. Perhaps the least successful mission was thus also the one with the strongest financial backing.

Overall, finances were an irritating problem for peacekeeping operations, but they were not a serious hindrance to the conduct or success of the missions. Anytime that a U.N. operation is deployed, there are likely to be financial difficulties. Yet the United Nations is able to muddle through these by various combinations of deficit spending, increased voluntary contributions, and some scaling back of the operation. Financial problems, at least at the level experienced so far by U.N. operations, are not a major factor affecting the success of peacekeeping operations. The MNF experience also demonstrates that financial stability is no panacea for other problems.

Political and Military Context

Kind of Dispute

We cannot expect peacekeeping operations to work successfully in all kinds of disputes. Specifically, one analyst argues that "peacekeeping has been less problematic and generally operated more smoothly when the danger has arisen from the threat to peace by external aggression."[28] One might also expect that peacekeeping is more successful when certain kinds of issues constitute the bases for contention.[29]

This sample of six cases reveals two interstate conflicts and four civil conflicts with international components. Confirming the foregoing suppositions, the two interstate cases (UNEF I and II) have been the most successful in limiting armed conflict, and violence was a more persistent problem in the cases of internationalized civil war (UNIFIL, ONUC, UNFICYP, and MNF). The findings clearly indicate that peacekeeping is most effective in disputes between state members of the international system.

Several explanations appear to account for the strong correlation between civil disputes and peacekeeping failure. First, civil conflicts often involve more than two identifiable groups in dispute; the civil component of the Lebanese conflict alone involved more than a half-dozen indigenous political factions, each with its own militia. This does not even consider the presence of terrorist groups, the PLO, Israel, or Syria. By definition, an internationalized civil war involves more than two actors. In contrast, interstate disputes have been overwhelmingly dyadic.[30] It is much more difficult to aggregate the preferences of more than two actors in a way that satisfies all parties with the outcome; indeed, "Arrow's paradox" shows that it may be impossible under certain circumstances.[31] Thus as the number of actors in the dispute increases, so does the likelihood that one or more of them will object to the cease-fire and the provisions for the deployment of the peacekeeping forces; they may take military action against other actors or the peacekeeping forces. A dyadic interstate dispute is much easier to control. Presumably both sides have agreed to the cease-fire, indicating that they at least initially support the peacekeeping operation.

Beyond the difficulty of aggregating multiple preferences in support of a peacekeeping operation, the geographic requirements, already found to be significant, differ in a civil conflict. Civil instability may mean that several groups are operating in different parts of the country, which could require the peacekeeping operation to cover a broader territory, opening up the possibility of more incidents. Furthermore, unlike an identifiable international border or cease-fire line, it may be impossible to demarcate a line or area that separates the many sides in the conflict. Being from the same state and often not wearing military uniforms (indeed, sometimes not being traditional military or paramilitary units at all), participants in a civil conflict are hard to identify, much less to separate, when they occupy the same geographic area. Interstate disputants are more easily identified and separated across internationally recognized borders or militarily defined cease-fire lines.

Peacekeeping always favors the status quo at the time of the deployment, a truism particularly important in civil conflict. A cease-fire and the imposition of peacekeeping forces relieves some pressure on the challenged government, which may also gain some political capital with the populace, who may long for stability in the country. In the eyes of the rebel groups, however, peace means continued domination of the government by the status quo elites. This is not to say that some rebel groups may not support peacekeeping forces. Civil conflict poses two unique problems, however. Not all rebel groups may find it in their interest to have a cease-fire. Even those that do agree with the peacekeeping deployment may support the cease-fire and the peacekeeping forces for only a short time. The threat of violence is their principal mechanism for forcing concessions from the government. Long-term deployment of peacekeeping forces and the limitation of armed conflict without political change is inimical to the interests of the rebels. In contrast, participants in an interstate dispute may be more willing to tolerate a freezing of the status quo over a longer time. In such circumstances, the government elites at least retain their domestic power and do not have to make meaningful concessions to their foreign enemies.

Other than the international/civil dichotomy, which itself has a number of correlates, the issues in dispute do not show much variation across cases. It may be that peacekeeping operations are deployed only in circumstances that have a high level of conflict over issues that are very salient. All cases involve some disagreement over territorial control, be the disputed area the Suez Canal, the West Bank, or a rebel province. There are religious and ethnic cleavages among the actors in all the situations. Perhaps peacekeeping operations might be more successful when the stakes are less salient or when reinforcing cleavages between disputants are not present. Yet such situations likely would not prompt the use of the peacekeeping strategy and, in the absence of empirical cases so far, cannot account for the variation we already find in success and failure among peacekeeping operations.

Behavior of the Host State and Other Primary Disputants

It may seem largely self-evident that peacekeeping operations should require the cooperation of the primary disputants in a conflict. We have already noted that the host states must grant permission for U.N. forces to be deployed on their soil. Furthermore, traditional peacekeeping operations have followed or been part of a cease-fire agreement between the primary protagonists—those states serving as hosts for the peacekeeping troops and those most directly and prominently involved in the dispute. Yet the initial agreement of the primary disputants is usually a given in the deployment of a peacekeeping force, a necessary condition for the peacekeeping strategy.

What concerns us here is more than the initial agreement to deploy the peacekeeping troops. Wainhouse notes that "where cooperation of the parties is not sustained and whole-hearted, a positive result will be difficult to obtain."[32] This continuing cooperation includes several aspects. First, the disputants should clearly observe the cease-fire provisions and not attack either their opponents or the peacekeeping forces. Less obviously, the disputants need to refrain from other acts that might undermine the purpose of the peacekeeping forces. Such acts include the buildup of military forces near the buffer zone, supply of weapons to other groups in the area, and failure to observe disengagement and withdrawal provisions of the cease-fire agreement. Finally, cooperation by the disputants includes the positive aspects of assisting the peacekeeping forces by providing information, maintaining friendly relations, and delivering other logistical support the commander of the operation might request.

The behavior of the disputants in the six cases under study provides some basis for optimism, but this does not go a long way toward solving the puzzle of why some operations succeed while others fail. The most successful operations in limiting armed conflict, UNEF I and II, received generally good cooperation from Egypt. That country complied with the provisions of the agreement and gave the peacekeeping force little trouble. Of course, Egypt asked UNEF I to leave in 1967 in order to facilitate an Arab attack against Israel, yet this was only a significant aberration in a pattern of strong cooperation. Israel was less supportive of UNEF I and II, sometimes having disagreements over troop movements and inspections. Nevertheless, those problems were generally minor, and in no case was the opposition violent or serious enough to jeopardize the mission (in contrast to Israeli behavior in UNIFIL). In these two cases, the initial cooperation of the host state and primary disputants continued, and the peacekeeping operations were largely successful.

UNFICYP has also received fairly good support from the host government of Cyprus and, since 1974, from the unrecognized Turkish Cypriot government on the northern part of the island. Although at one time the Cyprus National Guard blocked UNFICYP access to certain areas, now the peacekeeping operation is considered a normal part of life in the island.

The level of cooperation from the host state in the ONUC operation is somewhat problematic to gauge. Clearly, the Congolese government wanted the peacekeeping operation to do everything in its power to restore order in the country. Nevertheless, the government quickly splintered into factions, each with different ideas of what ONUC should do. Indeed, at one stage, ONUC was effectively supporting one faction over another. After Lumumba's death, a reunified Congolese government built a cooperative partnership with the peacekeeping operation.

The two operations in Lebanon, UNIFIL and MNF, had the most difficulty. The host Lebanon government in both cases was most supportive, but it was torn by factionalism and rather weak. The main protagonists, Israel and the PLO, tended to take actions that undermined each operation. Israel's refusal to turn over a "security zone" near its border to UNIFIL troops initially handicapped the operation. Instead, Israel assisted and supplied the Christian South Lebanese Army in that sector. In 1982, Israel invaded Lebanon through UNIFIL lines. Before and after that invasion, numerous disputes have arisen between the Israeli army and UNIFIL officials over Israeli actions in southern Lebanon. The PLO has been only slightly more helpful, encouraging the supply of weapons into the region and refusing to recognize UNIFIL activity in certain areas. With respect to UNIFIL, the Lebanese government has been largely irrelevant despite its support, and the primary combatants have provided only minimal cooperation at best.

The first stage of the MNF mission, in which the PLO was evacuated, revealed excellent cooperation by all sides. The second stage saw continued Lebanese government support and what might be described as Israeli indifference. These circumstances seemed to have little impact, as the MNF suffered numerous problems. Although one might point to lack of cooperation in the UNIFIL case as an important factor, this was not the situation with respect to MNF.

Overall, we can note that the cooperation of the host state and of the other primary disputants was fairly consistent across cases and within the time of each operation's deployment. With a few exceptions, the host states and primary disputants wanted the peacekeeping operation and cooperated in the venture. The UNIFIL experience shows that problems with the primary disputants can have a deleterious effect on the success of the mission.

It seems that continued cooperation of the host state and primary disputants is a necessary, yet far from sufficient, condition for the success of peacekeeping. Most of the operations studied here had that cooperation, but several had serious problems nonetheless. There are two explanations for this. First, cooperation of the host state means little if the government is very weak or is a secondary actor to the conflict at hand.[33] That the Lebanese government supported peacekeeping on its soil was largely irrelevant to limiting armed conflict by autonomous actors operating within its boundaries. Similarly, one of the main reasons for ONUC deployment was the weakness of the Congo government, which could give little effective assistance to the peacekeeping force. Second, and just as important, many of the conflicts involved more than the host state and primary disputants. It was often the cooperation of these third parties that affected the success of peacekeeping operations.

Third-Party States

Most analyses of international conflict focus on the two or three primary combatants. Yet states that are neighbors to the primary disputants or those that have regional power aspirations are in a position to influence the processes and outcomes of those confrontations. With respect to peacekeeping operations, one usually looks only at the primary disputants and ignores the regional context of the operation. Indeed, the legal requirement is only that the primary parties stop fighting and that host states grant permission to station the troops on their soil. Little consideration goes to how other states with a stake in the conflict might feel about the deployment of a peacekeeping operation. In many cases, these third-party states are intimately involved in the conflict, although they may not be its primary initiator or target.

Third-party states can influence the success of a peacekeeping operation in several ways.[34] Most obviously, they can directly intervene militarily in the conflict, causing a renewal of the fighting or jeopardizing the safety and mission of the peacekeeping operation. More subtly, they might supply arms and other assistance to one of the disputants or to a subnational actor that undermines the peacekeeping force's ability to limit violence. They might also bring diplomatic pressure to bear on one of the actors, disposing the actor to support or oppose the peacekeeping presence.

Third-party states might also indirectly influence the peacekeeping operation by virtue of their relationship to the primary disputants in other contexts. Conflict between a third-party state and one of the disputants over issues related or unrelated to the conflict in question can heighten tension in the area. The new conflict could spill over and poison the ceasefire between the primary disputants. Most dangerous would be a situation in which a primary disputant is aligned with a third-party state that becomes involved in a militarized dispute or war with the other primary disputant. In that case, the primary disputants are often dragged into renewed conflict through competing alignment patterns.

Third parties have the potential to play either a positive or negative role in the performance of peacekeeping operations. One suspects, however, that the latter is more likely, for there are potentially more ways to complicate a peacekeeping operation than to assist it. Furthermore, a third-party state that supports a peacekeeping operation will likely stay out of the conflict, whereas in opposition it will tend to take a more active role.

Among the sample cases, all but UNEF II involved significant intervention by third-party states. It is probably not because of a spurious relationship that this operation was quite successful both in limiting armed conflict and on the conflict resolution dimension. This is not to say that there were no other problems in the region. Syria and Jordan clashed with Israel on several occasions, but those confrontations had little impact on conditions at the Egyptian-Israeli border. The lack of direct third-party involvement contributed to the success of the mission.

At least for its first ten years, the UNEF I operation was again similar to its successor; tensions in the Middle East did not seem to affect the relative stability that existed in the zone patrolled by the peacekeeping force. Yet one can directly attribute the termination of UNEF I and its one major failure in 1967 to the actions of third-party states. The repeated clashes between Syria, Jordan, the PLO, and Israel brought the region to the brink of war. Syria and Jordan pressured Egypt into joining the coalition against Israel, and Egypt requested that the UNEF I troops be withdrawn from its soil. Without such pressure and the other conflicts in the region, it is unlikely that Egypt would have expelled the peacekeeping force and ultimately fought a war with Israel, at least in 1967.

Greece and Turkey are certainly key players in the UNFICYP operation. Greece has generally been supportive of the operation — except for its supply and support of irregular Greek troops there — probably because it freezes de jure control of the island in the hands of the Greek majority there. Yet that support has not had a major and overt impact. More significant has been the behavior of Turkey, who has consistently supplied arms and men to the Turkish community on Cyprus and in 1974 invaded the island, helping set up a separate republic. Since that incident, Turkey has been largely cooperative toward UNFICYP, or at least not overtly hostile. Nevertheless, the actions of third-party states lie behind many of the problems that the peacekeeping operation experienced.

The peacekeeping force in the Congo suffered most from the actions of Belgium. Belgian troops and mercenaries exacerbated the violence in the area. Belgium supported — some say initiated — the secessionist movement in Katanga. Until the withdrawal of its troops, Belgium seemed to place roadblocks in the way of ONUC's achieving its mission. Furthermore, as the former colonial power, Belgium used its remaining influence to frustrate U.N. efforts to arrive at a peaceful solution and a unified country. This is not to say that all of the armed conflict is traceable to Belgian complicity, but, at minimum, that country exacerbated and prolonged the conflict by its actions. Later in the operation, Belgium did show more cooperation toward ONUC. Neighboring African states were initially supportive of ONUC, even contributing troops to the cause. As controversy deepened around the operation, many of those states withdrew their support and their troops, relinquishing the opportunity to bring political and regional pressure on the warring factions.

Not surprisingly, the failed missions of MNF and UNIFIL each faced strong opposition from neighboring states. Syria played a critical role in the downfall of both. Syria gave weapons and other support to PLO fighters in southern Lebanon, helping them infiltrate UNIFIL lines and attack Israeli positions. Syria also built up its forces in the Bekaa Valley, threatening Israel and making those forces a target during the 1982 invasion. Similarly, Syria opposed the second stage of MNF through its allies among the factions in Beirut. It supplied weapons to them and pressured the Shi'ite and Druse factions not to accept a solution to the situation that involved the MNF. Excluding Syria from the MNF negotiations was a mistake that cost the country's cooperation in the peacekeeping operation.[35] There is also some evidence that Syria, Iran, and possibly Libya had a hand in supporting the terrorist attacks against the peacekeeping forces. The opposition of Syria to the two Lebanese operations was a critical factor in the problems they experienced.

The behavior of third-party states, often ignored when putting together a peacekeeping force, appears to be a critical factor in whether an operation will be successful or not. If a major state in the region actively opposes the operation or jeopardizes it by dealings with one of the primary disputants, then that operation is bound to experience problems. Most of the serious incidents in each of the operations can be traced at least indirectly to the actions of third-party states.

Subnational Actors

Just as third-party states might influence peacekeeping operations, so might subnational groups in the host or surrounding states.[36] They too may be ignored in the initial deployment of peacekeeping forces. The behavior of these groups could be especially important when peacekeeping forces are thrust into areas of internal instability. In some cases, subnational actors may actually control larger geographic areas than does the recognized government. Furthermore, there has been a trend toward such groups gaining more resources and autonomy over time, often at the expense of state power.[37]

Subnational groups that wish to undermine the extant government may view peacekeeping as hostile to their interests. Unlike third-party states, however, subnational actors affect peacekeeping operations primarily by direct actions of support or opposition. Their cooperation could be crucial in fostering a minimum level of violence in the area of deployment.

Internal groups played little or no role in either of the UNEF missions; the PLO and other groups did not operate in the area of UNEF deployment in the Sinai. Internal groups were also not of lasting importance on Cyprus, unless one counts the northern Cyprus republic and affiliated groups as internal, and even they have cooperated with UNFICYP over the past two decades. Early in the Cyprus conflict, irregular army units on both sides were responsible for some of the violence, but this has ceased to be serious problem. Once again, the three most successful peacekeeping operations (UNEF I, UNEF II, and UNFICYP) had few problems in dealing with internal actors.

The other three operations have faced active opposition from internal groups. ONUC was obviously a case in which subnational actors affected the operation. The Katangan independence movement was a cause of the deployment of U.N. peacekeeping troops. The Katangan secessionists clearly did not support an operation among whose purposes was the restoration of the central government's authority over all areas of the country. This situation relates to an earlier point: civil conflicts pose inherent difficulties for peacekeeping forces especially if subnational groups do not support their presence—and any support is likely to dissipate over time.

The PLO never really accepted UNIFIL, claiming that the Palestinians had a right to operate in the disputed area. Consequently, they smuggled weapons into the area and attacked Israeli positions, defeating the purpose of UNIFIL and eroding what little confidence Israel had in the peacekeeping force. Major Haddad's Christian militia in the area cooperated with Israel, which often did not translate into cooperation with UNIFIL. The actions of that militia often interfered with UNIFIL patrols and other activities and contravened UNIFIL's goal of limiting conflict. In this case, however, Sunni Muslims in the region did not hinder the peacekeeping operation.

Perhaps the best example of how subnational actors can ruin a peacekeeping operation is the tragedy of MNF. Lebanon consisted of a large number of well-armed and competing factions, few if any of which actually supported the MNF presence. Even the Christian Phalangists, who had the most to gain from the operation, were less than enthusiastic as they continued to battle Muslim factions. The Shi'ite and Druse factions opposed the MNF, feeling that the peacekeeping forces were a shield for the Gemayel government. Among their demands for a resolution to the conflict was the withdrawal of the peacekeeping forces. Terrorist groups also proved to be a deadly opponent to the operation. When third-party states acted in unison with subnational groups to undermine the peacekeeping operation, as they did in Lebanon, not even the support of the host state could save the mission.

Superpower Behavior

In almost any aspect of international relations between 1945 and 1990, but especially with respect to peacekeeping operations, the behavior of the superpowers requires examination. It is clear that the United States and the Soviet Union were key players in the authorization of U.N. peacekeeping missions. The Security Council has the primary responsibility for dealing with matters of international peace and security. By virtue of the superpowers' military capability and veto power, the Security Council was an important forum for the convergence and divergence of the superpowers' national interests.[38] U.N. peacekeeping operations are usually authorized through the Security Council; early efforts to move their authorization to the General Assembly seem to have petered out.

The superpowers also had a more subtle influence on peacekeeping operations, beyond their formal authorizing power. There is a strong correlation between superpower intervention in a conflict and the use of peacekeeping.[39] This demonstrates that the superpowers were an indirect stimulus for peacekeeping. Indeed, the establishment of UNEF II was largely at the behest of the superpowers. Despite the importance of the superpowers before and during the authorization of peacekeeping operations, we are concerned with operations already in existence and thus with superpower influence after authorization, which may be a very different matter.

The most tangible aspect of superpower support may occur when U.N. operations come up for reauthorization in the Security Council, as peacekeeping operations are authorized for a limited period, often for only six months at a time. Superpower support of the operation may become evident in the vote for mission reauthorization. Yet once authorized, most U.N. operations receive repeated reauthorizations with little dissent.

Beyond a formal vote of support, superpowers might affect the success of a peacekeeping operation in several ways. First, the superpowers could, by virtue of strong political support (as opposed to acquiescence), rally world opinion around the operation and pressure the disputants to cooperate with the peacekeeping force. This of course assumes that the superpowers already have some direct influence on the protagonists. Second, the superpowers will be called upon to provide much of the logistical and financial support for the operation.[40] This may influence the success of the mission, although the analysis of coordination and financing indicates that the effects may be minor. Finally, the superpowers might influence the local situation by actions they take in the area. These may include direct intervention or more subtle actions such as the supply of arms to the protagonists or third-party actors opposed to the peacekeeping presence. Thus, even though the superpowers may vote to reauthorize a peacekeeping mission, their other actions may undermine the effectiveness of that mission.

In the UNIFIL operation, both superpowers tended to ignore the situation following their initial support of the mission. Each regards the mission as largely ineffective but has not made a major effort to deal with the problems in the area, except with respect to MNF. The United States has not strongly pressured Israel to relinquish its security zone, nor has it provided the necessary funds for a stable financial base. The Soviet Union had until the late 1980s supported Syria with military aid and given political support to the PLO. The superpowers apparently have done nothing to directly undermine UNIFIL, but they have also contributed little positive activity to help the operation.

The same ambivalence is evident in the other long-term mission— UNFICYP. Again, the superpowers have allowed the operation to slide into debt and have done little for the mission. The Soviet Union has shown little interest in the situation, allied with neither Turkey nor Greece and not seeing its own interests affected. The United States has given aid to both Greece and Turkey but, other than not recognizing the independence of the Turkish republic on the island, has stayed uninvolved. Overall, one cannot attribute the successes or the shortcomings of UNFICYP to the actions of the superpowers.

The superpowers seemed considerably more interested in the UNEF operations, perhaps because their client states were the primary protagonists. Nevertheless, the success of both phases of that peacekeeping operation in limiting armed conflict probably cannot be attributed to superpower behavior. Although neither superpower was anxious to see a renewal of full-scale Arab-Israeli war and both supported UNEF I and II as being in their interests, the same financial problems appeared in the operations. More importantly, the United States continued to be a major arms and financial aid supplier to Israel, and the Soviet Union was similarly disposed toward Egypt. Their behavior was not substantially different with UNIFIL, and the results were considerably better.

The most active opposition to a peacekeeping operation was the Soviet dispute with Secretary-General Hammarskjöld over ONUC. The Soviets not only refused to pay their share of the operation but gave strong political support to Patrice Lumumba. This dispute clearly complicated the mission, as it was difficult for the peacekeeping troops to restore order and to negotiate an agreement among political factions. The United States did give critical support to ONUC by providing air transport and other material contributions. Without such support, ONUC's ability to operate effectively might have been diminished, but it was not enough to overcome the many problems of the operation.

The MNF is a unique case in that one of the superpowers, the United States, was the leading state in developing the mission and supplying it with personnel. Clearly, the United States made a strong financial, military, and political commitment to MNF, perhaps the greatest failure among peacekeeping operations; even the most supportive behavior by a superpower could not guarantee success. The Soviet Union's actions did not support the operation. The Soviets resupplied Syrian troops after their engagement with the Israelis, supported the PLO position, and vetoed a proposal in the Security Council to replace the MNF with a U.N. force. It seems, however, that MNF was too badly damaged already to conclude that the Soviet actions were decisive in any way.

None of the cases studied here involved the strong and active opposition of the superpowers, and it is therefore hard to assess what impact that might have. Furthermore, the end of the Cold War has apparently removed Russia from the ranks of the superpowers or, at very least, considerably diminished its role in global affairs. Other major powers such as Japan and the leading members of the European Community might be critical actors, much as the superpowers were, in future operations. Despite these changes, one might expect that no case of U.N. peacekeeping could ever reach a stage at which the United States or another major power would work strongly against the operation. Active opposition by a major power would probably result either in a Security Council veto, preventing the peacekeeping operation's authorization to start with, or the operation's premature termination; that a peacekeeping operation exists suggests some minimum level of major power support at the outset. The reluctance to repeat the Uniting for Peace strategy in the General Assembly makes this even more likely in the future.

It is also difficult to assess what would be the impact of strong and active support by major powers, although the MNF experience suggests that it may be enough to overcome other problems. The superpowers may never have had the influence over all the local actors necessary to pull the puppet strings and compel them to support the peacekeeping operations. The end of the Cold War, the increasing autonomy of local actors, and the lessening of Russian aid, in particular, may lessen opportunities for strong influence in the future.

What we are left with is modest superpower support of the six operations. The superpowers are in part responsible for some financial problems, and they occasionally supported actions that at least did not contribute to peacekeeping success and may have diminished its likelihood. Overall, though, the impact of the superpowers following authorization of the peacekeeping operations has not been great. In no case could one attribute a significant instance or degree of failure to superpower actions, direct or indirect. Similarly, the only operation that received strong and active support from a superpower, the MNF, was a failure by all standards.

The end of the Cold War has given rise to new expectations about the major powers' willingness to use the peacekeeping option.[41] Our analysis here suggests that warmer relations between the United States and Russia may mean that more peacekeeping missions will be authorized; as permanent members of the Security Council, they have the greatest influence at the authorization stage. Yet closer cooperation does not necessarily mean that those operations will be more effective. Other key factors in this chapter will have more to do with peacekeeping success than will the actions of major power states. To the extent that Russian and perhaps U.S. influence vis-à-vis other actors declines, the trend should continue in that direction.

Conclusions

International peacekeeping has had a mixed record of success in limiting armed conflict. The main reasons for the problems experienced by peacekeeping operations have been the opposition of third-party states and of subnational groups, respectively. By refusing to stop violent activity, and in some cases by attacking the peacekeeping forces, these two sets of actors can undermine a whole operation. The failure of UNIFIL and MNF can be largely attributed to the behavior of these actors, as can many of the difficulties experienced by other peacekeeping operations. This leaves us with something of a tautology: peacekeeping is successful only when all parties wish to stop fighting. Peacekeeping forces can take certain actions (e.g., remain neutral) to ensure that desire for peace continues. Nevertheless, peacekeeping will fail or be severely damaged if peace is not initially desired by all relevant parties.

Although the primary disputants and the superpowers each had a great deal of power to destroy a peacekeeping operation, this analysis reveals that neither group generally took strong opposing action. To set up a peacekeeping force, the host states must grant their approval and have some desire to stop fighting. A peacekeeping force organized by the United

Nations usually needs Security Council approval; major-power acquiescence is the minimum requirement for this. Therefore, a peacekeeping operation's authorization confirms that it is not opposed by the primary disputants or the major powers. Operations opposed by either of these two groups will likely never come into being. Of course, a sudden policy change by the primary disputants or the major powers to actively oppose the mission could damage the peacekeeping operation irrevocably.

The internal characteristics of a peacekeeping operation were generally found to have a relatively minor impact on the mission's success. A clear mandate was useful, but hardly critical in determining the outcome. When the mandate was vague, the underlying political consensus was already shaky, and the mission experienced problems with support from the various interested parties. The same conclusion is appropriate with respect to the financing and organization of the peacekeeping force. Problems with funding and command served to make the operations less efficient, but not necessarily significantly less successful overall. Budget deficits were ameliorated by voluntary contributions or ignored. Command, control, and coordination difficulties were never serious enough to jeopardize any of the operations.

Two aspects of the operations did have an impact on peacekeeping success: geography and neutrality. Peacekeeping operations performed best when their areas of deployment adequately separated the combatants, were fairly invulnerable to attack, and permitted easy observation. The absence of these conditions undermined confidence in the operations and allowed minor incidents to escalate. The neutrality of the peacekeeping force was also significant. If the peacekeeping force was perceived as biased, support from interested parties was likely to be withheld or withdrawn, which was often enough to sabotage an operation. Neutral behavior is not always linked with nonaligned force composition. The likelihood is much less, however, that a force composed of soldiers of nonaligned states will take action favoring one party or will be perceived as doing so.

From these findings, we can draw up a few guidelines regarding the use of peacekeeping forces. Peacekeeping is most appropriate in an interstate conflict in which all parties are willing to halt hostilities and accept a peacekeeping force. Beyond the two or three primary disputants, other interested parties and subnational groups deserve attention. In the face of opposition from them, the peacekeeping option might be reconsidered, unless the opposition is minor or would not involve violent actions. This criterion may confine peacekeeping operations to conflicts that involve relatively few actors, for the probability of consensus will decrease as the number of interested parties increases.

Once a peacekeeping operation has been authorized, the field commander must give special attention to ensuring a proper geographic deployment, as well as continuing the norm of neutral force composition. Although the issues of mandate, financing, and command should not be ignored, neither should problems with them hold up the operation.

The findings of this chapter do more than confirm the conventional wisdom about peacekeeping, although in some cases they do that too. The importance of the mandate and the role of the superpowers is considerably less than has been assumed. Analysts have also overestimated the importance of logistical concerns. The findings confirm the writings on international conflict and peacekeeping regarding the importance of third parties, neutrality, and geography.

Chapter IV

When Peacekeeping Does Not Lead to Peace: Peacekeeping and Conflict Resolution

THE PERFORMANCE of peacekeeping operations on the second criterion for success—promoting resolution of the underlying dispute following the deployment of peacekeeping troops—is considerably less impressive than even its mixed record on limiting armed conflict. The prospects for success are rather sobering.

Unlike the great variation across peacekeeping operations in their ability to limit armed conflict, there is virtually uniform failure in these same operations when it comes to conflict resolution. As one commentator noted, following deployment peacekeeping operations tend to "roll over and go to sleep."[1] Among all operations deployed prior to conflict resolution, only UNEF II can be classified as a success. Slightly more than five years after UNEF II deployment, Israel and Egypt signed the Camp David accords and subsequently a peace treaty, resolving many of the most serious outstanding issues between the former enemies.

The remaining five operations in this study were not able to promote longstanding peace among the disputants. The ONUC operation might be said to have achieved long-term stability in the Congo, but such success was largely the result of enforcement actions, not peacekeeping strategies. When that force acted as peacekeeping missions are designed to, little progress occurred toward peacemaking. UNEF I was abruptly terminated just before the Six-Day War, another in a series of Arab-Israeli military confrontations. The MNF seemed only to exacerbate the conflict among the major factions and other actors in Lebanon; one might conclude that the MNF impeded, rather than promoted, conflict resolution. UNFICYP and UNIFIL remain in place today, testaments to the long-term failure to achieve compromise solutions in two other troubled areas of the world.

The strategy in the last chapter, examining a number of factors along three dimensions in order to detect which might affect the ability of peacekeeping operations to limited armed conflict, is not suitable here. The concern is not with variation in outcome, as all but one of the missions failed to promote conflict resolution. Accordingly, here I explore the experience of UNEF II to discover what made that operation successful in achieving its second goal. Then, in light of the experience of all six operations, I examine four different explanations for why peacekeeping operations have had difficulty in achieving long-term peace.

UNEF II and Conflict Resolution

The signing of a peace treaty by Israel and Egypt was the culmination of a long series of dramatic events that started with the end of the 1973 Yom Kippur War. The UNEF II peacekeeping operation was the only one studied here that was *followed* by a major peace agreement between the disputants. A logical question is what role, if any, the peacekeeping operation played in this success.

If one explanation for the success of UNEF II in conflict resolution was the direct role that the peacekeeping force, and the United Nations in general, played in the peace process, one might attribute the peacemaking success to certain characteristics of UNEF II that perhaps were absent from the other operations. An examination of UNEF II, U.N. diplomatic activity, and events preceding Camp David, however, does not support this explanation. U.N. and UNEF II involvement in diplomatic activities was not substantial compared to other actors' efforts and produced few tangible results.

The United Nations was involved primarily at the earliest stages of the peace process, and then its main concern was with negotiating agreements over the conduct of the peacekeeping force, rather than with the broad underlying sources of dispute between Egypt and Israel.[2] Just after UNEF II was deployed, Egyptian and Israeli commanders met under the auspices of the peacekeeping operation to discuss preliminary measures concerning the cease-fire. Subsequent meetings produced agreements to allow the unrestricted flow of supplies to the trapped units of the Egyptian army as well as disengagement of the respective military forces. Although one could point to the instrumental role that UNEF II and the United Nations played in these talks, two strong caveats diminish the accomplishment. First, the agreements were mostly procedural in character and did not involve the substantive issues of dispute in the Arab-Israeli conflict (e.g., who would have ultimate control of the Sinai). Second, the success in those limited agreements came about only with extensive external involvement and pressure, most notably by the United States.

The failure of direct U.N. action to achieve more than procedural agreements does not mean that the U.N. made no comprehensive attempts at conflict resolution. The United Nations and its various organs continued to pass resolutions concerning the Arab-Israeli conflict, but with little impact on the politics of the region. Most significantly, U.N. Secretary-General Kurt Waldheim convened a Middle East peace conference in December 1973 in Geneva, the conference, under U.S. and Soviet leadership, included Egypt, Jordan, and Israel and adjourned the day after it began, with nothing substantive accomplished. Representatives of the participants remained in Geneva for further talks with the UNEF II commander, but these negotiations were also largely ineffective.

The primary facilitators of the Middle East peace process were third-party states, whose external intervention combined with a new willingness by the disputants to resolve the conflict. In 1975, Israel and Egypt came to sign what may have been their first substantive agreement. They agreed to the principle of resolving the conflict peacefully. They also defined various lines of demarcation that affected early warning stations, oil fields, and military deployments, and Egypt agreed to permit Israeli cargoes through the Suez Canal. The agreement was largely achieved by the intervention of the United States. President Ford held meetings with Egyptian and Israeli leaders, and Secretary of State Kissinger engaged in several rounds of his now-famous shuttle diplomacy. In addition, the United States made a number of guarantees and commitments to both sides in return for the agreement.

The major signposts of progress on the road to Camp David and beyond were also largely achieved by third-party mediators and go-betweens, although the United Nations was not one of those actors. In early 1977, the Israeli prime minister, Menachem Begin, indicated a desire to compromise with Egypt in order to promote peace. Using Romania and Morocco as intermediaries, the two sides exchanged proposals and indicated their willingness to negotiate. It is significant that neither state desired a renewal of the U.N.-sponsored talks in Geneva, as that would have involved the inclusion of other parties and thereby limited the opportunity for any agreement.

Egyptian President Sadat's dramatic visit to Israel in November 1977 was the catalyst that led to further progress on the diplomatic front. The

U.S. president, Jimmy Carter, brought Begin and Sadat together and me-
diated what would be known as the Camp David accords.[3] U.S. pressure
on Israel is often credited with wrapping up the agreement. Subsequently,
U.S. mediation helped conclude the other agreements between the historically bitter enemies.

Overall, the United Nations played little role in the process that led Israel
and Egypt to sign a peace treaty and foster better relations. On the one
hand, UNEF II was important in that its success in limiting armed conflict
may have contributed to an environment that made the dramatic events
just described possible.[4] In that way, we might say that UNEF II contributed
to conflict resolution. On the other hand, UNEF II was very little concerned
with the larger issues of the Arab-Israeli conflict. No explicit mechanism
tied to the peacekeeping operation was designed to help end the conflict.
International diplomacy was left to other U.N. initiatives, which proved
largely ineffective.

It is of course difficult, if not improper, to generalize from a single case.
Nevertheless, if one were to derive conclusions from the UNEF II experience
in conflict resolution, they would not necessarily favor the peacekeeping
strategy. Conflict resolution in this case appears to have had little to do
with the peacekeeping operation itself. More critically, the parties involved
showed a strong willingness to make concessions and peace. Without this
prerequisite, it is doubtful that any diplomatic efforts would have been
fruitful. The second key ingredient in the successful outcome was the
positive action taken by several states, most notably the United States, to
mediate the process and encourage resolution. Perhaps only a major power
with strong ties to one or both of the participants could have achieved this
outcome. In any event, one cannot attribute the success of the UNEF II in
conflict resolution to the characteristics or actions of the peacekeeping force.

The Failure to Achieve Conflict Resolution

The experiences of the five peacekeeping operations besides UNEF II in
conflict resolution vary, but the net results are similar: none promoted
conflict resolution between the primary combatants. Several of the operations, not surprisingly, met with little success because most of their efforts
were not directed at promoting long-term conflict resolution. The first
peacekeeping operation, UNEF I, had no real mechanism to deal with the
broader issues of the Arab-Israeli conflict. That operation concentrated on
what was regarded as its primary mission, achieving an "immediate peace"
(which it accomplished reasonably well), rather than on finding a per-

manent solution.[5] Thus, UNEF I had a short-term orientation and did not seek to deal with larger, long-term concerns.

UNIFIL also has devoted little effort to diplomatic activities, although it has been more active than UNEF I. Much of the U.N. focus has been on crises arising from the peacekeeping deployment, rather than on seeking long-term solutions to Lebanese instability. In 1979 and 1981, Secretary-General Waldheim and other U.N. officials worked feverishly to get all the protagonists to cooperate with UNIFIL on such basic items as withdrawing to designated zones and agreeing not to attack UNIFIL forces. Similar to UNEF I, these were immediate goals, and the most notable accomplishments were negotiated localized cease-fires that proved to be short-lived. Because the force—and perhaps the United Nations in general—has been preoccupied with various acts of violence in southern Lebanon, there have been few or no sustained efforts at conflict resolution. In that sense, both UNEF I and UNIFIL were victims, in part, of a lack of effort, although the sources of that inaction may differ.

Not all the peacekeeping operations can point to inaction for their failure to promote a peaceful end to hostilities. The remaining three peacekeeping operations made substantial diplomatic efforts at conflict resolution without success. UNFICYP has tried repeatedly to resolve the conflict between the Greeks and the Turks. The resolution creating UNFICYP provided for the appointment of a mediator charged with helping to draw up a peaceful solution to the conflict in consultation with the protagonists. In addition, Secretary-General Thant appointed a special representative to negotiate on his behalf. The mediator put out a report in early 1965 outlining the positions of all sides and setting the parameters for a possible final settlement. Rejecting the report because it foreclosed the possibility of partitioning the island, Turkey refused further cooperation with that mediator (who soon resigned) or any replacement.[6]

With the failure of mediation efforts, the secretary-general's special representative was given greater powers and was able to foster continued dialogue between all sides at various diplomatic levels. There were several renewed attempts at diplomacy throughout the history of the operation through both the special representative and the secretaries-general. Despite repeated efforts, often driven by crises such as the 1974 Turkish invasion, there have been no substantive agreements on resolving the conflict. The incompatible demands of the Greeks (complete control over the island or its unification with Greece) and of the Turks (partitioning the island) have confounded negotiations. Neither years of diplomatic intervention nor unilateral and multinational initiatives have affected the impasse. At best, the diplomatic initiatives have succeeded in achieving numerous and repeated formal meetings between all sides. In June 1992 the United Nations revived diplomatic attempts to resolve the Cyprus dispute, bringing together leaders of the Greek and Turkish communities on the island. There has also been an implicit threat to withdraw the UNFICYP force if no progress is made in the negotiations.

The secretary-general's special representative was also actively involved at several junctures in getting the leaders of the Congo factions together for talks.[7] These meetings produced few important results. More effectively, the United Nations forced a reconvention of the Congolese parliament; U.N. pressure led to a strengthened government under President Kasavubu, which achieved some measure of unity. Several attempts by the United Nations to broker a peace agreement between the factions, however, failed in the first two years of the ONUC operation.

Secretary-General Thant introduced a plan for national reconciliation that provided a blueprint for restoring peace to the Congo. The participants largely rejected it until the United Nations called for economic sanctions and eventually authorized the use of offensive military force by the peacekeeping troops. By early 1963, it might be said that the United Nations had achieved a measure of conflict resolution that was to permit ONUC's departure a year later. Conflict resolution did not follow, however, upon the creation of the proper environment for negotiations or upon traditional diplomatic efforts. It took some measure of coercion to force a resolution; because of that, ONUC cannot be considered a successful application of the peacekeeping strategy for conflict resolution.

U.N. peacekeeping operations were not the only ones that suffered problems in conflict resolution. The MNF, and particularly its U.S. component, had great difficulties in bringing peace and stability to Lebanon. U.S. envoy Philip Habib and the secretary of state, George Schultz, were successful initially in promoting negotiations between Israel and Lebanon over the conditions of Israeli troop withdrawal and on matters concerning relations between the two states. The negotiations led to an agreement that ended the state of war between them and clarified the status of Israel's presence in southern Lebanon. Beyond that agreement, however, there was little progress. Syria rejected all U.S. attempts at facilitating a withdrawal of Syrian forces, and as the fighting intensified in Beirut, diplomatic efforts concentrated on achieving short-term cease-fires rather than long-term conflict resolution.

The only major attempt at conflict resolution was a meeting in Lausanne, Switzerland, among the warring Lebanese factions in late 1983. In general, this conference represented a few steps back from resolving the conflict rather than any progress. First, the conflict achieved no substantive agreement beyond a temporary cease-fire. The MNF even became a sticking point in the negotiations, as some factions insisted that the peacekeeping force be withdrawn. The MNF thus became an obstacle to peace, rather than a facilitator. Second, the conference resulted in some backtracking on conflict resolution. Several factions insisted that the agreement with Israel be abrogated before further negotiations took place. The Gemayel government acceded to this demand. The net effect of the Lausanne conference was thus to undo the only success that had been achieved.

The United Nations was not intimately involved in the primary diplomatic initiatives. An attempt to replace the MNF with a U.N. peacekeeping force failed; the Soviet Union vetoed the authorizing resolution in the Security Council. The international body made no other noteworthy attempts at peacekeeping.

In general then, despite varying experiences, peacekeeping operations have been almost uniformly unable to promote conflict resolution.

Explanations for the Conflict Resolution Failure

With the success of UNEF II only doubtfully attributable to the peacekeeping force, the almost uniform failure of peacekeeping operations to promote conflict resolution lends itself to several explanations: (1) the failure to limit armed conflict, (2) the interconnection of peacekeeping and negotiation, (3) the creation of a counterproductive environment for negotiations, and (4) the inappropriateness of the peacekeeping strategy to the task.

Failure to Limit Armed Conflict

A simple explanation for why peacekeeping forces are unable to promote conflict resolution points to their inability to perform their supervisory function. That is, negotiations could not be successful if the cease-fire was repeatedly broken. Besides being the only operation that was able to promote conflict resolution, UNEF II was at least among the most successful operations in limiting armed conflict. One might credibly argue that an Israeli-Egyptian peace treaty would not have been possible in an environment in which the threat of renewed warfare was imminent or high, yet the threat of renewed warfare does not always prove to have negative effects of peacemaking.

An examination of the other five cases yields somewhat less compelling evidence in support of this explanation. On the one hand, when violence did erupt, there was a tendency to focus on restoring cease-fires and agreeing on withdrawal plans to the detriment of negotiations for long-term resolution. ONUC and UNIFIL, in particular, found themselves responding to various crises that sidetracked other efforts. The United Nations, similar to many other organizations, is crisis driven and only has limited attention and resources. Furthermore, the actors involved will be less receptive to settling their differences when immediate threats to their security are present; it may be politically impossible for them to negotiate a comprehensive agreement when they are still fighting with their enemy. Under these conditions, the failure to keep the peace will certainly harm attempts to solve the overall conflict, and all parties will have a short-term orientation. Thus, this explanation has some validity as a reason why peacekeeping forces *could* fail in conflict resolution, but it does not explain why the peacekeeping operations under study here *did* fail.

Those peacekeeping operations that were successful in limiting armed conflict had as much difficulty in conflict resolution as those that could not stop the violence in the area of deployment. Progress toward conflict resolution in Cyprus, for example, was no more evident at the outset of the deployment when shooting incidents were more common and during the Turkish invasion than when the situation was stable. Similarly, the MNF was as ineffective before the renewal of fighting as after the terrorist attacks on U.S. and French positions. Perhaps most damaging to this explanation is the experience of UNEF I. That operation was among the more successful ones in deterring violence, at least until 1967, yet it also was completely ineffective in promoting conflict resolution; had UNEF I been successful in peacemaking, it is likely that several of the other peacekeeping operations in the Middle East would have been unnecessary.

Judging from the six experiences, we might be able to say that stopping the fighting could be a necessary condition for success in conflict resolution. What is clear, however, is that it is far from a sufficient condition. The successful operations we noted in the last chapter were no better at achieving their second goal of long-term peace than those that were failures at limiting armed conflict. Other explanations must account for the different experiences in limiting armed conflict having the same outcome—failure to promote lasting peace.

The Interconnection of Peacekeeping and Negotiation

A second explanation for the failure to achieve conflict resolution centers on the connection between the efforts to limit armed conflict and those to negotiate an end to the dispute. A peacekeeping mission can either provide mechanisms for conciliation as part of the initial agreement to station troops or depend on other parties or chance to facilitate a settlement. Some analysts argue that the former will result in serious problems, others cite the latter as the cause of failure.[8] Our sample of cases provides examples of both approaches, yet analysis reveals that peacekeeping encounters something of a two-edged sword in seeking to stimulate negotiations or mediation; both options are fraught with pitfalls.

Providing no mechanism for negotiation runs the risk that nothing will be done. No guide to how to initiate the peace process means heavy reliance on the initiative of states who only recently were fighting with one another. This does not necessarily bode well, as is evident in the experiences of UNEF I and UNIFIL. The United Nations and its peacekeeping operations made little effort to bring the Arabs and Israelis together for anything other than consultations about the procedures of the peacekeeping operations and troop withdrawal. UNEF I performed well in limiting the armed conflict, but the Six-Day War is powerful evidence of the ineffectiveness of not providing mechanisms for conflict resolution. Placed in southern Lebanon to separate Israel from Palestinian units, UNIFIL has not been able to stimulate any dialogue between opposing sides. The United Nations has offered no strong initiatives to solve the problems.

Reliance on third parties, in the absence of international initiatives or mechanisms, is also far from an effective strategy. In support of this approach, one might cite the effectiveness of the United States in facilitating the Camp David agreement as well as most recently in arranging Middle East peace negotiations between Israel and her neighbors. Yet in other cases third-party intervention has not worked. Various initiatives in Cyprus and Lebanon have produced no promising results, despite the best of intentions. There is also the risk that third-party intervention could hamper progress in conflict resolution. An interested third party may stifle movement toward reconciliation if that state tries to serve its own interests in the course of promoting a solution to the conflict. The introduction of a third set of preferences into the negotiations may make it impossible to achieve an outcome acceptable to all parties.[9] Thus, third-party intervention is most helpful when it is relatively disinterested, and even then it has no strong record of effectiveness.

As problematic as not providing mechanisms for conflict resolution can be, there may be no alternative for some peacekeeping operations. In U.N.-sponsored operations, the Security Council may find it difficult to achieve consensus on the form or substance of the mediation efforts. In the Congo, the Security Council was split over the role of the peacekeeping forces and their relation to the Lumumba government. Some council members also became increasingly dissatisfied with the amount of power given to the secretary-general to pursue a settlement. A stalemate in the council forced the General Assembly to assume responsibility for ONUC. Similar problems could arise in the future, given, for example, the divergent policy preferences among U.N. members vis-à-vis the Arab-Israeli and Indo-Pakistani conflicts, which make it unlikely that the Security Council will grant the secretary-general sweeping powers or that the General Assembly will supersede the council by its actions. The result is likely to be the establishment of a peacekeeping force without any corresponding mechanisms for resolving the conflict.

As problematic as no explicit mechanism for conflict resolution can be, the alternative does not appear to have a better empirical record. The United Nations was actively involved in trying to promote peace in the Congo and in Cyprus. Special representatives of the secretaries-general, as well as the secretaries themselves, worked actively for a negotiated settlement. The agreements were not forthcoming in the case of Cyprus, and only with the use of military force in the Congo. In Cyprus, the mediator and the peacekeeping force commander held parallel positions in the operation's hierarchy, and there was close cooperation between the two. Although such an arrangement was administratively successful, the mediator was unable to forge consensus between the disputants. Thus, even under the best of circumstances, combining the supervision and conciliation efforts did not produce a settlement.

Besides no strong evidence of effectiveness, a close association between the supervisory and conflict resolution functions could have negative side effects. Negotiations for conflict resolution may be complicated by their association with the peacekeeping mission, or vice versa.[10] States may find it difficult to regard the peacekeeping troops as neutral when they are aligned with the personnel that must make controversial decisions and proposals in the search for an acceptable compromise. Initial failure in conciliation may spill over and cause problems for the troops' function of preserving the cease-fire.[11] The disputing parties may begin to question the neutrality of the troops, or they may withdraw their support for a process that might be perceived as counterproductive to their interests. On the other hand, problems with the peacekeeping mission may distract peace efforts from their central purpose. If all efforts are spent on keeping the peace and related concerns, little attention may be left over for peacemaking. When the MNF's role in Lebanon began to dominate the discussion between the various warlords in that country, the MNF actually became an obstacle to conflict resolution.

The analysis here does not support the contentions of either side concerning the relationship of the peacekeeping force to the conflict resolution efforts. Peacekeeping forces had problems whether they were closely associated with conciliation efforts or were involved in no diplomatic initiatives. This explanation does not bring us any closer to understanding why peacekeeping forces cannot conflict resolution, nor does it offer many guidelines for success; different variations of conflict resolution efforts met with the same unfortunate fate.

A Counterproductive Environment for Negotiation

Until now, we have accepted the assumption that peacekeeping improves the environment for negotiation and reconciliation between disputants.[12] A third explanation for peacekeeping's conflict resolution failures argues the opposite: peacekeeping operations actually inhibit negotiation or lead to its stagnation.

Negotiations appear to be more successful when there are significant time pressures on the parties involved.[13] Concessions are more often forthcoming when there is pressure to reach an agreement; it is not surprising that conciliatory actions tend to increase as a deadline for settlement approaches. States will also make concessions when they believe the situation might adversely change in the near future or when they tire of the political, economic, or human costs of war. Peacekeeping, according to this explanation, removes much of the immediacy from the situation and thereby takes away some of the incentive for negotiations or concessions.[14] A cease-fire dissipates internal political or moral pressures to end the conflict. In the absence of these pressures, states could fear that opponents will view offers of concessions or conciliatory actions as signs of weakness and fail to reciprocate.

Once peacekeeping forces are in place, bargaining positions may harden, precipitating a stalemate.[15] The status quo becomes an acceptable alternative to serious negotiation or renewed fighting; the status quo entails no bloodshed, as well as no need to offer concessions that affect national interests or are difficult to sell to a domestic political audience. A patient strategy of doing nothing thus yields some benefits and preserves the hope for a more favorable set of circumstances at a later time. We noted in the last chapter that the preservation of the status quo and a reluctance to negotiate by the extant government was a reason that peacekeeping was not well-suited to civil conflicts. It is now apparent that one or both parties' tolerance (if not preference) for the status quo provided by a cease-fire can also cause problems.

UNIFIL, MNF, and ONUC never reached the stage in which the military pressure for action was eliminated; the peacekeeping force was preoccupied with violations of the cease-fire. Yet this explanation has a ring of truth for the other operations in our study. The UNEF operations for Egypt and Israel tended to take few risks before the Sadat visit; as the state most served by the status quo, Israel had and continues to have few incentives to negotiate seriously except on its own terms. Similarly, Egyptian and other Arab leaders risk political suicide or worse if they accept those terms. In Cyprus, the peacekeeping force seems to have reinforced the stalemate, especially after the Turkish invasion. Greeks on the island still control most of the territory and do not want to offer special status to Turkish residents. Having their own enclave, the self-proclaimed Turkish Republic of North Cyprus, the Turkish Cypriots also feel little urgency to deal with the bitterness on the island. The peacekeeping forces have done such a good job in limiting armed conflict that the fear has lessened, but so has the perceived need to take some action in the situation.

One might suggest avoiding this trap by stationing peacekeeping troops for only a predetermined amount of time or making the disputants pay for the operation.[16] Indeed, most U.N. operations are authorized for only limited periods, yet these deadlines have proven ineffective. Peacekeeping mandates are regularly renewed or extended, so the approach of a deadline does not have the same effect it would if the operation were really to cease at that point. Decision makers in the United Nations and in national capitals face the options of mandate renewal or peacekeeping force withdrawal and possible recurrence of warfare. Historically, they have opted for the risk-averse choice of continuing the peacekeeping mission; they view stalemate without fighting as preferable to possible military conflict. As long as rivals know that peacekeeping deadlines are essentially meaningless, however, they will have little incentive to hurry negotiations or work for a settlement.

War has many undesirable qualities, but it can pressure combatants to seek solutions and focus world attention on the dispute. Peacekeeping operations have many desirable qualities, not the least of which is to stop the widespread killing of human beings. Yet they also may remove the urgency from the situation and thereby contribute to the protraction of conflict. Paradoxically, decreasing the level of hostility may make it more difficult to arrange a final resolution to the conflict.[17] This accounts, in part, for some peacekeeping operations' failure to promote conflict resolution.

Inappropriateness of the Peacekeeping Strategy

The preceding explanations for the failure of peacekeeping operations to promote conflict resolution relate, to a great degree, to the framework or functioning of the operation. The final explanation goes to the heart of the peacekeeping philosophy: peacekeeping has failed to promote conflict resolution because it is an inappropriate mechanism for doing so. Variations in context and implementation strategies cannot overcome this fatal flaw.

Peacekeeping is an inappropriate strategy for conflict resolution because its basic design is not geared toward the requirements for effective peace-making.[18] Most of the peacekeeping strategy and organization is consistent with achieving the first duty of limiting armed conflict. The quasi-military setup and composition of the force favors truce supervision and not diplomacy. One could study the *Peacekeeper's Handbook* or any of the more philosophical writings on the subject and note that peace*keeping* is relatively unconcerned with peace*making*.[19] When peacekeeping operations do include mechanisms for conflict resolution, as was the case with UNFICYP, they are limited and not always a logical extension of the peacekeeping operation.

More often than not, the peacekeeping operation does not have provisions for peacemaking and must rely on diplomatic initiatives by the sponsoring organization or group of countries. Most of those efforts are not in any but a nominal way connected to the peacekeeping operation; furthermore, there is little evidence that they are more effective when tried during a peacekeeping operation, despite the claims that peacekeeping offers a more beneficial climate for negotiation. That is, peacekeeping operations cannot take much credit for conflict resolution, even when negotiated peace settlements occur on their watch, as was the case with UNEF II.

Peacekeeping is also built on the notion that the force is neutral and should not be actively involved in the dispute. Yet active involvement and perhaps passing judgment on the viability or validity of disputant positions is contrary to the noninvolvement standard. It may not be surprising that ONUC settled the conflict in the Congo only after it violated peacekeeping practice, specifically supporting one side in the conflict, and became actively involved.

The essence of this argument is thus that limiting armed conflict and peacemaking are two fundamentally different missions. Peacekeeping operations are designed to limit armed conflict and do not have the mechanisms necessary to make peace, if indeed peace could be achieved at all in some cases of intractable conflict. We might expect that any time operations try to achieve goals for which they are not designed, they will fail more often than not.

Conclusion

Regarding the role that peacekeeping operations play in conflict resolution, what is abundantly clear is that they are not very successful. Four of the six operations were undeniably ineffective in resolving the underlying dispute between the principal actors. The ONUC operation achieved success in the Congo, but only through the use of enforcement and other military actions contrary to the peacekeeping philosophy. The sole case of a peacekeeping operation followed by a substantive agreement between the disputants is something of a chimera; the Israeli-Egyptian rapprochement was found to owe little of its triumph to UNEF II, except perhaps with respect to providing a suitable military and political environment for reconciliation, and even that assertion is subject to some debate.

Four explanations for the persistent failure of peacekeeping operations were explored. First, peacekeeping operations could not achieve conflict resolution if they were unable to stop the violence; some missions were preoccupied with short-term problems with keeping the peace and therefore did not devote much attention to long-term resolution efforts. Even those operations that did limit violence had difficulties in peacemaking. A second explanation centered on the extent of the connection between the peacekeeping efforts and the diplomatic efforts to resolve the dispute. Failure occurred in a variety of scenarios; it seemed not to matter whether the peacekeeping operation had extensive diplomatic initiatives or no mechanisms at all for finding a peaceful settlement to the dispute. A third possibility was that peacekeeping actually inhibits negotiations by removing some of the urgency from the situation. This was found to have some validity, although one could not offer it as a general explanation for why peacekeeping operations fail. The final explanation, the inappropriateness of peacekeeping operations for conflict resolution, although not negating the utility that parts of other explanations may have, is one that is able to account for all operations' experiences. Regardless of the circumstances of the peacekeeping operation—type of conflict, actors involved, and other elements of context—the end result was failure. It may be true that no diplomatic efforts can resolve two or more fundamentally incompatible positions, yet it appears that peacekeeping is not the mechanism to achieve satisfactory diplomatic outcomes.

The failure of peacekeeping operations to resolve conflict should not imply that the peacekeeping strategy should be abandoned. Rather it suggests that the situations in which it is applied, the expectations it generates, and the supplemental mechanisms needed must undergo some alteration. Peacekeeping operations may be best suited for use *after* some measure of conflict resolution, rather than the traditional preresolution deployment.

Chapter **V**

Permanent, regional, or multinational peace keeping force.

Institutional Alternatives to Traditional U.N. Peacekeeping Operations

PEACEKEEPING operations have performed some valuable functions in mitigating armed conflict. At the same time, they have not fulfilled all the expectations of the founders of the peacekeeping strategy. There are several notable instances in which violence in the area of deployment persisted or escalated despite the presence of peacekeeping forces. In addition, peacekeeping has been largely unsuccessful in promoting the long-term resolution of conflict. In the face of these imperfections, there have been various alternatives proposed to existing arrangements.

I have defined traditional peacekeeping operations to be those organized by the United Nations on an ad hoc basis to act as an interposition force following a cease-fire, but before the disputants reach any agreement resolving major issues in dispute. Previous peacekeeping operations share most or all of these characteristics. Alternatives to this arrangement represent variations on the institutional arrangements and on the functions of peacekeeping operations.

Institutional alternatives can be divided into two categories. First are those suggestions that seek to address the problems associated with the ad hoc method of organizing and directing U.N. peacekeeping operations, which can be viewed under the umbrella of plans for a permanent U.N. peacekeeping force. Second are those that shift the responsibility for peacekeeping away from the United Nations to other entities; most commonly these are either peacekeeping operations organized by regional organizations or multinational forces not under the control or direction of an international organization.

A Permanent U.N. Peacekeeping Force

U.N. peacekeeping operations today must be organized on an ad hoc basis. There is no permanent force, and the United Nations must rely on the voluntary troop contributions of its members. Only a few states (most notably Canada and the Nordic states) have made any efforts to identify and train troops for possible peacekeeping duty. Coordination and supply of peacekeeping missions occur after the authorization of the operation, with the mode of organization varying each time, not entirely because of the situational requirements of the mission. There have been few major changes in the structure of U.N. observer and peacekeeping operations over the last fifty years.[1]

Historical Background

The idea of a permanent peacekeeping force has extended roots in the post–World War II era. According to article 43 of the U.N. Charter, members were to make available to the Security Council troops and material to be used in the organization's enforcement actions. The inability of the superpowers to agree on the details of the plans meant that the provisions of article 43 never reached fruition. Although such forces were intended as military units rather than as peacekeeping troops, the concept of an international force was envisioned by the framers of the charter. Later proposals for a peacekeeping force resembled those charter provisions, except that the mission assigned the forces no longer involved military enforcement.

Recognizing the need for an international force, but also understanding that the superpowers could not agree on one that involved collective security, Trygve Lie, the U.N. secretary-general, offered a pathbreaking proposal in the late 1940s.[2] He suggested that an international force be created, based upon the model of observer groups then operating in the Middle East. This was the beginning of the movement for a permanent international force that was not designed for collective security purposes. Even such a limited plan, however, failed to gain the approval of the Security Council, and of the Soviet Union in particular. Shortly thereafter, the General Assembly did approve a "shadow force" consisting of names of potential recruits for international observer missions; the collection of such names, however, never took place. It is notable in this instance that plans for a permanent force quickly gave way to a less far-reaching proposal. This scenario was to be repeated several times over the next decades.

The excitement surrounding the initial success of UNEF I in the late 1950s inspired a new wave of proposals for a permanent force ready to go in the event of another crisis. Many ideas, including those of Secretary-General Dag Hammarskjöld, focused on standby forces, akin to military reserves, that could be activated on short notice. Although many sources expressed support for the general concept, disagreements between the superpowers again negated any possibility for the creation of such a force.

In the early 1960s, Lester Pearson, who was instrumental in the formation of UNEF I, proposed creating standby forces, perhaps through the joint efforts of several states.[3] Again, this represented a concession to the reality that more ambitious proposals would fail. This suggestion called only for a stand*by* force, not a stand*ing* force. Furthermore, the proposal suggested that the United Nations might not have a primary role in the formation of peacekeeping units, a job left to a consortium of interested states under a multilateral agreement. Pearson undoubtedly had the Nordic countries in mind, as they were already involved in joint efforts at training peacekeeping personnel.

With the deployment of UNEF I, ONUC, and UNFICYP, there was some recognition that the United Nations should develop regular procedures for such operations. The initial result was the Special Committee on Peace-keeping Operations.[4] Throughout its history, this committee has been a forum for disagreement between various states with differing conceptions of the mission and conduct of peacekeeping operations. Consequently, the committee's progress has been minimal, similar to the inability to reach agreement that has plagued disarmament efforts at the United Nations.

Over the past two decades, various proposals for improving peacekeeping force readiness have been quite limited, but even so they have gone unadopted.[5] Many plans have advocated that states earmark troops for peacekeeping duties, with those troops available on short notice should they be required; this is one step below the level of readiness achieved with standby forces. This arrangement would still necessitate a U.N. mission organized on an ad hoc basis, but the troops would presumably have had some training in peacekeeping techniques and would also be more readily available. Still, the individual states control most of the training and supply aspects of the force, and such proposals belie the earlier formulations of a permanent peacekeeping force. In 1992, U.N. Secretary-General Boutros-Ghali revived the idea of an international standing force that could assume peacekeeping and other duties.

Characteristics of a Permanent Peacekeeping Force

Describing the characteristics of a permanent peacekeeping force as laid out in various proposals might be compared to integrating the descriptions made by the proverbial blind men about an elephant. The various proposals just noted as well as those in the academic literature represent a wide range of ideas.[6] While some stress an international army that may have some enforcement responsibilities, others advocate only troops that are earmarked for international duty. Furthermore, some proposals are highly detailed, including troop size and cost estimates for all aspects of the force; other proposals are unrefined and merely lay out general guidelines. Despite such wide variation, all of these ideas emanate from similar sets of assumptions and rationales. To single out any one of these proposals as the basis for evaluation might imply that possible praise and criticism apply only to that proposal, when they may apply equally to the range of plans that fall under the general category of permanent peacekeeping force proposals. Instead, identifying six dimensions of a permanent peacekeeping force covered in the various proposals (structure, training, administrative staffing, logistics, financing and authority), describing the breadth of suggestions and drawing comparisons with current practice, should establish what a permanent peacekeeping force might entail and provide a base for judging the utility of such a force.

Structure

Currently, contributions of peacekeeping personnel are solicited from member states, following authorization of the mission by the appropriate U.N. organ. The process of forming the peacekeeping contingent is somewhat chaotic, with little advance planning concerning which states will contribute how many troops. For the most part, these troops must be assembled in national units before they are sent to the crisis area. Indeed, even the troops themselves may be unaware until the last minute that they will be assigned peacekeeping roles.

The most ambitious proposals include provisions for a peacekeeping force that is truly international in character. The force would be composed of international civil servants who are trained jointly, stationed together, and immediately available for duty; such an international army might roughly parallel national efforts at defense, except that peacekeeping units would have less of an enforcement role, or none at all. Less extensive proposals advocate standby peacekeeping troops. In practice, this would involve forces that may or may not have joint training but would include predesignated national troops for rapid deployment to any area of the world. A less formal commitment is the idea of earmarking troops for peacekeeping duty. Here, a state would plan ahead so that a set number of its military personnel would be available for peacekeeping duty.

The range of options differs in the degree of coordination needed in the final formation of a force, as well as in the level of commitment that states must demonstrate. Yet the intent of each variation is to make troops available for peacekeeping duty on short notice.

Training

Some proposals dictate that U.N. soldiers undergo a rigorous training regimen under international auspices. Specialized training for peacekeeping is necessary because the attitudes, methods, and tactics of peacekeeping differ significantly from conventional military doctrine. Proposals range from a training center for national units run by the United Nations to a regular training schedule pursued by a standing international force. Joint multinational training, such as that presently done by the Nordic countries, is another possibility. The most limited form of training would involve national training for peacekeeping assignments as a part of every soldier's training, or at least for those who might be assigned peacekeeping duties.

At present, some national and multinational training programs do exist, but no training program directed by the United Nations.[7] The closest approximation to an international program is the series of seminars and materials sponsored by the International Peace Academy. Generally, the training of most peacekeeping troops takes places in their own military establishments, if they receive any special training at all. Any specific training in U.N. peacekeeping operations is likely the result of service experience in prior peacekeeping operations.

Administrative Staffing

Members of the Secretariat have directed and coordinated all U.N. operations, yet, there is no ongoing staff effort to formulate scenarios for peacekeeping, conduct simulations, or arrange for operation services, should a mission suddenly be authorized. Because of prior and current missions, the U.N. staff has some experience in these and related areas but undertakes no long-range planning.

Proposals for a permanent peacekeeping force all include an expanded role for the Secretariat or some other international body to provide for advance planning and coordination of any future operation. Common to the proposals is a larger staff assigned full-time to peacekeeping operations and an increase in staff scope and authority, with planning the most notable new function.

Logistics

To fulfill its mission, a peacekeeping operation requires a great deal of technical and material support, including transportation, communication, and basic supplies. Currently, peacekeeping troops receive most of this logistical support through the donations of the U.N. member countries or their own states; immediately following the authorization of the mission, the U.N. staff must determine and request whatever is needed. Clearly the requirements of each mission differ according to the locale and circumstances encountered. Still, no provisions exist for identifying potential donors of needed items, much less for keeping an inventory of food or supplies, although some equipment is stored in Italy.

A permanent peacekeeping force requires a well-developed infrastructure for logistical support. Various proposals advocate warehouses that can store necessary equipment and material. A more limited idea would be for the U.N. staff to secure prior commitments from states to supply certain items or assistance; for example, an industrialized state might be well suited to provide assistance in setting up a communication network. Some proposals are so detailed that they even discuss how to provide soldiers with their native foods. All the plans that address the logistics issue emphasize enhanced preparedness.

Financing

There are many innovative ideas on how a permanent U.N. peacekeeping force might be financed. Although the type of financing of course depends partly on the size and organization of the force, we might identify two broad categories of ideas. One involves U.N. members bearing the costs of the peacekeeping force, either through the regular budget or some special provision. The second is the creation of a permanent fund based on contributions from states, philanthropic organizations, businesses, or private individuals. In either case, the concern is to ensure an ongoing source of funding and avoid the heavy reliance on ad hoc special accounts and voluntary assistance that characterizes most current U.N. missions, although the United Nations has funded some peacekeeping and observation expenses out of the regular budget.

Authority

Any peacekeeping operation must address the question of what agency authorizes and directs the mission. The historical record shows that both the Security Council and the General Assembly have authorized peace-keeping operations, with the secretary-general maintaining great latitude in directing some missions and very little in others. Ideas for a permanent force mirror historical experience, with the authorizing body varying as does the organizational scheme for overseeing the mission. Some have suggested that a new committee or working group, perhaps composed of Security Council members and modeled on the Military Staff Committee, should direct missions. Recent experience suggests that the Security Council would be the authorizing body for future peacekeeping operations.

Rationale for a Permanent U.N. Peacekeeping Force

Most of the alleged benefits from a permanent peacekeeping force stem from the advantages attendant to increased preparedness. In this way, most advocates emphasize the operational, rather than the political, benefits of such a force. We might roughly place the advantages cited into four categories: professionalism, reaction time, efficiency, and financial stability. Basing this analysis of benefits on an ideal type—an international standing force and a well-developed support structure—we can be aware that the advantages of more limited proposals (e.g., earmarking troops) are cor-respondingly less. If the advantages are insufficient to justify creating a permanent peacekeeping force along the lines of the ideal type, then the case will be even less compelling for the other, more limited alternatives.

Professionalism

A major component of permanent peacekeeping proposals is extensive training for the troops, on the assumption such training will produce sol-diers familiar with basic peacekeeping philosophy and tactics. The impor-tance of special training in peacekeeping techniques derives from the in-adequacy of traditional military training for peacekeeping duties.

The ONUC and MNF operations reflect the impact of improper training. In the former, an officer who disobeyed or failed to receive orders not to conduct a particular maneuver jeopardized part of the mission.[8] The re-action of the MNF to sniper fire—using heavy artillery to bombard the surrounding hillsides—was compatible with a military mission, but not a peacekeeping one. It undermined the credibility and neutrality of the MNF, and future attacks on its positions resulted.

According to permanent peacekeeping force advocates, training results in professionalism that produces better organizational discipline and fewer mistakes in the conduct of an operation. In particular, training may prevent incidents such as an overreaction to attack or initiation of military force by peacekeeping troops and thus stave off a renewal of hostilities between the disputants.

Reaction Time

A second advantage attributed to enhanced preparedness is the improved reaction time between the authorization of a peacekeeping mission and the actual deployment of troops. Instead of the United Nations having to request troops from member states in various parts of the world, the troops will be immediately available in preorganized units; presumably the only lag time after authorization will be that needed to transport the troops from their bases to the site of the dispute. With bases around the world, this time could be very short. The United Nations has had some difficulties with reaction time in the past: the UNFICYP mission was not operationally complete for the first three months of its existence, and ONUC's staff was still forming six months after its authorization.[9] A permanent force would not have had these difficulties.

The ability to deploy a peacekeeping force quickly represents more than symbolic advantage. Rapid deployment can permit an interposition force to be in place at a critical juncture of the conflict—just after the agreement for a cease-fire.[10] The ability of the peacekeeping force to deploy quickly and efficiently also inspires confidence from the hostile parties and the surrounding population. Because UNIFIL was not able to deploy enough troops in its early phase, for example, it was the target of harassment by local groups.[11] This confidence is an essential component of a successful peacekeeping mission; if the disputants doubt the peacekeeping force's ability to deter armed conflict, they may decide to use military force to protect their interests. The 1982 Israeli invasion of Lebanon can be traced, in part, to this lack of confidence.

Efficiency

Many of the hypothesized benefits from a permanent peacekeeping force stem from the bureaucratic efficiency of such an arrangement, at least relative to the current ad hoc approach. Generally, peacekeeping missions under the new arrangement would be better coordinated. First, there is provision for an increase in staffing at U.N. headquarters, as well as for expanding staff functions to include primary responsibility for planning and implementing the operations, a quantum leap over present arrangements. Furthermore, planning mechanisms should allow staff and field officers to react more effectively to various contingencies that may arise. Finally, the immediate availability of logistical support and supplies should alleviate much of the disorganization and inefficiency that has complicated some U.N. peacekeeping missions.[12] One might expect fewer violent incidents between the peacekeeping force and the disputants, as well as less controversy over the duties and performance of the force.

Financial Stability

A permanent peacekeeping force involves a predetermined and secured source of funding. The mission should not have to worry about supply of funds or other support once it has received its authorization. Initial refusals of support would not jeopardize or slow down the mission. Thus one might hope to avoid the kind of financial haggling that led to a delay in UNTAG's deployment in Namibia with a smaller force than thought necessary. Perhaps more importantly, national withdrawal of financial or material support during the mission would no longer complicate performance of the force's duties; unlike the experience in the Congo, the recall of national troops (here they would be international civil servants) or the withholding of funds would not be an option. In addition, the large debt that has accumulated from peacekeeping operations may become a thing of the past. A permanent peacekeeping force, it is argued, will minimize disruptions and complications arising from funding.

Evaluation of a Permanent U.N. Peacekeeping Force

There are certainly some attractive features to a permanent U.N. peacekeeping force, but few studies have explored the extent and importance of those benefits. Indeed, the assumption is that a permanent peacekeeping force is, a priori, a good idea, a line of thought reflected by James Boyd: "It is difficult to argue against the intrinsic value of having a permanently constituted force."[13] Yet on closer inspection, the advantages of such a force are less significant than advocates have assumed. This is not to imply that a permanent force is not preferable to the present ad hoc arrangement, but rather that the benefits may not be dramatic enough to justify the expense and effort.

One result of a permanent U.N. peacekeeping force is the improved professional character of the unit. Although current forces do not receive the kind of training proposed under the most ambitious plans, they are not necessarily inexperienced in peacekeeping matters either. Many peacekeeping troops receive suitable training in their own countries. The Nordic countries have extensive training programs and, perhaps as a consequence, have contributed a disproportionate number of troops to past peacekeeping efforts. Furthermore, there have already been enough peacekeeping operations to create a large body of soldiers with prior experience now available for future peacekeeping duty. Training and experience among peacekeeping soldiers varies widely at the time of deployment, yet mistakes have been infrequent; only the MNF, a mission conducted outside U.N. auspices and in some ways contrary to U.N. principles, had any serious problems as a result. Individuals designated as commanders of the peacekeeping operations have had considerable experience, in some cases as commanders of earlier peacekeeping operations or observer missions. Given a choice, one would always prefer a well-trained unit or commander to one with less experience or training. Nevertheless, with respect to peacekeeping, the marginal advantage over the current system is not great. Until the use of peacekeeping operations expands, which indeed appears likely, there already are enough experienced personnel to form a significant portion of any new force.

Another feature of a permanent peacekeeping force is rapid deployment following mission authorization. If one assumes the maximum efficiency of such a force, then this point holds. Yet, once again, the performance of the troops under the present ad hoc arrangement is not as far from that standard as one might imagine. Experience has shown that, barring disagreements over financing or other matters, some troops are on the ground and in place between the combatants only a few days after authorization. Indeed, Canadian troops arrived in Cyprus within twenty-four hours of UNFICYP's approval. A symbolic presence is perhaps all that is needed in the first days of a cease-fire anyway. Even a full contingent of peacekeeping troops cannot prevent renewal of hostilities by a determined party. Maintenance of the cease-fire ultimately depends on the willingness of the parties to refrain from fighting. A symbolic deployment in the first few days, using troops from extant operations, thus far has not jeopardized that willingness. A complete staff may not be ready in a timely fashion under the current system, but the most critical step of deploying peacekeeping troops has gone forward remarkably well, given the constraints under which the United Nations must operate. The International Peace Academy, a foremost proponent of peacekeeping, is even so bold as to say that U.N. operations have not been substantially delayed because of the ad hoc system.[14]

A permanent U.N. peacekeeping force backed up by advance planning and a full-time staff would undoubtedly be more efficient that the present system. Nevertheless, there needs to be more than a comparative advantage to justify a permanent force on this point. A more stringent criterion is that the advantage gained must be critical to the success of the mission. In the case of improved efficiency, there is no evidence that this is true. Problems with command, control, and coordination in previous operations have been relatively minor, relating to problems over communication with troops with different native tongues and establishing lines of command across national contingents (see chapter 3); inadequate staff has never caused a peacekeeping operation to founder.[15] Those difficulties have never seriously complicated the ability of peacekeeping troops to perform their duties or jeopardized the overall mission.

The final pillar on which the argument for a permanent U.N. peacekeeping force rests is financial stability. Such reasoning, I believe, is flawed because it assumes that financial problems are separable from all other peacekeeping problems. In actuality, the willingness or reluctance of states to contribute to the support of a particular peacekeeping mission is a reflection of their political support for the operation. Historically, states' withholding or withdrawing their financial support or troops signaled an erosion of political support for the mission among key parts of the U.N. membership. An alternate and autonomous method of funding, besides member contributions, does not address the underlying problem of dissatisfaction or opposition from some significant states. The resulting hardships from financial instability have not been severe; even the accumulation of a large debt from peacekeeping operations has not seriously hindered the conduct of existing operations or the authorization of new ones.

The limited value of a permanent U.N. peacekeeping force also becomes evident if we look back to the most important factors in the success of a peacekeeping operation. A sometimes insurmountable obstacle to this success is the politically charged authorization process. In some instances, such as the ill-fated attempt to replace the MNF with a U.N. force, the Security Council has been unable to reach agreement on the need for a peacekeeping operation or on the conditions of deployment. Political disagreements can prevent a mission from ever being authorized. Even with agreement on the need for a peacekeeping operation, working out the final details and approval may take weeks or months, resulting in a delay in stopping the bloodshed far longer than the time lag in organizing an ad hoc peacekeeping force. The immediate availability of a permanent peacekeeping force is irrelevant to the fundamental need for political consensus among the members of the United Nations and the Security Council. As Morgenthau aptly noted, peacekeeping operations cannot be more reliable or efficient than the political interests and capability of nations allow them to be.[16]

A permanent peacekeeping force also does not address the need to have the support of third-party states and subnational actors in a dispute. On the one hand, a permanent force might behave in a more neutral fashion and thereby engender more support and cooperation from the disputing parties. Nevertheless, some conflicts are intractable, and the maintenance of a cease-fire does not serve the interests of all parties. Neither a permanent nor an ad hoc force can address such problems; yet it is exactly these concerns that are the most significant barriers to the effectiveness of a peacekeeping operation. A permanent peacekeeping force also cannot contribute to the resolution of underlying conflict. We noted in the previous chapter that past U.N. missions have been largely unsuccessful in facilitating the end of serious conflict between the disputants, even if they have made some progress in mitigating the most violent aspects. A permanent peacekeeping force alone cannot solve the unique dilemmas posed by enduring conflict. Enhancing the prospects for conflict resolution requires using additional mechanisms.

The case for a permanent U.N. peacekeeping force rests on grounds other than solving the most serious problems of this approach to peace. On that basis, a permanent peacekeeping force has some advantages, but its marginal utility is not substantial. As is evident from the historical record, the present ad hoc system has performed reasonably well given the difficult circumstances. Indeed, this ad hoc arrangement offers the advantage of flexibility and adaptability in organizing operations.[17] Most of the problems it has encountered have been minor or the result of factors that cannot be resolved by the imposition of a permanent force arrangement. A permanent force would be more efficient and professional, and its reaction time would be improved. Surely, given the choice, most would favor such a force over current arrangements. Nevertheless, the resulting benefits are not great. Indeed the ultimate success or failure of any peacekeeping mission does not seem likely to be affected by the adoption of a permanent peacekeeping force proposal. It might also be pointed out that the benefits of a fully developed permanent force are only slightly greater than the current system; comparing the present system to more limited proposals, such as those advocating standby troops, narrows that gap.

Too many analysts treat a permanent U.N. peacekeeping force as a panacea for threats to international peacekeeping and security and for the flaws of existing peacekeeping strategy. It is essential to remember that improving peacekeeping operations requires more than creating a permanent force. Perhaps one should view such a force as a culmination of tension reduction between states, rather than as a precursor to it.[18]

Regional Peacekeeping Operations

Beyond internal changes in the framework of U.N. peacekeeping operations, institutional alternatives include conducting the operations outside that organization. The most common suggestion is that regional organizations conduct the operations. Such proposals are based on the logic that regional organizations are better able to limit conflict by not expanding the arena to the global stage and are better attuned to the needs of the disputants and the parameters imposed by the local situation.

The overall record of regional organizations in security matters, and in comparison with U.N. actions, is mixed. The United Nations' frequency of handling threats to peace and security is comparable to that of the average regional organization; this indicates that states are not more likely to go to regional organizations than global ones and that the former are not necessarily more responsive to security concerns. Furthermore, on interventions that range from mediation to more operational functions such as peacekeeping and collective security, the rate of effectiveness was similar for regional and global international organizations. Some regional organizations, however, have enjoyed comparatively more success than international organizations of all types. The Organization of American States (OAS) was very successful in dealing with threats to peace in the Western Hemisphere until 1965; since that time, however, the decline of U.S. hegemony and the lack of consensus in the organization has precipitated a drop in that effectiveness. In contrast, the League of Arab States has consistently been ineffective in dealing with security matters in the Middle East. In most other cases, regional organizations are either underdeveloped or non-existent, and thus have little impact on regional security matters.[19]

Characteristics of Regional Peacekeeping Operations

Not all regional organizations are capable of conducting a peacekeeping operation. One might first expect such operations to fall under the purview of regional organizations that have some concern with security matters, at least in the broad sense, which narrows the range considerably. One can also exclude military alliances in the form of regional security organizations, such as the North Atlantic Treaty Organization (NATO), primarily designed for collective security against external attack. They lack the training, equipment, mandate, or inclination to assume peacekeeping duties, a situation that may change with the end of the Cold War. NATO is already considering alternate uses of its troops, and the Western European Union (WEU) has authorized the use of its members' forces for peacekeeping duty if necessary.

More likely, though, regional peacekeeping operations will arise from general purpose (including security matters), comprehensive membership regional organizations.[20] One might thus expect organizations such as the OAS, Organization of African Unity (OAU), the League of Arab States, and perhaps even the European Community (EC) to conduct peacekeeping missions. In 1992, the Conference on Security and Cooperation in Europe (CSCE) agreed to supply peacekeeping troops to the United Nations and perhaps to its own peacekeeping operations. The Commonwealth of the Independent States (states of the former Soviet Union) have also taken steps in this direction. Few other such regional organizations in existence at this time are capable of conducting peacekeeping operations.

It is easier to identify organizations that are likely to conduct a peace-keeping operation than it is to specify the provisions under which each would authorize and direct such a mission. Much like the United Nations, none of the regional organizations have provisions in their charters for authorizing peacekeeping missions, and none as yet have a permanent force available for duty. Some organizations, such as the OAU, have only minimal provisions for action by the organization in security matters. (The intent at OAU's inception was that it would only take actions such as mediation or conciliation when threats to peace arose.) The OAS has much better developed machinery for action, although that organization was envisioned primarily as a collective security agency under the Rio Treaty. It too has little direct constitutional basis for peacekeeping operations. Regional organizations thus mirror U.N. operations in their ad hoc character and their lack of established provisions.

One can further expect regional peacekeeping operations to operate in a manner similar to U.N. operations in almost all ways. There are thus few advantages or risks associated with regional peacekeeping operations that stem from changes in function or philosophy. One notable difference, however, may be in force composition. Traditional U.N. operations draw troops from neutral countries that have no close ties to the disputants. This is more difficult in regional operations; the disputants' closest allies, strongest trading partners, and often most bitter enemies are in the same region.

To ensure the neutrality of the force under these circumstances, a regional peacekeeping operation might limit troop contributions to those states that do not share a border with the disputants; this is what the OAU did in its operation in Chad. Although far from an optimal solution, it does help to mitigate some potential problems.

Although the provisions for a regional peacekeeping operation appear scanty and seem to differ little from U.N. operations, there are several empirical cases of regional peacekeeping operations. Regional groupings, especially the OAS, have a long history of conducting observation missions, so the idea of a regional peacekeeping force is hardly novel. Yet many of the most prominent regional organizations have conducted only one peace-keeping operation apiece, according to the strict definition used in this study.

The OAS launched a peacekeeping operation in the Dominican Republic in 1965, following the intervention of U.S. Marines into the civil unrest of that country.[21] The operation had a broad mandate to restore normal ac-tivities in the country, promote the observance of human rights, and work toward the development of democracy. The Inter-American Peace Force (IAPF) was withdrawn the following year and might be considered a success according to the criteria in this study. The situation was stabilized and the elected government of the Dominican Republic eventually requested that the force depart. Nevertheless, the operation remains a sore point in re-lations among OAS states. Some consider the operation only a legitimizing vehicle for U.S. intervention into the internal affairs of a member state. The force was successful because of the large U.S. presence (the United States supplied 85% of the troops), and because the initial U.S. Marine invasion crushed any opposition. Thus, the IAPF may not qualify as a wholly neutral force, and its deployment followed some resolution of the dispute by force of arms.

The OAU's only foray into peacekeeping took place in 1981 when it sent forces into Chad.[22] Chad was experiencing a civil war, and this conflict was interwoven with a dispute between Libya and Chad over the Aouzou Strip. The operation terminated in less than a year, amidst general failure, unable to stop the fighting and indeed subject to attack itself. It also did little to promote peacemaking, as the conflict continued in various violent and nonviolent forms over the next decade.

The League of Arab States authorized a peacekeeping force to help Lebanon in the midst of a civil war in 1976.[23] This force, with a prominent and disproportionate Syrian component, went beyond some of the limi-tations of peacekeeping philosophy, and it is questionable whether one could label this a true peacekeeping operation at all. For example, the operation used military force in situations other than those requiring self-defense. The troops also seemed to function as an occupying force that served Syria's regional designs. In any event, the force brought only a temporary respite to the factional fighting in Lebanon, requiring unilateral Syrian intervention at various times afterward to reestablish a minimum of order.

Finally, the most recent example of regional peacekeeping was the operation sponsored by the Economic Community of West African States (ECOWAS) in Liberia.[24] Liberia was also in the midst of a bloody civil war, and the ECOWAS force went into the country to protect civilians, gain a cease-fire, and restore law and order in the face of the government breakdown. The force was not able to impose a cease-fire (again, this is an inherent limitation of peacekeeping forces), despite some military actions that seem to have exceeded the peacekeeping philosophy. Its long-term effect cannot yet be judged.

Regional peacekeeping does not have an inspiring record, yet many of the problems encountered by those operations may result from the kinds of conflict into which they were deployed (e.g., civil wars with significant subnational actors hostile to the force). Below we look at the possible benefits and risks of a regional peacekeeping force, relative to those of the United Nations, that inherently derive from the organization of the operation on a regional level rather than from the conflicts themselves.

Possible Advantages of Regional Peacekeeping Operations

Although one might expect regional peacekeeping operations to experience success and failure for many of the same reasons as U.N.-directed operations, they may have some unique advantages, including greater consensus in the organization, broader support from the disputants, more control over third-party states, and heightened chances for conflict resolution.

Greater Consensus

One of the primary problems of U.N. peacekeeping operations stems from the inability of the permanent members of the Security Council to agree on authorizing a mission. In the 1950s and 1960s, this often meant going to the General Assembly in order to get a peacekeeping operations approved, as was the case with UNEF I. Later it meant that no operation was possible, as was the case after the failed attempts to have a U.N. force replace the MNF in Lebanon. The diversity of states in the United Nations has combined with superpower tensions to create little consensus in trying to take concerted action in response to threats against international peace and security.

One might expect regional organizations to have an advantage over the United Nations because their membership is more homogeneous.[25] States in a regional organization are more likely to be at the same development level, share historical, ethnic, or tribal roots, and have similar political outlooks flowing from facing common regional problems. These commonalities are supposed to provide more consensus among the members and make authorization of peacekeeping operations easier, as there will be fewer disagreements blocking strong action. Thus, one might expect regional organizations to be better able to meet threats to peace; this means more frequent peacekeeping operations, as well as operations authorized in a more timely fashion, with fewer conditions imposed on the missions.

In practice, these expectations have gone unfulfilled. Regional organizations have authorized few peacekeeping operations (and very few operations of any sort) in their histories. One often finds great splits among members of regional organizations when dealing with regional conflicts. For example, the League of Arab States was virtually paralyzed during the Iran-Iraq War and the Iraqi invasion of Kuwait because its members were strongly divided in their loyalties to the protagonists. Regional animosities also tend to hamper regional organizations' actions. Unity from homogeneity comes in response to threats to security external to the organization, such as Arab unity against Israel or African support for decolonization in Angola. The most common threats to regional peace—internal threats—are exactly those least likely to generate consensus.

Although superpower tensions have dampened U.N. involvement in some conflicts in the past, the United Nations may still be a better peacekeeping institution at times than regional groupings. Even during the Cold War, the superpowers were able to cooperate in regional conflicts in order to limit escalation.[26] For example, the superpowers worked to establish UNEF II as a part of the termination of the 1973 Middle East war. With the significant lessening of Cold War tensions, one might expect that further superpower cooperation is possible, as the peace agreement in the early stages of implementation in Cambodia in 1992 attests. It is doubtful whether regional organizations have the consensus or influence to achieve lasting peace in those areas, at least without external assistance.

It is of course conceivable that for certain conflicts, regional organizations may be able to achieve more consensus and act more swiftly than the

United Nations. Nevertheless, regional groupings have no inherent advantage on this point, and one might suggest that a disinterested global organization in a post–Cold War world may actually better to authorize a peacekeeping operation to limit local conflict.

Greater Support

A second possible advantage for regional peacekeeping operations is that the support given them by the disputants and the local population will be greater than that given U.N. operations. This argument relies on the notion that the people and governments in a region have a natural affinity with those in that geographic area and an inherent suspicion of what they perceive as outside intervention. Thus, there are frequently calls for "Arab" or "African" solutions to regional conflicts before international forces intervene. Disputants may be more accepting of actions by a regional organization, but, just as important, subnational groups and others in the conflicting states may see such actions as more legitimate. Thus, one might expect the operation to run more smoothly and the peacekeeping force to be less subject to controversy and attack.

The experience of African states in the ONUC operation soured those countries on global peacekeeping operations. They believed that the organization was not sensitive to their situation, and many withdrew support from ONUC amid claims that it was serving imperialist interests. Similarly, the Arab states tried to find an Arab solution to the Iraqi invasion of Kuwait, rather than rely on U.S.-led activities in the United Nations. In general, states and their people will prefer to localize conflict rather than expand it to the global arena.

To the extent that regional peacekeeping operations can generate more support than U.N. missions, they have an important advantage. Yet they must clear two hurdles that may frequently trip up such attempts. First, the organization must reach sufficient consensus to authorize the mission, in order to give it legitimacy, far from a foregone conclusion in most cases. Secondly, and more directly to this point, the regional organization and its peacekeeping forces must be accepted as honest brokers in the conflict. This again may be difficult to achieve. For example, an OAS operation that is led by the United States and that may serve U.S. interests will have less legitimacy than a U.N. force. A Syrian-led force in Lebanon would encounter similar difficulties. If the conflict at hand causes splits in the region as a whole, then an operation is unlikely to receive authorization and, even if approved, may not be perceived as neutral or fair by all parties. Thus, while the advantage of greater support is true in theory, it is less likely to be manifest in practice.

Conflict Resolution

Regional peacekeeping operations may also be better at promoting conflict resolution than is the United Nations, which has tended to put peacekeeping operations in place as Band-Aid solutions to security problems, with limited follow-up diplomatic efforts. Regional organizations may be more concerned with resolving the underlying conflict because the implications are much greater for the states in the area. Furthermore, they may more closely tie the stationing of peacekeeping troops to a mechanism such as negotiations or to an actual plan such as elections for resolving the dispute. In this sense, regional organizations may have more incentive and opportunity to address the major weakness of U.N. operations—conflict resolution.

In theory, this contention offers little to quibble with. In practice, much depends on the success of those regional diplomatic efforts and the form that they take. Regional organizations such as the OAU and the Arab League have followed peacekeeping efforts with extensive diplomatic initiatives, yet reconciliation attempts in Lebanon and Chad, for example, have not always been successful in the long run. Intervention by regional organizations is not necessarily any more successful than global efforts, even though it may be more frequent.

When regional efforts at conflict resolution have been successful, they have taken a form that may be incompatible with the philosophy of peacekeeping. The IAPF was successful in allowing the transition to democratic elections in the Dominican Republic, but only after the United States intervened militarily and crushed opposition forces. IAPF did help stimulate negotiations between the disputants, as it prevented each side from attaining a military victory.[27] The Arab force in Lebanon used enforcement actions to stabilize the situation, albeit temporarily, and consequently this form of conflict resolution is contrary to peacekeeping ideals and certainly not unique to regional organizations. The use of military force also does not guarantee success, as the ECOWAS force in Liberia learned. The empirical record, therefore, does not lead one to an optimistic conclusion about regional peacekeeping efforts at conflict resolution.

Restraint of Third Parties

A final possible advantage of regional peacekeeping forces is that they may be better able to secure the support of the interested third-party states, who will almost assuredly participate in the debate and authorization of a regional peacekeeping operation, whereas they may not in a U.N. operation. In this way, the third-party state has a better chance of modifying the operation according to its views and is more likely to support it. More importantly, it is less likely to sabotage the peacekeeping operation, a major cause of the failure of U.N. operations. One might also presume that active third-party opposition to a peacekeeping force would prevent that force's approval by the regional organization, thus avoiding the embarrassing failures experienced by some U.N. operations.

Although this advantage is by no means guaranteed, the support of third-party states is a definite benefit for regional peacekeeping operations and constitutes the primary advantage of those operations over missions run by global organizations or multinational configurations. Yet one must recognize that there may be instances in which a third-party state is not cooperative with the peacekeeping force (e.g., South Africa in any OAU operation), and regional groups still have to contend with potential opposition from subnational actors, much as the United Nations does. Third-party opposition might also prevent the regional organization from taking any action.

Possible Risks of Regional Peacekeeping Operations

Several problems unique to the mode of the organizing agency are inherent in regional peacekeeping operations, among them possible difficulties with resources, organization, and neutrality. Regional peacekeeping forces may also face situational constraints when dealing with external threats to regional peace and the involvement of regional hegemons.

Resources

There is a strong risk that the difficulties the United Nations has experienced in paying for peacekeeping operations and soliciting contributions for equipment and other supplies would be magnified in a regional operation.[28] A regional peacekeeping operation would incur expenses similar to a U.N. operation but would have fewer states to draw upon for contributions. Each member would have to pay more than if the costs were borne on a global level; an organization with a small membership could find the burden crushing.

One may not need to worry as much about funding and supplying a peacekeeping operation if the regional organization is composed of wealthier, developed states, as is the EC, although it also has financial constraints.

Yet an organization of less developed countries, such as the OAU, cannot rely solely on its members to pay for the operation. Even setting aside the financial aspects, many of these organizations' members are not sufficiently advanced technologically to provide equipment such as helicopters or personnel carriers to the peacekeeping force. Thus, regional organizations in some cases may have the willingness but not the means to authorize a peacekeeping force.

Resource constraints were most prominent in the OAU operation in Chad. Many states failed to follow through on promises to support the peacekeeping force with troops and financial contributions. Indeed, the OAU had to appeal to the United Nations and external states for assistance in paying for the operation. It is doubtful that the OAU or a similar grouping of poor states could sustain a peacekeeping force for an extended period without outside aid. Other regional groupings might fare better. The League of Arab States may be able to rely on oil-rich members as benefactors of an operation. Similarly, the OAS would not encounter resource difficulties if the United States were to bear a disproportionate share of the burden in providing money and equipment. Nevertheless, resource constraints may determine which organizations can carry out peacekeeping operations and for how long they can do so.

Organization

A second problem associated with regional peacekeeping operations is their organization. The regional organizations that are structurally under-developed, with a small and weak secretariat, such as the League of Arab States, would have difficulty managing an operation.[29] The OAU, for example, had to rely on an ad hoc monitoring commission headed by the secretary-general to direct the operation in Chad. The bitter experience with ONUC has made the OAU reluctant to grant much power or latitude for initiative to the secretariat.

Even the best developed of the regional groupings may have to adapt to using peacekeeping forces slowly. The EC is a highly developed economic and political organization but currently has few institutions that could provide the framework for conducting a peacekeeping operation. Similarly, the OAS has a well-developed structure for security matters, but these were designed for collective security operations and diplomatic consultation. Even assuming that these might be adapted for directing peacekeeping operations, there may be some initial problems until the appropriate structures evolve.

Even if regional organizations have some structures that could direct peacekeeping operations, most, if not all, lack procedures and precedents for organizing and operating a peacekeeping operation. The United Nations is successful in its ad hoc arrangements in part because of its experience in running previous operations. Regional organizations have little experience, and in some cases the precedents established, such as the OAU operation in Chad, did not provide methods that should be repeated. Until the regional organizations explicitly plan for peacekeeping operations and gain some experience in the task, they will be at a comparative disadvantage vis-à-vis the United Nations.

Neutrality

A key requirement for peacekeeping success is that the troops be composed of personnel from nonaligned states and that the combatants perceive them as impartial. Regional peacekeeping forces will have difficulty meeting the neutrality standard established by the United Nations.[30] First, with the exception perhaps of the Nordic countries, most regional groupings have no personnel trained in peacekeeping techniques and philosophy. This means that a peacekeeping force would likely be composed of regular soldiers from national armies; indeed, this was the case in previous regional peacekeeping efforts. These personnel are more likely to go beyond the limitations imposed by the peacekeeping strategy and become embroiled in the conflict. Of course, this scenario could change with experience, but many plans for a regional force designate using the same force in enforcement and peacekeeping duties.[31]

Beyond limited training in peacekeeping philosophy and tactics, regional peacekeeping forces may have difficulty in drawing troops from nonaligned countries. U.N. operations will often draw the bulk of their troops from outside the region of conflict, believing that these states are more disinterested in the conflict than those in the immediate area. Regional organizations do not have that luxury. The OAU tried to limit troop contributions to states that did not share a land border with the area of conflict. This practice certainly helps promote the neutrality of the force, but it does not exclude other states who have economic or political ties—or who desire them—to the area involved (e.g., Iraq or Syria in the Middle East). The smaller the area and the fewer the members of the regional organization, the more difficult it will be to put together a neutral force.

Even if a regional organization is successful in acquiring properly trained forces from neutral states, it still must deal with the disputants' perceptions of the forces. A force composed of personnel from regional states may be viewed more suspiciously, regardless of its behavior—the OAU force in Chad was subject to attack by both sides in the conflict. It is possible to put together a neutral regional force, but the task is much easier on the global level.

Meeting External Threats

An inclusive global organization by definition has no limitations on the geographic scope of its actions (except those set by national sovereignty) or on its theoretical capability to deal with threats to international peace and security. Regional organizations, in contrast, may have problems with conflicts that involve external intervention.[32] On the one hand, there may be more consensus in the organization when external threats are present. The OAU was designed in part to eliminate colonialism and extraregional interference in African affairs. The OAS is in some ways an extension of the Monroe Doctrine and its solidarity against external attack. One might anticipate fewer problems with internal consensus in such cases.

A peacekeeping operation, however, depends on more than consensus in the authorizing organization. All disputants and relevant third parties must acquiesce or cooperate if the mission is to be successful. Unfortunately, regional organizations do not have the political influence, moral suasion, or means of coercion to convince external powers to cooperate in a peace-keeping operation. The United Nations had enough difficulties convincing Belgium to refrain from hostile acts during the ONUC operation. It is inconceivable that an organization such as the OAU would have been able to pressure Belgium into compliance. Similarly, the League of Arab States could do little to ensure Israeli cooperation in any conflict in the area. Only a global organization can deal effectively with external threats to peace when deploying a peacekeeping operation. The advantage that regional organizations have in bringing in interested third-party states disappears if those states are at the heart of the conflict and are external to the region.

Dealing with a Regional Hegemon

A consistent theme in the analysis of regional organizations is their inability to take concerted action against their most powerful members.[33] Regional peacekeeping operations are unlikely to be authorized in conflicts that directly involve the global powers or regional powers in the area. The organization has neither the political clout nor the resources to mount an operation opposed or not actively supported by those states. A regional hegemon would be able to resist pressure to support a peacekeeping operation. Even were one authorized, the hegemon could effectively sabotage the mission through direct action or covertly through intermediate actors. This condition necessarily confines regional peacekeeping operations to conflicts between or within smaller states.

The problem of dealing with a hegemon is most evident in the Western Hemisphere. The OAS has been unable to mount any effective operational action that was not supported by the United States. Its one peacekeeping operation, the IAPF, was possible only as a denouement to U.S. intervention in the Dominican Republic. Although the United Nations might also face difficulties in gaining U.S. cooperation for a peacekeeping operation in Panama, for example, the possibility seems foreclosed in the case of the OAS. Other regions may have fewer problems, at least given current power configurations. The OAU is composed primarily of weaker states and perhaps is not as limited by this factor. The League of Arab States, however, could not conceivably mount a peacekeeping operation opposed by any of several well-armed members.

In general, only the United Nations offers the potential to restrain a regional power, although perhaps not a superpower. The United Nations has the resources, even without the cooperation of some states, and it has the political power to pressure states such as India to accede to its peacekeeping operations. The inability to restrain regional hegemons is a major disadvantage to regional peacekeeping initiatives.

A Tentative Assessment of Regional Peacekeeping Operations

The experience of regional peacekeeping operations does not inspire great confidence in this institutional alternative. Nevertheless, such regional operations have been thrust into the most difficult situations—civil conflicts—in which even U.N. operations would have had a hard time limiting the fighting and promoting conflict resolution. A review of the potential for regional peacekeeping operations, however, shows little more promise. Although much depends on which regional organization is involved and the circumstances encountered, regional peacekeeping operations have serious limitations. They will undoubtedly have difficulty with organizing, directing, and conducting a mission with the efficiency and neutrality of the United Nations. Such disadvantages may dissipate over time as regional organizations develop or adapt new structures and gain experience in running peacekeeping operations.

Nevertheless, some inherent problems will not go away with time. Regional organizations may be limited in their effectiveness to conflicts between small states that do not involve external intervention or a major state in the region, which necessarily restricts the scope and importance of regional peacekeeping efforts. There are few corresponding advantages to such operations. The ability to garner the cooperation of third-party states achieves little if that third-party state is a major actor.

All this is not to say that regional peacekeeping forces cannot be effective but that U.N. peacekeeping will have a comparative advantage in most circumstances. Regional peacekeeping operations have not proven to be viable substitutes to current U.N. arrangements, yet they may work well as supplements to those efforts. A best-case scenario, at times, may be for joint peacekeeping operations between a regional organization and the United Nations, if consensus exists in both organizations. Regional organizations could make some troops available and be intimately involved in gaining the agreement of the disputants and third parties for a peacekeeping force. The United Nations may provide additional troops, resources, and administrative assistance for the operation. The net effect may be to capture the advantages gained by a regional peacekeeping mission with the strengths of a U.N.-organized operation.

Multinational Force Arrangements

A third institutional alternative to current U.N. peacekeeping operations involves the substitution of organized collections of national troops for U.N. peacekeeping forces. Multinational forces differ from U.N. and regional arrangements in several ways. First, multinational forces are drawn from private groups of states and as such have no ties to an international organization, regional or global. This means that the primary responsibility for directing the operation is outside existing supranational bodies and procedures. Second, it is presumed that the troops are from countries outside the region of conflict; indeed, they are likely to be from several continents. This circumstance eliminates from consideration unsanctioned and largely unilateral efforts at intervention under the label of peacekeeping. The interventions by Syria into Lebanon and India into Sri Lanka represented enforcement actions that violated many of the principles of peacekeeping and lacked any multinational character in force composition. Finally, multinational forces are deployed with the authority of agreements negotiated with the disputants.

There appears to be some disagreement on the value of the multinational alternative vis-à-vis existing U.N. arrangements. Some suggest that multinational peacekeeping operations can be as good as, and in some cases better than, U.N. missions. This logic is often stated as "As long as the job gets done, does it matter who does it?"[34] Other analysts suggest that such multinational operations are inherently inferior to those directed by an international organization.[35]

Structural Characteristics of Multinational Force Arrangements

Unlike proposals for permanent and regional forces, there are no set plans for what a multinational force might look like. Indeed, one might expect that the composition, logistical deployment, and modes of operation would vary widely across time and the kind of conflict encountered, largely because the arrangements of such a force will by necessity be ad hoc. Nevertheless, some precedents shed light on how a multinational force might operate. Beyond some observer missions, the two empirical examples of multinational peacekeeping forces are the MNF and the MFO.

The failure of the MNF may suggest that multinational peacekeeping operations are doomed to failure (see chapters 2 and 3). Yet, the experience of MFO tells a different story. Deployed between Israel and Egypt, the MFO ultimately succeeded UNEF II after the signing of a peace treaty. Israel felt that an observer mission in the form of UNTSO was inadequate to oversee the implementation of the peace agreement. The MFO has been deployed in the area since 1982, monitoring military movements and ensuring that some conditions in the peace agreements are fulfilled.

According to this study's criteria, the MFO continues to be successful. In limiting armed conflict, the MFO has benefitted from having most of the necessary conditions for success outlined in chapter 3. The strong support of the disputants and the absence of third-party states and subnational actors have made the operation a model for multinational peacekeeping. Promotion of conflict resolution, the second criterion for success, is not an issue here, for the peacekeeping force was deployed following a peace agreement, rather than as a precursor to one. In that sense, the MFO, unlike most other peacekeeping operations, was introduced into a situation in which hostilities were already diminished. As suggested in chapter 4, the tasks of peacekeeping are less complex if they involve the implementation of an agreement resolving outstanding issues between the disputants. The success of the MFO provides a distinct contrast to the difficulties of MNF.

Of course, any future multinational peacekeeping force could have almost any set of political concerns, logistical needs, and states involved. Nevertheless, one might suspect that the MNF and MFO experiences offer some insight into how a multinational force might be organized. In contrast to U.N. operations, both operated under open-ended mandates, rather than relying on specific time points for renewal. With no authorizing agency or precedent to set time limits, one might expect a similar scenario in a future multinational force. Further enhancing this prospect is the relationship of the force to the disputants. A multinational peacekeeping force would still need the consent of the host states, but the expectation is if one can judge from MFO experience, that the peacekeeping force serves at the pleasure of all parties, withdrawn only with the permission of all sides.

Beyond the conditions of authorization, one might expect a multinational peacekeeping force to consist of personnel from no more than a few countries. The MNF had only four states providing troops, and the MFO only ten. With no ongoing structure for soliciting troop contributions, a multinational force will rely on existing diplomatic contacts of the disputants, or more likely of the leading states organizing the force, which will necessarily confine troop contributors to countries with which those leading states have close relations. This also may mean that the multinational force will not have broad political or geographic representation. Nevertheless, one might expect that no contributing states will be from the conflict's immediate geographic region nor will they have a strong and direct interest in the conflict, although they may not meet the general U.N. standards for neutral force composition.

When it comes to the actual operational activities of a multinational peacekeeping force, the standards are less clear. For example, the MNF did not operate under a central command but instead had loosely coordinated national units linked through liaison. The MFO has a strong central command with a U.S. officer at the helm. It might be presumed that a multinational peacekeeping mission would resemble a U.N. operation in tactics, strategies, and most methods of operation. Yet the lack of guidelines and clear expectations about what the force might look like and what conflicts could be involved make firm predictions infeasible.

It is difficult to draw any generalizations about the usefulness of multinational peacekeeping, as the two empirical cases lead to wildly divergent conclusions. More important for the purposes of this analysis is how well multinational operations compare with those of the United Nations. Many of their positive factors (such as the MFO being deployed following an agreement) and their negative experiences (such as the opposition of subnational groups to MNF) spring from circumstances that are not peculiar to the multinational arrangement; one might expect U.N. operations to have met similar fates. Nevertheless, some supposed advantages and risks attend to multinational as opposed to U.N. forces.

Possible Advantages of Multinational Force Arrangements

Alleged advantages to the use of multinational over U.N. forces include improvements in authorization and operation, financing, logistics, and promotion of conflict resolution.

Authorization and Operation

One of the common themes in analyses of the MFO is the advantage of not having to thrust the peacekeeping troops into the political context of the United Nations.[36] With respect to authorization, it may be easier to get approval for a multinational mission, for only the disputing states must agree to the operation; of course, there must be states ready and willing to lead the operation and supply troops. Such conditions are necessary but not sufficient for authorization of a U.N. mission, which must await approval by the Security Council or, on increasingly rare occasions, the General Assembly. This means that a state with no direct interest in the conflict can block—unilaterally if it is a permanent member of the Security Council—any U.N. action. In contrast, only those states most directly affected by the peacekeeping force can stop a multinational operation.

The two multinational forces, MFO and MNF, both operated with open-ended mandates and could therefore undertake long-range planning and maintain some autonomy. U.N. operations are renewable at six-month intervals and subject to changes in their operations according to the prevailing political winds in the United Nations, rather than the needs of their missions. Throughout its life, a multinational operation must satisfy the interests of the disputants. In contrast, U.N. operations must serve the interests of many masters and receive their formal approval at regular intervals. Some argue that multinational operations will be easier to authorize and will operate more smoothly than those in the sphere of international organizations that represent many and divergent political positions.

This claim seems to have strong validity, as multinational operations are able to satisfy the desire of the disputants for peace without allowing outside states to interfere with that goal. Yet having the United Nations stand behind an operation offers greater assurance that the authorization will represent the viewpoints of third-party states and subnational actors, whose approval or acquiescence is critical to the success of peacekeeping (see chapter 3). For a bilateral conflict such as the one that MFO encountered, the multinational force benefited by not being involved in U.N. politics, for many Arab and Third World countries did not favor the peace agreement. In contrast, the multiple actors that the MNF faced show that the approval of the primary states (here Israel and Lebanon) may not be enough to guarantee the success of the operation. The United Nations, representing many of those other interests, was not able to authorize a U.N. operation to replace the MNF.

Financing

One of the primary advantages of a multinational force cited by several analysts is the financial stability of the operation.[37] Unlike a U.N. operation, in which the membership of the organization provides the bulk of the monetary resources, expenses of multinational forces are generally borne by the countries involved. In the MFO, this meant that Egypt and Israel, the disputants, as well as the United States, the leader of the operation, paid for the peacekeeping force. A handful of other states provided troops. With respect to the MNF, each of the four states contributing troops was responsible for its own expenses; the host government of Lebanon did not provide any direct financial assistance.

The multinational force financing places the burden on those states that have a direct interest in the success of the operation, on the presumption that they will be more forthcoming in meeting the expenses of the operation and less likely to withhold funds for political or economic reasons. A logical inference from this argument is that multinational peacekeeping forces would be unlikely to run up the large debts incurred by U.N. operations.

As with the plans for a permanent peacekeeping force, the financing for a multinational force appears superior to current arrangements. Nevertheless, this analysis has demonstrated that financial problems have not presented serious hardships to U.N. operations; thus, the financial advantage of the multinational arrangement would be small. Moreover, the multinational force carries with it some unique financial risks. If the costs are primarily borne by the small number of troop-contributing countries, as in the MNF, high costs might force those states to scale back or withdraw troops, which may leave the force with less than an effective number of troops. Although similar problems could arise in the United Nations, the tendency there is to rely on debt accumulation and other devices, rather than be at the mercy of any one contributing state.

The alternative of having the disputants bear the costs, a fairer proposition in the minds of some, may be no better. Putting financial control of the operation in the hands of the disputants opens the way for one of them to use that control for leverage in the conduct of the operations or in negotiations with its enemy. The multinational force may be in the unenviable position of having its funds withheld in order to extract a change in operations that might be said to favor the disputant withholding the funds. The United Nations may have experienced some problems in paying for peacekeeping operations, but they have generally maintained financial autonomy from the disputants, the lack of which could open the peacekeeping operations to blackmail and manipulation.

Overall, the financial stability advantage of multinational peacekeeping forces over U.N. operations is clear. Yet the importance of that advantage is not high, and there are attendant political risks to relying on financial support from troop-contributing countries and the primary disputants to the conflict.

Logistics and Supply

Whereas the United Nations ad hoc system has some problems with logistics and supply of peacekeeping operations, multinational forces can rely on existing military systems for deployment patterns, supply of materials, and modes of operation.[38] This means that when the peacekeeping force is authorized, the operational components already exist, preventing any delays and ensuring that the mission runs smoothly. U.N. operations must request supplies from a variety of countries after the mission is authorized, and patterns of distribution and organization vary tremendously according to the operation.

In the absence of a permanent U.N. peacekeeping force, a multinational force will be more likely to ensuring a smooth peacekeeping operation. Because multinational forces rely heavily on national military units for organization, they are assured of established patterns of supply and organization, with set plans for a variety of contingencies. National units do not have to make many adjustments to their normal operations in order to supply the peacekeeping operations. Furthermore, because they rely on military units, the peacekeeping troops can call upon other parts of the national military establishment (such as to request helicopters or other equipment) on short notice as the need arises. Of course, multinational forces offer no inherent advantage over U.N. operations in coordinating activities between different national units of the peacekeeping operations.

Linking Conflict Abatement with Conflict Resolution

Finally, some analysts contend that a multinational force might better be able to connect peacekeeping and peacemaking, linking the two criteria for success defined earlier.[39] It is clear from the analysis in chapter 4 that U.N. operations have difficulty assisting the conflict resolution process, although they may be effective in limiting armed conflict. It is not clear, however, exactly how multinational peacekeeping forces might be better at promoting conflict resolution. Many of the mechanisms to tie peacekeeping to conflict resolution that would be unique to a multinational force involve the force playing an active role in the conflict. Such intervention will likely violate the principles of peacekeeping, and the peacekeeping force runs the risk of becoming "just another partisan actor in the conflict."[40] In that sense, the link with conflict resolution implies something of an enforcement role and further exacerbates some risks associated with the neutrality of the force.

The experiences of the MNF and MFO do little to support the contention of a linkage advantage. The MNF had no real mechanism for conflict resolution built into its operation. Its assistance in strengthening the Lebanese army led it to violate the principle of neutrality, which intensified the conflict in the area and undermined support for the operation. In negotiations over the conflict, the MNF became an issue in the dispute rather than a facilitator of reconciliation. The MFO was put in place *after* significant conflict resolution took place. It had nothing to do with the peace agreement several years earlier. Certainly, there is no unique advantage to having a multinational rather than a U.N. peacekeeping operation in place following conflict resolution. Yet, no benefits appear to adhere to using the multinational alternative before that resolution.

Possible Risks of Multinational Force Arrangements

Although multinational peacekeeping has some attractive features, significant problems and risks attend it, including problems with organization and neutrality, domestic political constraints, and undue influence by the leading peacekeeping state.

Initial Organization

That multinational peacekeeping operations have a smoother time with logistics and supply is an advantage apparent only after the force is initially organized. Multinational forces do not have a corresponding advantage in constructing the force and indeed may be at a considerable disadvantage. The United Nations requests troop contributions and organizes a peacekeeping operation on an ad hoc basis, a scheme with its own disadvantages, but at least the United Nations has extensive experience and preestablished contacts with potential contributing states; the result is that problems and disruptions are surprisingly minimal. Multinational forces also are formed as the need arises, but with no corresponding experience to facilitate the initial organization of the mission. The problems of multinational peace-keeping forces are thus the same type that U.N. operations face, only to a greater degree.

A multinational force will be able to rely on the leading or organizing state to form the centerpiece of the operation; the United States clearly played this role in the MFO. Yet there may be some delay in getting other states to contribute troops. The traditional suppliers of U.N. operations may be unable or unwilling to support a private peacekeeping force. Some states are constitutionally prohibited from contributing troops to non-U.N. organizations.[41] The MFO experienced such difficulties in its initial stages, and only strong U.S. leadership overcame these hurdles; one cannot assume that such leadership will exist in all contexts.

Multinational forces must also organize themselves with what, up until now, has been little or no precedent, a circumstance that the success of the MFO may change to some extent. Without that background, multinational forces will be inefficient in their initial deployment and may even be delayed considerably in that deployment. The advantages of logistics and supply for multinational forces appear to be offset by potential problems in or-ganizing the force, especially in the first days of the operation. In either case, however, such problems do not have a major impact on the success of the operation.

Neutrality

A second risk associated with multinational peacekeeping forces is that they will not behave in a neutral fashion, an important ingredient in peace-keeping success according to our earlier analysis. Multinational peacekeep-ing troops would not necessarily be drawn from countries that are non-aligned or have no stake in the outcome of the dispute. (Both the MNF and MFO were dominated by the United States, which has a close association with Israel.) This nonneutral composition may call into question the actions of the troops. Further problems may ensue if the peacekeeping forces are linked to diplomatic actions of their home country that one or more of the protagonists finds objectionable. That the disputants would have to agree to the troop contributions at the outset eliminates some of the concerns. Yet even with that initial approval, there is a greater chance that the multi-national troops will be considered biased than would U.N. forces.

Beyond the perception of bias, there also seems to be an increased risk that the troops will actually act in a biased fashion. Multinational peace-keeping troops may have no prior experience and training in the principles and practices of peacekeeping, where U.N. operations draw from personnel pools with extensive experience, and some regular contributing states have peacekeeping training programs. In the case of the MNF, U.S. troops behaved more like a military unit than a peacekeeping one. The use of excessive force and their support of the Lebanese government made them an inviting target for terrorist acts.

The risk of a multinational force being perceived as biased or actually behaving in a non-neutral fashion is significant; in contrast to some of the other advantages and disadvantages, this is a factor that could make or break a peacekeeping mission. This is not to say that a multinational force is incapable of neutrality; the MFO has performed admirably in this regard. When contributing countries have more experience in peacekeeping and institute the kind of specific training programs that currently exist in the Nordic countries, fears should diminish. Furthermore, there may be some circumstances in which the disputants are *more* willing to cooperate with a non-neutral than a U.N. force. Such would be the case when at least one of the involved states does not trust the United Nations; Israel's insistence on a strong U.S. presence in the MNF and MFO stems from distrust of the international organization that regularly condemns Israeli behavior. All things being equal, however, the U.N. force probably has an advantage in preserving the impartiality of the peacekeeping operation.

Domestic Political Concerns

U.N. peacekeeping operations depend on continued support from the U.N. membership as well as from the troop-contributing states. Yet the deployment of peacekeeping troops under the U.N. flag differs psychologically from troops deployed in a foreign land under a national flag. The former seems insulated from critical public opinion; the operation is under U.N. control and less identifiable as the act of a particular state's foreign policy. There generally is also a greater acceptance and less controversy inside a state that contributes to U.N. operations. In multinational operations, the deployment of troops must be justified or legitimized on the home front much the same as any stationing of troops abroad. This may lead to problems in obtaining the consent of some states to contribute troops, or it may result in the premature withdrawal of some forces because of public pressure.

The record of MNF confirms this risk. The uncertain mandate and the danger of violence against the troops undermined public support for the operation in the troop-contributing countries. It is noteworthy that the operation was terminated, in part, because of public pressure to bring the military personnel home.[42] MNF might have reorganized, changed its deployment locations, sought to broaden the composition of the force, or adopted a host of other changes in the short term. Other than trying unsuccessfully to have a U.N. operation take its place, though, the MNF retreated very quickly in 1984.

Yet one should not assume that multinational forces automatically incur problems from an unsupportive public. The MFO has gone more than a decade without much public controversy. It may even be that people in the home countries of the troops are largely unaware of the MFO presence in the Middle East. The operation had a clear mandate at the outset that the public could understand and support. Furthermore, the risk of violence for the troops was considerably less than in most peacekeeping operations, given that the force was deployed following the resolution of key points in the conflict. To the extent that other multinational peacekeeping operations have clear, popular mandates with little chance of loss of life, domestic political factors should not constitute a disadvantage.

Close Identification with One Contributing State

In a multinational enterprise of any kind, unless there is broad representation from many states and decentralized power, the operation will become identified with one or two states. If a multinational peacekeeping force is sponsored by one state, involves troops predominantly from that state, and is directed by that state, it begins to resemble a national operation. The legitimacy of the force under those conditions begins to come into question, thereby undermining its ability to perform its mission. The force may also be subject to attack (verbal and otherwise) as jingoistic or nationalistic appeals carry more credibility. Claims of imperialism are also possible if the area of deployment is in the Third World and the leading state is a major power. Local actors and interested third-party states may also actively oppose the operation if one country dominates the force.

A U.N. operation is not subject to the same problems. Control is largely in the hands of the United Nations. Its troops are from nonaligned countries, and no one state contributes a significant portion of the personnel. The U.N. force thus cannot be accused of promoting the foreign policy interests, in any specific sense, of the contributing states by virtue of its mere presence or behavior.

Overall, the risk of this disadvantage, according to one analyst, is overrated.[43] The first stage of MNF and MFO included a strong role for the United States, particularly in the MFO, for which the United States has acted as a political and financial guarantor. The second stage of the MNF also included strong national roles, exaggerated by the separate deployments and lack of coordination between national peacekeeping units. In that instance, however, the problem was more the non-neutral behavior of the troops than the domination of the operation by any one state. It may be that a multinational peacekeeping operation led by one state is more likely to act in a biased fashion or to be perceived as biased by the relevant actors. Nevertheless, it does appear that the risk may be overstated, and that in any case a peacekeeping operation can be quite successful despite its identification with one state.

Multinational and U.N. Forces Compared

An overview of the differences between multinational and U.N. forces shows the gap separating the two to be quite small. Multinational forces are better able to obtain authorization, can supply and organize the troops in a preestablished pattern, and have fewer financial worries. These benefits make multinational peacekeeping operations more efficient in many ways than their U.N. counterparts. Little evidence indicates, however, that multinational forces address the major concerns that seem to have a strong impact on the success or failure of those missions. Multinational forces offer no inherent advantages in assuring the cooperation of subnational actors or third-party states. Of course, they also face the same geographical obstacles and opportunities as peacekeeping forces organized under any other mode. There is also little reason to believe that multinational forces enhance the likelihood of conflict resolution between the disputants. Abandoning U.N. operations for multinational alternatives thus seems inadvisable.

Multinational peacekeeping forces also carry with them some serious risks. Without established procedures and existing contacts, multinational forces may have even more difficulty soliciting troop contributions and initially deploying the operation than the ad hoc U.N. system. Maintaining domestic popular support for the operation in troop-contributing countries may also be a problem. Yet the greatest risk appears to lie in the neutrality of the troops. Multinational troops are not necessarily drawn from non-aligned countries and may not be trained in the principles and practices of peacekeeping. Thus, they may not act or be perceived as neutral forces. This critical risk could undermine the whole peacekeeping operation, leading to its failure, and is more likely to arise in multinational operations than in U.N.-sponsored missions.

If there are few serious differences between the two structural modes, when might multinational forces be the more desired option? Gregory correctly notes that multinational forces are not substitutes for U.N. operations where the proper conditions for peacekeeping success are not present.[44] Thus, if there is significant opposition from local actors or third states and the consensus for authorization is not present for a U.N. operation, these should be taken as warning signals for caution, rather than as a go-ahead for creating a multinational peacekeeping alternative. The MNF experience certainly illustrates this point.

Multinational operations may be a good alternative when one or both of the protagonists prefers or insists on such an arrangement vis-à-vis relying on a U.N. operation. The disputants may feel more comfortable with states that are trusted friends than with the United Nations, which may have a clear and objectionable record in the conflict in the eyes of the disputants; Israel and South Africa would fit this profile. In these circumstances, a U.N. operation may not be possible because of the disputant's opposition, even though the other objective conditions for success are present. Multinational peacekeeping forces under those circumstances, and with the strong support of the disputants, have a good likelihood of success and are viable alternatives to the traditional U.N. operation.

Conclusion

Overall, despite its faults, the current ad hoc method of conducting U.N. peacekeeping operations holds up rather well in comparison to institutional alternatives. The permanent peacekeeping force was the most desirable alternative, but its comparative advantages to present arrangements were not as great as one might suppose. Furthermore, a permanent force cannot address the major problems that previous peacekeeping operations have encountered. Because regional and multinational peacekeeping operations have the potential to succeed or fail for many of the same reasons that U.N. operations do, they might be appropriate substitutes. Yet they also carry some unique risks and problems that make their applicability much more limited. Multinational operations might be best used when one or more of the disputants objects to the participation of the United Nations or wishes to have a major power guarantee. Regional peacekeeping efforts may be desirable when carried out jointly with the United Nations or when confined to conflicts involving small states in the region.

The most prominently suggested substitutes for U.N. peacekeeping arrangements thus reveal that the current system is among the best available. The conclusion that other alternatives can systematically substitute for or replace U.N. operations is unfounded.

Chapter **VI**

Functional Alternatives to Traditional U.N. Peacekeeping Operations

TRADITIONAL peacekeeping operations act as an interposition force after the institution of a cease-fire but before disputants have resolved the underlying conflict. In looking at peacekeeping functions that deviate from this norm, our concern is not so much with improving the performance of existing peacekeeping missions, but rather with exploring how such missions might expand their duties to further the goal of international peace and security.

Functional alternatives differ from the traditional mode of operation in all or some of the following ways. First, and most obviously, the peacekeeping mission may be assigned duties dramatically different from those of an interposition force; for example, duties in drug interdiction involve a more active role than the passivity required in traditional peacekeeping. Second, the form of the peacekeeping operation may differ. This means the peacekeeping operation may be composed of civilians or technocrats rather than soldiers with light arms; an arms control verification team is an example. Finally, the timing of the peacekeeping deployment may deviate from the post-cease-fire, preresolution mode. Functional alternatives include deploying peacekeeping troops while fighting persists in the area, as well as deployment following the termination of fighting and the resolution of major sources of dispute; providing humanitarian assistance during a civil war is an example of the former, and election supervision illustrates the latter.

Any number of tasks, some wholly unrelated to peacekeeping, might be assigned to U.N. peacekeeping forces. Rather than giving a cursory glance to a large number of primarily bureaucratic missions wrongly classified under the rubric of peacekeeping (e.g., a collection of statistics on human rights abuses) the focus here is on a set of the most often mentioned specific proposals for using peacekeeping troops in new ways. In general, these alternatives represent extensions of current peacekeeping ideas and institutions to new areas of expertise; in particular, many of the ideas are among those summarized by former peacekeeping commander Indar Jit Rikhye.[1]

Trip-Wire

The first functional alternative to traditional U.N. peacekeeping involves the placement of troops as a trip-wire against surprise attack from any disputant in a conflict.[2] In this role, U.N. peacekeeping forces would serve at or near a defined border area to monitor military movements in the area and act as a mediator for disputes that arose. Surprise attacks by any protagonist would have to pass through the peacekeeping forces, thereby sounding the alarm for the international community and the target of the attack, as well as taking the moral high ground away from the attacker.

This description of peacekeeping forces as a trip-wire sounds remarkably similar to their traditional role as an interposition force, yet it differs in two important ways. First, the troops would be deployed before the initial onset of conflict, rather than following a cease-fire agreement that halts a war. In this way, peacekeeping forces exercise preventive diplomacy to head off international crises, instead of acting as Band-Aids for those that have already occurred. The presumption is, of course, that peacekeeping troops would be deployed between states that have an ongoing rivalry, such as India and Pakistan or Libya and Chad. The second difference is that this functional alternative applies only to conflicts between states, not to those within states. It seems unrealistic to place peacekeeping troops in a civil conflict before it has begun. How would one know when to place those troops in a given country? Furthermore, peacekeeping troops in those circumstances would function as an internal security force in support of the status quo government, not a role that the United Nations should or wants to play.

There are several potential benefits to the use of peacekeeping troops as a trip-wire. First, the troops provide a deterrent to attack, they remove some of the moral and political incentives for states to use military force to resolve disputes.[3] Second, in providing such a deterrent, the peacekeeping forces may be superior to traditional military forces performing the same function. As a lightly armed, neutral force, a U.N. peacekeeping operation neither poses the threat to the disputants of a heavily armed military force of another country nor favors one side's position over the other. U.S. forces in the demilitarized zone in Korea may be an effective deterrent, but they do not have the attendant advantages of a peacekeeping force performing the same function. Early satellite detection of hostile troop movements could also serve the trip-wire function, but this would not be as effective a deterrent as a U.N. peacekeeping force; visible ground troops offer a greater physical and moral barrier to armed conflict than does a distant satellite. Third, trip-wire peacekeeping forces are actually better for the disputants than relying exclusively on their own military establishments. Peacekeeping forces are considerably less expensive for the disputants than stationing their own troops in the area. With peacekeeping troops, whose expenses are primarily borne by the United Nations, the hostile states could demobilize, pull back, or reassign troops that might normally be stationed near the border area. Even if the disputants paid for the operation themselves, costs would be less in that the number of peacekeeping troops would be fewer than the number of military personnel stationed in the area. Finally, peacekeeping troops assure that accidental engagements (which by definition neither side desires) do not occur or are reconciled without escalation.

There is little precedent for this use of peacekeeping forces. Perhaps the closest analogy is with the 1991 deployment of U.N. personnel in southern Iraq near the Kuwait border to deter another Iraqi invasion of the territory. Clearly, however, such an operation followed a war (not preceded one), and some measure of coercion went into gaining the acquiescence of the parties involved.

Trip-wire peacekeeping troops will likely experience the same difficulties as traditional operations. In particular, there needs to be some mechanism to permit, encourage, or facilitate peaceful change and resolution of disputes. Otherwise, the peacekeeping force will freeze the status quo, which may inherently favor one side or the other. In the long run, the absence of conflict resolution could lead the peacekeeping force to come under attack by one of the parties, to be asked to withdraw in preparation for an attack (similar to the Egyptian request for the withdrawal of UNEF I), or to be forced to linger for an indefinite period (as is the case with UNFICYP). Of course, trip-wire peacekeeping troops serve only as a moral deterrent and therefore cannot stop a determined aggressor from seizing a disputed piece of territory. Similar to traditional peacekeeping operations, this alternative depends heavily on the cooperation of the parties involved and the power of world opinion. Nevertheless, there appear to be few disadvantages to the concept, and trip-wire troops could be an important extension of the peacekeeping strategy. The net result could be the avoidance of several wars. The use of trip-wire troops only in interstate disputes also enhances the prospects for a successful operation.

Naval Peacekeeping

If the alternative of trip-wire alters the timing of peacekeeping deployment, naval peacekeeping represents a different form of intervention and several new duties. Traditional peacekeeping operations involve the stationing of land forces between disputants, yet sometimes the geographic separation between opponents is a body of water; for example, any war in the Middle East may involve military actions in the waters surrounding the region. The United Nations could thus commission naval units to act as an interposition force that supplements or substitutes for land units, depending on the geographic configuration of any cease-fire agreement.

Presumably, the United Nations could solicit national contributions for ships and personnel much as it does for ground units. Yet, under these circumstances, maintaining the neutrality of the force would be more difficult. The states that have the military hardware to contribute to a naval peacekeeping force are the major powers of the world or interested regional powers. The ships might have to fly the U.N. flag, and the United Nations might have to assume more direct control of the operation than is common in traditional peacekeeping operations. In that sense, the use of naval peacekeeping forces might necessitate a more truly international operation, including strong U.N. direction and the consideration of peacekeeping personnel as international civil servants.

Because most traditional uses of peacekeeping will continue to require land forces, naval peacekeeping has more potential if it takes on new roles beyond interposition. One such role would be as an escort service for neutral shipping. In this application, U.N.-flagged vessels would escort neutral shipping through dangerous waters during a war. According to international law, neutral shipping is supposed to be free from attack during a war, but not all belligerents abide by that standard. Furthermore, warring states may fire on foreign shipping that is conducting trade with one of the belligerents. U.N. escorts discourage belligerents from attacking neutral shipping or conducting illegal searches and seizures in international waters. U.N. forces might also conduct mine-sweeping operations in the area.

The deployment of U.N. troops as naval escorts represents a fundamental departure from traditional modes of operation. U.N. peacekeeping would be deployed *before* the end of fighting and well ahead of any efforts at conflict resolution. The main goal of naval peacekeeping would be not to prevent armed conflict between the disputants but to limit the conflict to the warring parties, and to prevent it from expanding its area or the number of its participants. Thus the concern is much more with the protection of other states and much less with the primary disputants.

With respect to naval peacekeeping during an ongoing war, a U.N. operation might be preferable to any multinational operation or no international effort at all. The disputants would not suspect U.N.-flagged escorts of performing strategic roles that might exceed the immediate peacekeeping requirements, which would not be the case, for example, if the U.S. Navy assumed the escort role. In addition, a U.N. naval force would be less likely, given its acceptance by all parties, to raise issues of national sovereignty by incursions into territorial waters. The international community as a whole benefits from the continuation of commerce in a war-torn area and from keeping the war in bounds. The combatants avoid a situation in which both sides lose by having supplies cut off and their economies more adversely affected by the war.

The United Nations has never tried naval peacekeeping but it was first suggested during the Iran-Iraq war. When attacks by Iran and Iraq against each other's naval targets and tankers escalated (irrespective of the tankers' registry), Kuwait appealed to the United Nations for the protection of neutral shipping. The United States and other countries responded unilaterally to this request by reflagging ships and providing escorts for them through the Persian Gulf. The Soviet Union and other states in the immediate area grew apprehensive of the large Western naval presence and unsuccessfully argued for a U.N. force to replace national navies in the area. Among the unfortunate incidents was the shooting down of a civilian Iranian airliner by a U.S. Navy ship that alleged it was under attack. Had U.N. naval peacekeeping forces been in the area, it is likely that this incident and other attacks on Gulf shipping would not have occurred, or would at least have been fewer.

A naval peacekeeping force might also play a role in the verification of arms control treaties. For example, it could verify those provisions of the Sea Bed Arms Control Treaty that prohibit the placement of nuclear weapons on the ocean floor. It could play a similar role with regard to regional arrangements, such as the Treaty of Tlatelolco, which established a nuclear-free zone in Latin America; the peacekeeping force could verify that signatory states did not place nuclear weapons in the sea bed beneath their territorial waters.[4] A naval peacekeeping force might also verify compliance with international environmental regulations.[5]

Supervising arms control agreements may be a valuable service, but the likelihood of treaty violations at this time is small. More significant could be the monitoring of nuclear submarines through remote sensing or observation of ports, especially if new states deploy the technology.[6] These confidence-building measures could reduce the risk of nuclear war or accident and save money for all interested parties by limiting the need for expensive new antisubmarine warfare technologies.

Naval peacekeeping certainly has great potential to expand the scope of U.N. activities in peacekeeping and other security-related matters. The major problem with this alternative is the possible hostile reaction of the primary disputants. In traditional peacekeeping, one could generally assume the acquiescence of the main state parties. In naval peacekeeping, this may not be the case. If naval peacekeeping forces are deployed during a war without the cooperation of the warring parties (despite some incentives for them to cooperate), the naval forces could be involved in heavy fighting; unlike peacekeeping ground troops, naval peacekeeping forces would be a larger target and would likely have high-powered defenses. Thus, any violence (e.g., missile or rocket attacks) is likely to be rather serious. Naval peacekeeping forces may also have some problems with patrolling the area of deployment, beyond acting as an escort service. The area covered by the operation is likely to be greater than for a land operation; unless the naval force is supplemented by air support or includes a large fleet, there is a greater chance for some actors to plant mines without detection or cause other disruptions. Other than these greater risks, a naval peacekeeping force should be subject to the same limitations as conventional peacekeeping forces. Nevertheless, this functional alternative appears viable.

 Arms Control Verification

Another new role for peacekeeping forces that expands their duties is arms control verification. An essential part of a modern arms control agreement is the assurance for each party that the other signatories will live up to the terms of the agreement. Not surprisingly, it has often been disagreements over the verification procedures that have sidetracked or derailed arms control agreements, not conflicts over substantive provisions of those agreements. Beyond disagreements over specific provisions, the SALT II controversy included U.S. concerns over Soviet cheating and what were perceived as inadequate means for verifying Soviet compliance.

Peacekeeping forces offer the potential to be the verifying agency for arms agreements. Most conventionally, peacekeeping forces might verify troop reductions or withdrawals within a given area. Traditional peacekeeping operations have performed this role in the past, as in UNEF II's monitoring of Israeli and Egyptian disengagement following the Yom Kippur War. A more innovative activity could have peacekeeping forces performing on-site inspections; they might supervise the destruction of weapons or verify that troops levels and weapons deployment are within prescribed limits. The most ambitious use of peacekeeping personnel in arms control verification involves aerial surveillance.[7] Peacekeeping forces would be equipped with their own planes, satellites, radar, and other intelligence-gathering mechanisms to verify arms agreements through technical means. Less ambitiously, U.N. peacekeepers could collect and analyze information provided by national authorities.[8]

Using peacekeeping troops to verify agreements offers several advantages over national verification. One might expect that reaching arms agreements, in the self-interest of all parties, will be easier if the option of peacekeeping verification is available. Furthermore, all sides receive unbiased estimates of arms control compliance, not having to rely on what may be varying, politically motivated internal reports (e.g., the phantom "missile gap" between the Soviet Union and the United States of the late 1950s and early 1960s). Accordingly, there are likely to be fewer disputes over verification (which may jeopardize continuation of the agreement), and the peacekeeping operation could provide mechanisms to resolve those disputes when they do occur.

Peacekeeping troops in arms control verification also lessen the fear of espionage that accompanies the gathering of information in another country. National on-site inspectors might be tempted to gather other strategic information during visits to military installations. National technical means may also be used to collect information in addition to that related to verification. Not surprisingly, many countries are suspicious of verification schemes that allow an opponent to gather additional strategic intelligence. Peacekeeping-controlled verification eliminates that possibility, as information gathering is in the hands of neutral parties and involves only matters related to the arms control agreement—assuming, of course, that the United Nations could find inspectors with the needed expertise from countries all sides regard as impartial.

Peacekeeping forces have already performed this role in a very limited fashion by monitoring troop withdrawals as part of a cease-fire agreement. U.N. observation forces have also supervised arms agreements; in 1989, an observation force in Angola, the U.N. Angola Verification Mission

(UNAVEM), monitored the Cuban troop withdrawal from that country. Successful international arms verification has also occurred in a limited fashion. The International Atomic Energy Agency (IAEA) inspects nuclear energy facilities under provisions of the Nuclear Non-Proliferation Treaty to verify that nuclear materials are not diverted for weapons purposes. U.N. officials also attempted to inspect Iraqi military facilities after the Persian Gulf war. Peacekeeping forces might also supervise proposed bans on chemical weapons production. In these and dozens of more hypothetical situations, peacekeeping forces could insure the faithful execution of the agreement as both sides desire without the intrusion common to national means of verification.

The promise of success for peacekeeping troops in arms control verification is high. The peacekeeping forces would be used in the implementation of an agreement—in the post–conflict resolution phase—rather than before the end of fighting or before the underlying dispute is settled. Furthermore, arms control verification would also include a narrow set of duties and, in most cases, a set time frame for deployment, avoiding the indefinite length of deployment that has been the case with several U.N. operations. Peacekeeping forces in arms control verification are probably subject to the same advantages and risks as any other peacekeeping mission. In that sense, it might be presumed that peacekeeping verification is not necessarily appropriate to all arms control agreements; there may be superior multilateral alternatives in some cases.

Assuming that the function of arms control verification is promising, U.N. peacekeeping forces cannot continue as currently configured. First, verification efforts in many cases cannot be handled by traditional peacekeeping personnel. Although traditional peacekeeping troops can monitor troop withdrawals from an area or the creation of a demilitarized zone, such is not the case with other types of arms control verification. Peacekeeping units will need to include technical experts to assess the evidence encountered, for example, to ascertain whether the possession of certain chemical compounds constituted a violation of any chemical weapons ban.

Second, the United Nations lacks the infrastructure to conduct more sophisticated kinds of verification. Technological requirements for verifying some arms control agreements could include seismographic equipment and satellites, as well as more mundane equipment such as aircraft. The United Nations has neither this type of equipment nor the personnel to operate it. If the United Nations is to engage in this activity on a continuing basis, especially in its more technically sophisticated aspects, then it would be appropriate, if not necessary, for the United Nations to have its own independent verification capability through a permanent U.N. agency,[9] rather than to rely on ad hoc contributions from member nations—in some cases it may be impossible to integrate national contributions, or utterly impractical, for example, to loan space on a satellite. All this requires a large supply of funds, complex organization, trained personnel, and experience in verification matters. As the United Nations is apparently not prepared to take on these duties in the near future, one can more credibly expect it to be confined to verification of disengagement agreements.

Finally, the use of peacekeeping troops in arms control verification makes the need for a mediation mechanism to resolve disputes more critical. Without a forum to discuss and, one hopes, resolve the disagreements that are bound to arise over the verification procedures and findings, the arms control agreement may come apart. In that way, the peacekeeping force might be responsible for the collapse of the agreement. Clear procedures for dispute resolution need to be defined as part of the peacekeeping deployment, rather than relying on the good offices of the secretary-general or the force commander.

Humanitarian Assistance

For peacekeeping troops to provide humanitarian assistance might involve their deployment in a civil conflict or following a natural disaster.[10] During many civil conflicts, control over the country is split between the central government and various rebel groups. Combined with the disorder caused by the civil war, this prevents essential services such as food supply and medical care from being delivered to the population and creates a flood of refugees fleeing battle zones. International agencies such as the International Red Cross are responsible for providing emergency assistance to these victims, yet their efforts are often hindered by the challenged government or by rebel groups, who fear that relief supplies might fall into the hands of their enemies' troops and perhaps contribute to the war effort.

For peacekeeping forces to deliver food and medical supplies to wartorn areas means commissioning cargo planes under U.N. auspices. Once on the ground, U.N. troops would guard the convoys that transport the food to the areas of greatest need. It is conceivable that peacekeeping troops would also be involved in the actual distribution of food and medical supplies to affected populations, but one could more sensibly envision those duties being handled by other international agencies—the International Red Cross, World Health Organization, and U.N. High Commissioner for Refugees.

There are several potential benefits from the use of peacekeeping troops in providing humanitarian assistance during civil conflict. U.N. peacekeeping forces might provide protection for relief agencies, ensuring that the supplies reach the affected populations without interference from the disputants. This may benefit all sides in the conflict, as well as being the optimal solution for the distressed population. It relieves the central government and the rebels of the burden of providing food and other assistance to those in the areas they control—and also of the bad publicity attendant to pictures on Cable News Network (CNN) of starving children and emaciated adults. Such protection not only guarantees that the affected population receives the supplies it needs but increases the likelihood of more assistance, as international donors will be more generous when they know that supplies will reach their intended destination. The disputants will also have less incentive to attack supply convoys headed to their opponent's sector; they no longer have to fear that those supplies will be diverted to military personnel. The assurance that food and medical supplies will go to affected populations prevents both sides from being worse off from attacks that disrupt the supplies.

Beyond their role in civil conflicts, peacekeeping forces might also be called upon to supply humanitarian assistance in the aftermath of natural disasters, such as earthquakes, floods, and famine. In those circumstances, a host government incapable of meeting relief demands with its own resources and distribution system would invite a peacekeeping force into the country to safeguard the distribution system for humanitarian aid in the midst of probable civil disorder. To prevent the theft or misappropriation to the black market of food and medical supplies, peacekeeping forces would be available to guard warehouses and distribution centers as well as protect the transportation distribution system for the aid. Beyond the benefits gained from assuring safe distribution of humanitarian aid, the presence of the peacekeeping troops again may actually serve to increase the volume of that aid. International donors may be more willing to contribute to relief efforts if they are more confident that the aid is getting to the people most in need of assistance.

The idea of using peacekeeping forces for humanitarian assistance is a good one only if all the affected parties agree to the operation. In civil conflicts, peacekeeping forces may experience problems similar to those encountered by interposition forces (see chapter 3). Those opposing the government, especially terrorist groups, will have maximum incentive to disrupt the operation of everyday life in the country; the strategy is that the resulting chaos will be blamed on the government, making it more

vulnerable to a takeover or collapse. Preventing food and medicine shipments to government-held areas may force the ruling group to devote more
of its own resources to humanitarian aid rather than to military efforts.
Rebel groups also do not want to see food supplies and assistance go to
those who support the government. Part of their strategy is to demoralize
the population and persuade them that a viable alternative to government
authority and inefficiency exists. Thus it is conceivable that some rebel
groups will oppose the establishment of peacekeeping forces to distribute
food and medical assistance, although they bear some costs in bad publicity
by doing so.

Even the status quo group may have reason to oppose the distribution
of food and medicine to its population. The government may want to punish
people who live in areas controlled by rebels and, in the view of some,
therefore support the opposition. To the extent that the civil war mirrors
ethnic, tribal, or other national divisions, there may be little feeling of
obligation on the part of the government to feed its citizens. The government
may also resent what could be viewed as a violation of its sovereignty;
many governments insist on being involved in the distribution of supplies
in their territory, which opens up the possibility of diverting those supplies
to military purposes.

There are also some logistical problems associated with providing humanitarian assistance. Unlike traditional peacekeeping operations, those
distributing food and medicine might have to operate in a war zone. Even
with the best wishes of the protagonists, which cannot be assumed, the
peacekeeping troops may find themselves in the line of fire. One might
thus expect casualties even under the best of circumstances; as part of their
assignment, peacekeeping troops will have to venture into the most dangerous areas. (The U.N. force in Yugoslavia [UNPROFOR] is finding it very
difficult to distribute humanitarian aid in the middle of a civil war, despite
verbal assurances of cooperation from the parties to the conflict.) Furthermore, not being deployed at fixed positions in a neutral area increases a
peacekeeping force's vulnerability. In the air and on the ground, a peacekeeping force will move frequently and cannot secure the areas in which
it travels, which again requires the cooperation of the combatants and
perhaps some changes in the normal procedures of U.N. peacekeeping.
Indeed, one analyst argues that NATO, a traditional military group, is a
better institution than a U.N. peacekeeping operation for this kind of mission.[11]

Of course, both sides in a civil conflict may find that the advantages of
humanitarian assistance, without diversion to military purposes, outweigh

the risks and disadvantages to one's own position. The moral imperative might also be enough for all sides to agree to a peacekeeping operation, especially in the face of famine and widespread starvation. It would be suicidal for a peacekeeping force to intervene without the approval of all relevant actors. Neutral organizations such as the International Red Cross have already experienced problems with noncooperation in Ethiopia and the Sudan. A U.N. peacekeeping force could be the subject of attack by surface-to-air missiles or by armed units on the ground. Thus, a peacekeeping force supplying humanitarian assistance during a civil conflict is a risky proposition.

Traditional U.N. peacekeeping operations have provided humanitarian assistance to local populations, but such a role was secondary and in some cases peripheral to their main missions.[12] Making humanitarian assistance the primary role of peacekeeping forces appears to present some serious problems when those troops are deployed in the middle of a civil war. This functional alternative seems more promising in the context of the aftermath of a natural disaster, although the cooperation of host government and subnational actors is still a prerequisite for success.

Drug Interdiction

U.N. peacekeeping forces involved in stopping the production and distribution of narcotics could search for and destroy fields of opium and coca; this could include aerial surveillance as well as ground operations.[13] Presumably, the troops would work in conjunction with local authorities. Peacekeeping forces might also monitor air and sea traffic in and over international waters that are known corridors for drug transit.

The use of peacekeeping forces as drug enforcers could have a positive outcome for countries that grow most of narcotics as well as for those that provide markets for the products. Host countries frequently cannot eradicate illegal crops of their own, yet getting direct assistance in the form of personnel and equipment from narcotics-consuming states can cause serious domestic political problems, and drug lords are able to make nationalistic appeals against drug eradication efforts.

U.N. peacekeeping troops can provide the assistance necessary without the political costs associated with outside intervention. U.N. intervention carries greater moral authority, and one likely to generate more domestic support than efforts sponsored by a drug-importing country. The symbol of the world community conducting the operation blunts jingoistic appeals by the opposition. Furthermore, drug interdiction and eradication efforts by the United Nations are less likely to be linked to other controversial issues, such as criminal extradition, that might undermine those efforts.

Similarly, states with a large drug market may not want to devote resources to drug eradication efforts in other states. Furthermore, efforts to stem the flow of drugs in or over international waters pose legal and jurisdictional problems. Even without those barriers, the military establishment in those states is often ill-trained and reluctant to assume drug interdiction missions far from home. A peacekeeping force offers a professional cadre of drug fighters armed with international legal authority. Drug market states are also spared the criticism that often stems from their efforts to curb the supply of drugs when little corresponding effort is made to temper demand.

The use of peacekeeping troops to fight drug trafficking is certainly one of the more interesting applications, but it is also one fraught with peril. The drug war has some of the characteristics of an internationalized civil war. Although it is important that the host country and interested external states support the operation, it is equally clear that the drug-trafficking groups will not. Thus, a peacekeeping force will immediately face subnational groups opposed to its mission. Many drug lords are well armed, with as much firepower as a small army. In addition, many of the drug-processing facilities and growing areas are heavily guarded and booby-trapped. The chances that peacekeeping troops would be involved in combat are high; drug barons have little reason to cooperate in the mission.

Opposition from drug lords is only one problem. Farmers who grow the coca plant or opium poppies may also turn against the force. These people depend on growing the crops used to make narcotics for their livelihoods. Unless some program in conjunction with the peacekeeping operation provides price supports for alternate crops, the farmers will assist the drug lords or even take violent action themselves. Furthermore, some drug lords have made alliances with rebel or guerrilla groups operating in the host country; the drug lords receive protection, and those opposed to the government gain access to money and weapons. Such has been the case with the Shining Path rebels and drug producers operating in Peru. When this occurs, peacekeeping forces would be thrust into the middle of a civil war in which one side and its allies are determined to defeat peacekeeping efforts at drug eradication. One might suspect that peacekeeping operations would meet a fate similar to that of UNIFIL or the MNF, which had to deal with civil conflict situations.

The problems of peacekeeping and drug interdiction are not confined to the hostility of internal groups. Drug-growing areas are in rural, not easily accessible areas. The peacekeeping forces will be operating at a disadvantage in rugged terrain against an enemy familiar with the territory. Furthermore, in order to have any chance of success, the peacekeeping force will need specialized training in drug eradication and will almost assuredly abandon restrictions on carrying only light arms and using force only in self-defense—the alternative might be suicide. Yet in relaxing those limitations the force begins to lose its character as a peacekeeping force, and one begins to wonder whether a traditional military unit with specialized training might not be more effective than a mutated peacekeeping force.

Perhaps drug interdiction might work best if the peacekeeping forces patrol the high seas and monitor air traffic, working with national officials. In those circumstances, they may still come under attack, but the chances are much less with no indigenous forces to aid the drug smugglers. Nevertheless, it is next to impossible to detect all or most of the illegal land or sea traffic in narcotics, and one would either have to accept a low rate of detection (already a problem with national entities such as the U.S. Coast Guard) or be prepared for a peacekeeping force larger than the air forces and navies of the largest states in the world, clearly an unrealistic expectation. Therefore, although the use of peacekeeping forces for drug interdiction has some attractive features in theory, its application appears doomed to failure.

Combatting Terrorism

Terrorism as it has been practiced over the past three decades is a classic example of a transnational phenomenon that is not under the purview of any one state. International efforts at preventing or dealing with terrorist incidents, however, are somewhat isolated. Several U.N. resolutions and legal conventions on the subject have had little impact on the problem. Furthermore, few international organizations other than the International Civil Aviation Organization (ICAO) are designed to deal with terrorism, and ICAO's concern lies only with airline highjacking, an interest subordinate to the many other purposes of the organization. This vacuum opens the way for the idea that peacekeeping forces might play a role in combatting terrorism.[14]

One possibility is that peacekeeping forces could coordinate and disseminate intelligence information about terrorist activities. Such information is currently provided bilaterally, and therefore unevenly, with little international coordination. One might assume that a neutral agency that facilitates maximum coordination will be better at providing information about possible terrorist attacks or about the location of wanted terrorist suspects. The net effect would presumably be the prevention or preemption of terrorist incidents, or, if incidents do occur, the apprehension of those responsible.

Another function might be the use of special peacekeeping troops as an elite negotiation and hostage rescue team during any terrorist incident involving the seizure of civilians. The most likely scenario involves an airline or ship hijacking when hostages are seized to achieve some set of demands. The peacekeeping force would attempt to act as a neutral party in brokering an agreement that involved the resolution of a protracted terrorist act. Another unit of the forces might be charged with taking forceful action to free the hostages, should negotiations fail or should circumstances suggest dramatic action (e.g., if terrorists have begun executing hostages).

Finally, peacekeeping forces might be deployed to assist in security at those airports that handle a significant amount of international travel. The peacekeeping force would screen all baggage and passengers on those flights, utilize the latest in bomb and weapon detection, and provide various other forms of security in the airport area.

The suggestions on how peacekeeping forces might be used in combatting terrorism represent very different types of functions, although all presume the establishment of uniform standards across all states, ensuring that terrorists cannot exploit national differences in security, intelligence, and military expertise. Furthermore, the peacekeeping forces would fill a void in international coordination in the form of organizations or other structures in this area of concern. It is difficult to dispute the need for greater international coordination in security, intelligence, and hostage negotiations. The key question is whether peacekeeping troops are best suited for the tasks.

Intelligence coordination presents no problem, assuming the cooperation of the member nations in the consortium, and might be accomplished with a relatively small number of personnel and limited expense. Yet one wonders whether this function is related at all to the basic notion of peacekeeping or whether some newly created U.N. agency might do an equal or better job. The intelligence function involves no inspection and no direct monitoring of activities; any neutral (or nonneutral) agency could perform it. Intelligence coordination to combat terrorism has its merits and drawbacks, but none of the most significant advantages or disadvantages seem to be unique to having peacekeeping troops carry out this function. In that sense, there is little compelling reason to assign peacekeeping forces these duties.

Similarly, one might question the use of peacekeeping forces in hostage negotiation and rescue. The training necessary for such a unit is quite different from, and in some cases inimical to, traditional peacekeeping training (e.g., assault techniques to rescue hostages). Furthermore, peacekeeping forces have been ill equipped to promote negotiated settlements directly, instead relying on stabilizing the situation in the long run, a duty that is the opposite of resolving a hostage crisis quickly. There is also the sovereignty issue: how much control over the operation is given to the local authorities on whose territory the terrorist act has occurred? One might suspect that problems could arise from disagreements between those authorities and the leaders of the peacekeeping operation.

A further problem is the difficulty of reconciling the twin roles of hostage negotiation and rescue. Negotiation may play to the strength of U.N. peacekeeping forces in that the neutrality of the peacekeeping unit may allow it to broker an agreement. It is significant that the hostage takers in Lebanon requested the assistance of U.N. Secretary-General Javier Pérez de Cuéllar in working for the release of all hostages in the Middle East. Yet the possibility that the peacekeeping force might undertake a hostage rescue mission undermines its credibility as a neutral party in the process. Terrorists may not trust a peacekeeping unit that may become its enemy depending on circumstances, at which point peacekeeping forces differ little from national authorities. Although the peacekeeping force could easily be assembled for hostage missions, the peacekeeping strategy seems ill-suited to the task.

Perhaps the most promising function for peacekeeping troops in preventing terrorism is in strengthening airport security. Such a role is closest to the traditional operation in that the forces are lightly armed, monitor activities, and work in harmony with the interests of the host government. The specific duties involved, such as searching individuals and vehicles, are similar to some conducted by traditional peacekeeping troops at various checkpoints. The major drawbacks are the specialized training that would be necessary and, depending on how many airport sites would be involved, the tremendous expense. Nevertheless, the peacekeeping force would be valuable in establishing international standards and would represent another layer of protection beyond national efforts. There is clearly a need for more airport security, and a peacekeeping force appears to be a plausible choice to meet it.

Overall, peacekeeping forces could contribute to the global battle against terrorism only in a very limited fashion, perhaps by assisting in airport security. Other possibilities would seem to require a fundamental reorientation of the peacekeeping strategy, and even then the new roles could be performed equally well or better by other international entities specifically designed for those functions.

Election Supervision

That peacekeeping forces could supervise elections that resolve internal conflict is not a new idea—League of Nations observers monitored plebiscite elections in the past. In addition, U.N. observer teams have played a role in assisting democratic elections; in 1989 and 1990, the U.N. Observer Group in Central America (ONUCA) monitored the military disengagement of opposing forces before and following elections in Nicaragua.[15] Yet the idea of using U.N. peacekeeping forces to supervise elections has received renewed attention.

An increasingly popular way to resolve factional conflict in a state is through democratic elections, allowing popular sentiment instead of force of arms to decide which groups will control the government. U.N. peacekeeping forces would be charged with several tasks in the process. First, they would patrol the area in which the election is held, seeking to limit the campaign violence that has become common in many parts of the world. Second, and most importantly, the peacekeeping forces would monitor the election process to ensure that fair and regular procedures were followed; in effect they would be on hand to report and thereby deter any ballot tampering or irregularities on election day. Peacekeeping forces might also be called upon to assume certain governmental functions (e.g., to provide a police force) before the election.

The use of peacekeeping troops as election supervisors is a solution to conflict that offers several advantages. Presumably both sides desire an end to bloodshed, hence the agreement to hold elections. Peacekeeping forces help ensure that the fighting will not be renewed, thereby preserving the peace agreement and perhaps saving the lives of thousands of supporters on all sides. Similarly, the presence of peacekeeping troops preserves the integrity of the election, preventing opponents from manipulating the election results or from using claims of fraud to invalidate or ignore those results should they lose. In effect, peacekeeping troops guarantee the legitimacy of the election. Without them, conflict could be renewed during or after the election, and both sides (even the election winner) would be worse off; the whole purpose of the election is to establish order and prevent extraconstitutional challenges to the government.

Peacekeeping troops served in this capacity in Namibia as the U.N.

Transition Assistance Group (UNTAG) and were scheduled to do so as of 1992 in Cambodia and possibly Western Sahara.[16] The Namibian experience illustrates both the potential for success of this function as well as some possible problems.[17] On the one hand, one can consider the UNTAG operation a success. Free and fair elections, a judgment shared by all or most observers, resulted in Namibia's gaining its independence in 1990 with its first majority-rule government. Given Namibia's long and sometimes violent history as a dependent territory of South Africa, this is quite an accomplishment. On the other hand, violence was not absent from the election process, with clashes between the South African Defense Forces (SADF) and troops loyal to the South West African People's Organization (SWAPO). At times the U.N. troops were powerless to stop the bloodshed.

The Namibian experience offers several lessons for the use of peacekeeping troops in election supervision. The first is a need for a dispute resolution forum to supplement the peacekeeping operation. Without mechanisms in place to help work out disagreements that arise between the parties in the implementation of the election process, one or more of them may use military force to "resolve" a dispute. In Namibia, the SADF believed that SWAPO forces entered Angola in violation of the peace agreement. South Africa wanted to retaliate and threatened to withdraw from the agreement. Without any means of verifying the claim and with no mechanism to discuss the dispute, the United Nations stood by as South African troops invaded Angola, killing over two hundred people.[18]

There were also various claims that South Africa was trying to manipulate the election outcome, seeking to deny SWAPO the two-thirds majority it needed to write the new constitution unimpeded. UNTAG was powerless to investigate these charges, and the peacekeeping force was not designed to deal with disputes between the parties. Yet charges of tampering arise in any election campaign, even in longstanding democracies. A U.N. peacekeeping force must include mechanisms to investigate rival claims of improper behavior and to reconcile disputes between the competitors before they escalate to violence.

A second difficulty in election supervision is the size of the peacekeeping force. Traditionally, peacekeeping forces have ranged from a few thousand to ten or fifteen thousand strong. Election supervision requires that troops be deployed throughout a country to monitor activities, and ideally at every polling site on the day of the election, which means a force considerably larger than in traditional operations—the exact size will vary according to the size of the area, the number of people in the territory, and the potential severity of the conflict. For election supervision the United Nations would

thus need to solicit more contributions to meet those increased requirements. The UNTAG force was supposed to number 7,500, but financial
haggling in the United Nations delayed its deployment, and the number
eventually put in the field was only 4,000.[19] This strength was not sufficient
to monitor the actions of 1.5 million Namibians, not to mention South
African security forces in the country.

A problem related to force size is the geographic area that the troops
must monitor during the election. Traditional missions are deployed in a
narrow geographic area, often at a few fixed points. For example, the
UNFICYP operation is concentrated along the line separating the Greek
and Turkish communities. Potentially, a peacekeeping force might have to
supervise elections and disengagement activities over hundreds of thousands of square miles. This area may make it impossible to detect violations,
even given an expanded force. Because of the enormous area UNTAG had
to cover, it was often unable to verify that South African forces had been
confined to their bases, relinquished their weapons, or released political
prisoners. In some cases, the South African forces moved troops, weapons,
and prisoners from location to location, several steps ahead of a peacekeeping force that could not monitor the whole country. The problems
with geography experienced by traditional peacekeeping forces are thus
likely to be magnified when a force has the task of supervising an election.

Another potential problem unique to the function of election supervision
concerns the control of the election machinery and the preservation of
order. If an interested party (in Namibia, this was South Africa) controls
the election machinery, then there is great room for abuse. The controlling
party can manipulate the process by making it difficult to vote in areas
where opposition forces hold sway and may deny or grant voting privileges
unjustly. If that same interested party is responsible for maintaining the
government functions of law and order until the election, it may use police
forces to intimidate voters. Disengagement and disarmament agreements
among the parties are useless, because one party still has the police force
or army to influence the election outcome. Not surprisingly, this arrangement is most likely to generate disputes, and a fraudulent outcome to the
election will only renew the violence the election agreement was designed
to stop. Under these conditions, success for the peacekeepers will be difficult to come by.

In Namibia, South Africa maintained some control over the country until
election day. South African troops acting under the guise of police forces
intimidated the public and passed weapons to groups opposed to SWAPO.
South African officials also manipulated the voter registration process, at

one time recruiting residents of Angola to vote in the Namibian election.

As problematic as these conditions may be, an alternative is to have the U.N. peacekeeping force assume the municipal functions until the election in a trusteeship arrangement. This has the advantage of ensuring the neutrality of the process, but it imposes several new burdens on the peacekeeping force. First, it places a large number of administrative functions (e.g., designing and implementing elections) on the shoulders of the peacekeeping force, hardly their normal duties. More significantly, the cost of the operation and the number of troops required would dramatically increase, although a successful operation would be cheaper in the long run than peacekeeping operations in stalemated conflicts, such as that in Cyprus. The added numbers required only add to the burden.

Most importantly, if the peacekeeping troops must assume police functions, they will have to perform enforcement actions. Unless peacekeeping troops were specifically recruited with this expertise in mind, it would be difficult to put together an efficient force; it might also be impossible to separate the peacekeeping from the enforcement duties. The experience of peacekeeping troops in the Congo does not provide much confidence for the arrangement.

Finally, peacekeepers as election supervisors will be most vulnerable to the opposition of subnational actors. Before deploying troops, the United Nations must be sure that the election has the support of all the relevant parties. An election held under other circumstances will likely encounter violence and fail to lead to the long-term stability of the country. All the disadvantages associated with peacekeeping in a civil war are potentially present with the function of election supervision.

Although the obstacles to the use of peacekeeping forces in election supervision may seem impassable, such troops could be a valuable mechanism in the crafting of solutions to civil wars, internationalized civil wars, and proxy wars over disputed territory and sovereignty. The plebiscite, almost extinct in international relations, might even make a comeback if peacekeeping forces are available to ensure its legitimacy. Election supervision requires some major changes in the size of the forces and their breadth of expertise. Although UNTAG might be considered a success, future operations must be better designed and more attuned to the particular needs and risks associated with monitoring elections.

Enforcement

Many of the suggestions for the use of peacekeeping forces in enforcement roles can be dismissed as largely irrelevant to this book; as noted in
chapter 1, the term *peacekeeping* has often been applied in blanket fashion
to all proposals for international intervention, when the terms *collective
security* or *collective defense* might be more accurate. More to the point is the
idea that true peacekeeping forces, as we have defined them, should be
allowed to initiate military force and restore order.[20] Most notable would
be the possibility that peacekeeping forces could intervene in a conflict,
perhaps without the consent of the parties involved, to stop the fighting
and impose order in the situation. The failure of collective security and
other enforcement actions by the United Nations is well documented, and
the employment of peacekeeping forces in those roles is not likely to change
that outcome. The litany of problems inherent in performing those functions
does not need repeating. More important here is the impact that such efforts
may have on the strategy of peacekeeping.

In my view, the inclusion of any enforcement functions in a peacekeeping
operation's mandate has serious detrimental consequences. First, it clouds
the international perspective on what peacekeeping is and how it operates,
which may undermine support for the strategy, as people and governments
object to various enforcement actions taken by the peacekeeping troops.
Furthermore, it may make states less likely to accept even a traditional
peacekeeping force, perhaps fearing that the troops might take actions
against national interests and in violation of sovereignty.[21] Years of precedent in establishing the neutrality of the force may be lost when enforcement actions are undertaken. The stature of peacekeeping, and therefore
the likelihood that it will be adopted by international and other organizations, will be diminished by the failures likely to accompany the expansion
of peacekeeping roles to include enforcement.

Second, and equally important, enforcement actions by the peacekeeping
force may complicate its ability to perform monitoring duties. Will training
or participation in enforcement duties contaminate the ability of the force
to exercise restraint in other contexts? Will troops know when to draw the
line between offensive and defensive use of military force? Will peacekeeping forces have to be armed with more sophisticated and more deadly
weapons? Will the protagonists be more likely to attack the peacekeeping
force because of fear of those weapons and the relaxed limits on the use
of force? These are significant risks that cannot be tolerated within the
peacekeeping framework. If enforcement actions are to be taken and jus-

tified, they are best done by a different force under U.N. authorization, rather than by mixing those incompatible functions with those of peace-keeping. The alternative is not likely to be successful, and the result could jeopardize the positive benefits yielded by traditional peacekeeping.

Conclusion

The current mode of U.N. peacekeeping operations has held up quite well under scrutiny through this book. Despite the vitality of the model, however, the analysis in this chapter reveals that U.N. peacekeeping operations can be applied to contexts beyond post-cease-fire arrangements. An exploration of eight of the most prominent functional alternatives to traditional U.N. peacekeeping reveals that U.N. peacekeeping forces can play valuable roles in several new areas, furthering the goals of international peace and security.

The most promising functional alternatives include use of peacekeeping forces as a trip-wire, in election supervision, in arms control verification, and as naval peacekeepers. In each case, peacekeeping forces offer inherent advantages over the status quo, and their neutral character makes them superior to many other possible arrangements. In all instances, however, these new roles require adapting existing peacekeeping institutions to the tasks. Election supervision may involve, in part, the dramatic increase in the number of troops needed for the mission. Arms control verification may require specialized training and the inclusion of technocrats in the peacekeeping force. New equipment and procedures would have to be in place before deploying a naval task force in a peacekeeping role. Each of these new roles is also not without certain unique risks. For example, the trip-wire peacekeeping troops may be subject to attack by hostile parties. Nevertheless, these new operations have the potential to be at least as successful as traditional peacekeeping operations and could be valuable additions to the U.N. repertoire.

Several other functional alternatives for U.N. peacekeeping appear less promising. These include roles in humanitarian assistance, drug interdiction, combatting terrorism, and enforcement actions. In each case, the use of peacekeeping troops resembles the proverbial square peg in the round hole. Peacekeeping operations would have to undergo dramatic revisions in order to perform the prescribed duties; for example, they would have to be trained in specialized drug eradication techniques. Combatting terrorism or engaging in enforcement actions would mean abandoning such basic tenets of peacekeeping philosophy as neutrality and the use of force only in self-defense. In all cases, other existing or proposed institutions appear more appropriate than peacekeeping forces for carrying out these duties. Serious problems could result from adapting peacekeeping forces to these functions.

It seems that using peacekeeping forces in unconventional ways works best when some or all of certain conditions are fulfilled. First, the best functional alternatives are those that represent incremental deviations from the traditional model, rather than dramatic changes in modes of operation. Naval peacekeeping and election supervision, for example, include many of the same basic activities as traditional peacekeeping (e.g., monitoring movements and detecting violations), but in different forms and contexts. In contrast, combatting terrorism seems far afield from traditional peacekeeping and is probably best handled by other means. Second, promising functional alternatives include those that involve deployment following a significant degree of conflict resolution. We have noted throughout the book that traditional peacekeeping operations encounter difficulties in promoting conflict resolution. Yet, as with the MFO, peacekeeping forces are quite successful in implementing agreements; functional alternatives that involve implementation of an agreement between the disputants, such as an arms control pact, have a good chance of being successful. Not surprisingly, the alternatives most lacking in promise not only involve deployment prior to conflict resolution but include circumstances in which a temporary cease-fire is not even in place. Finally, functional alternatives, much like their traditional counterparts, operate best in contexts other than civil conflict. The incentives for noncooperation by subnational actors can lead to violence and other problems just as easily for new applications of the peacekeeping strategy as they can for traditional interposition forces.

Although functional alternatives for U.N. peacekeeping include many interesting ideas, peacekeeping is not a panacea for all global problems, and new applications of the strategy must be done judiciously rather than in blanket fashion.

Chapter **VII**

The Prospects for
International Peacekeeping

THERE ARE several reasons to expect that international peacekeeping will become more common as the century ends. First, the end of the Cold War will undoubtedly make the United Nations better able to authorize peace-keeping operations. Cold War animosities have precipitated deadlocks in the Security Council, thereby preventing the authorization of new peace-keeping operations. Even in the early Gorbachev era, however, the Soviet Union was beginning to show a new willingness to rely on the United Nations for dealing with international threats to peace.[1] This was manifested in Soviet proposals for naval peacekeeping forces and for reviving the Military Staff Committee. Furthermore, the U.N. Good Offices Mission in Afghanistan and Pakistan (UNGOMAP), which monitored Soviet troop withdrawal from Afghanistan, represented the first time that the United Nations supervised superpower actions.[2] All indications are that Russia, as successor to the permanent seat of the Soviet Union on the Security Council, will be even more cooperative in U.N. efforts. The breakup of the Soviet Union also means that the Cold War will no longer limit the types of disputes that are suitable for international peacekeeping.

Second, and perhaps more important, changes in the world over the past few years have lessened the intensity of regional conflicts; disputants have become more amenable to international intervention as a means of stopping military conflict and assisting in the resolution of its underlying sources. Regional conflicts, such as the civil wars in Angola and Afghan-istan, are less exacerbated by arms shipments and other assistance by the superpowers and other states than they once were. Furthermore, the United States and Russia have pressured the protagonists in those regional conflicts to enter dialogues for peaceful resolution. The peace agreement in Cambodia owes much of its impetus to the cooperation and pressure of the major powers. Of course, the United Nations has been designated to play a major role in the peace agreement and elections in that country.

Third, the United Nations is beginning to assume new roles in a variety of conflicts on various continents. In 1992, proposals and preliminary steps for U.N. intervention involved Cambodia, Western Sahara, Angola, El Salvador, Yugoslavia, Somalia, and elsewhere. In the absence of a well-defined collective security system (and one is not visible on the horizon), the United Nations will apparently rely on variations of its most prominent operational alternative—peacekeeping.

Although peacekeeping may be a more frequent and salient approach to international security problems, it may not always be an appropriate or successful strategy. One of the primary purposes of this book has been to identify the conditions under which peacekeeping operations are successful, and, by implication, to develop some suggestions on how to use the technique effectively, while avoiding mistaken and costly applications. The two criteria developed to assess the success of peacekeeping operations are: their ability to limit armed conflict and their ability to promote resolution of underlying sources of conflict in a dispute. Because peacekeeping operations in the future are likely to go beyond traditional missions (defined as interposition forces deployed after a cease-fire, but before significant conflict resolution), the viability of various institutional and functional alternatives was also explored. Institutional alternatives refer to changes in the mode (ad hoc) or organization (United Nations) of peacekeeping operations. Functional alternatives concern the assumption of new peacekeeping roles, beyond acting as an interposition force.

Success in Peacekeeping: Some Guidelines and Applications

A review of six of the most notable peacekeeping operations reveals a variety of experiences in conflict abatement, with less variation in matters of conflict resolution. The findings suggest some guidelines for the deployment of peacekeeping troops, which differ considerably for the two goals of peacekeeping—limiting armed conflict and promoting conflict resolution.

Limiting Armed Conflict

Some peacekeeping operations, both phases of UNEF, in particular, did a fine job of preventing and deterring violence in their zones of deployment.

In contrast, other peacekeeping missions, such as UNIFIL, have been largely ineffective in controlling the conflict that has pervaded their areas of operation. The authorization of the peacekeeping operation seemed to have little to do with the outcomes; problems with financing or mandate clarity were not fatal and often only symptomatic of broader concerns with the political context. Characteristics of the peacekeeping operation itself, especially its neutrality and locus of deployment, significantly influenced the conduct and success of the missions. Yet more than any other set of factors, the political context into which the peacekeeping forces were sent affected the success or failure of the operation; support from host and third-party states, as well as subnational actors, was also critical.

There is a tendency, heightened by recent global changes, to advocate the use of peacekeeping forces in response to almost every conflict in the world. Most recently, the civil war in Somalia led a few of the participants and some U.N. members to call for a U.N. peacekeeping force. Peacekeeping operations should not, however, be seen as the panacea for all international conflict problems. The United Nations and the global community have a host of other diplomatic mechanisms that might be used in conjunction with, or instead of, the peacekeeping option; these include mediation, arbitration, adjudication, peace observation, fact-finding, and more coercive mechanisms such as economic sanctions and military enforcement action.[3]

Peacekeeping should only be employed in circumstances in which less intrusive mechanisms (such as mediation) have not been successful or because time pressures do not permit other measures in the short run—for example, when a mechanism is needed to achieve a cease-fire agreement immediately. Equally important, peacekeeping operations should be deployed only when a high probability exists that the force will be successful in limiting armed conflict; this means sending peacekeeping forces to disputes that have those characteristics (or can be altered to have those characteristics) that are conducive to a successful operation.

One line of argument assumes that peacekeeping forces are desirable in any circumstance in which they are even marginally better than inaction. The rationale is that if peacekeeping forces can prevent the loss of one life or lessen the likelihood of conflict escalation to even a small degree, then their use is justified. In this view, even the UNIFIL operation is a desirable one in that it has prevented some violent incidents, although it has failed miserably to stop others—almost any peacekeeping operation is a good peacekeeping operation.

This argument raises several problems. First, the choice in the hands of decision makers is not usually confined to either a peacekeeping operation or no action. Indeed, the deployment of a peacekeeping operation may preclude the adoption of some other alternatives, such as economic sanctions, that may be more appropriate to the situation and possibly more successful. Peacekeeping operations remove the immediacy of the conflict not only for the disputants but for the community of nations. Thus an ineffective operation such as UNIFIL not only fails in its primary mission but has the additional undesirable quality of lessening the chances for other, possibly more effective actions.

Second, the assumption of only two options implies that any action is better than no action. This may not always be the case. Even though peacekeeping operations may limit some of the violence in an area, they may cause more serious conflict to occur. The civil war around Beirut did not dissipate appreciably with the presence of the MNF, and the fighting became more intense in spots because of that peacekeeping operation. The shelling of Lebanese villages by U.S. peacekeeping units may have cost more lives (not to mention those lost in the terrorist bombing attacks) than were saved by the peacekeeping presence.

Third, a largely ineffective peacekeeping operation may save a few lives only at great cost. The United Nations, other international organizations, and the states that support peacekeeping operations do not have unlimited resources and should not be asked to spend large sums of money for small gains. Furthermore, one can assume that money saved by not deploying an ineffective peacekeeping operation may be spent for any number of activities that would have a more positive impact on international security and well-being, for example, more International Atomic Energy Agency inspectors or increased disaster relief.

Thus, the view taken here necessitates a much narrower application of the peacekeeping strategy than as a response to all threats to international peace. Only when conditions are favorable should peacekeeping forces be sent to limit armed conflict. The following are policy-relevant guidelines for the deployment of peacekeeping operations:

Securing Support

A precursor to any other concern is that the peacekeeping operation must have the support or acquiescence of the relevant actors in the general area of deployment. Most obviously, the host states must agree to the stationing of the peacekeeping troops on their soil. Just as importantly, their primary enemies must also support the idea of a peacekeeping force after a cease-fire. No peacekeeping operation (as opposed to an observation mission) has yet been deployed with the support of only one side or without the cooperation of the host state. There appears to be no reason to suggest otherwise in the future. The support of the primary protagonists has usually not been a problem, but that support is so critical that mere acquiescence is not enough. The peacekeeping operation could be destroyed if the luke-warm support of a principal disputant gives way to hostility. Ideally, the request for peacekeeping forces should come from the main parties to the conflict, rather than the United Nations or major power states having to coerce their approval.

Support for the peacekeeping operation by the primary protagonists is not sufficient. It must also have the backing of other key actors in the area. In most cases, this means states that are geographically proximate to the site of deployment and have the means and willingness to exercise military influence there. The most obvious example is that no peacekeeping force should be sent to Lebanon without a guarantee that Syria will not under-mine the force through overt military actions or through support of inter-mediaries. Legal approval is not needed, but appropriate diplomatic con-tacts must be made to these third-party states in order go gauge their views. The more they are involved in the process of stopping the conflict and setting up the peacekeeping operation, the more prospects for a successful operation increase.

In civil conflicts and some interstate conflicts, subnational actors such as rebel groups and local militias will also need to be supportive of the peacekeeping force. Although they may have less capacity to damage the operation than states have, they still can cause serious problems. Again, the leadership of the United Nations and the primary state actors must be careful to consult local groups, lest the approval of a peacekeeping force by the host government be a thin veneer covering significant domestic opposition. Similarly, major power states must acquiesce in the peace-keeping force. Any peacekeeping force must avoid the opposition of a powerful state that can directly or indirectly undermine its mission. Of course, no U.N.-sponsored operation is likely to be authorized if one of the five major powers opposes it. Yet the diffusion of global military power and advanced technology has made the permanent members of the Security Council less important; the behavior of emerging regional powers must also be considered.

Although this guideline restricts the application of the peacekeeping strategy, it does not constitute an implicit unit veto by any actor in a given dispute. That peacekeeping operations cannot and should not be authorized without the consent of the primary disputants does imply that every one of the other relevant actors must also support the operation, although this would be the ideal. The opposition of any actor must be weighed according to the intensity of that opposition, the actions likely to follow from it, and the capability of that actor to cause serious damage to the peacekeeping operation's efforts to preserve the cease-fire. It is conceivable that peacekeeping operations can go forward despite some groups or states opposing the mission. To the extent that those states or groups are central to the dispute, will work to destroy the cease-fire, and have significant military capability, however, going forward with a peacekeeping operation is ill-advised.

Emphasizing Interstate Conflicts

A second policy consideration is that peacekeeping forces should be primarily directed at interstate, as opposed to civil, conflicts for reasons noted earlier, including geography and the status quo being more acceptable to both disputants. Furthermore, the charter of the United Nations and the persistence of state sovereignty (albeit somewhat weaker than in earlier eras) make it questionable whether international organizations, regional groupings, or other collections of states should even be playing a leading role in civil wars, unless they have or are likely to spread to neighboring territories.

The emphasis on interstate conflicts for peacekeeping deployments does not mean that intervention in civil conflicts should not occur, but rather that it should be approached with some trepidation. Civil conflicts that seem most amenable to peacekeeping forces are those that already have a peace agreement between the main parties and need a peacekeeping force to implement parts of that accord. In the absence of conflict resolution, peacekeeping might be appropriate for secessionist struggles in which all sides agree to a cease-fire and an identifiable boundary separates the warring parties (more likely in secessionist struggles than in general civil wars).

Geography

An effective peacekeeping operation must be deployed in such a way as to maximize its ability to supervise a cease-fire. The three geographic elements identified were that peacekeeping operations should be relatively invulnerable to attack, able to patrol an area to detect violations easily, and able to separate the combatants at a safe distance. As peacekeeping operations cannot simply rearrange borders and terrain to meet the guidelines outlined here, the geographic component is not easily subject to manipulation by decision makers.

Nevertheless, this does not mean that the peacekeeping mission is helpless in promoting desirable geographic conditions. U.N. or other peacekeeping officials may have some input into the configuration of the ceasefire lines. They certainly have a great deal of influence (although they cannot dictate terms) regarding where the peacekeeping force will be located. Appropriate precautions can lessen the chance that the force will come under attack. These operational decisions can enhance already favorable geographic conditions or mitigate those that are problematic.

All things being equal, peacekeeping operations should be placed along a clearly defined international border, preferably in a thinly populated and relatively flat area. Any sudden troop movements will be easily detected, and the international border will make clear to each side the lines of demarcation. In contrast, peacekeeping troops should avoid being deployed in urban areas, where it is difficult to monitor activities and to protect themselves; mountainous regions, where covert actions might go undetected, are also problematic. Regardless of where they are deployed, however, peacekeeping troops must form a wide enough buffer zone to prevent accidental or less than accidental engagements that could escalate to war. One only has to consider the experience in the narrow demilitarized zone between the two Koreas to see the potential problems.

Neutrality

The final central guideline for the deployment of peacekeeping troops is that they be an impartial force. The key element is that their actions neither favor nor be perceived to favor any side in the dispute. Failure to achieve this will erode whatever cooperation had been garnered from the relevant actors in the conflict.

In some ways, it is very difficult *before* the deployment of peacekeeping troops to ensure their neutral behavior *after* deployment. Furthermore, the achievement of impartiality also depends on the perceptions of the conflicting parties, a component largely beyond the control of the peacekeeping force. Nevertheless, the authorizing agency or the peacekeeping force can take several steps to ensure the best possible chance of achieving neutrality. The first is to avoid assigning to peacekeeping operations functions that directly serve the interests of one protagonist to the detriment of the others. Operations like ONUC need to be avoided. Similarly, the MNF's policy of training the Lebanese government army should act as a negative precedent for peacekeeping operations, either multinational or United Nations directed.

A second proposal related to neutrality is to train peacekeeping soldiers in peacekeeping techniques and philosophy, and, if possible, to place them under a strong central command. These ideas help remove the troops from their orientations as national military personnel. The International Peace Academy and several national governments have training regimens for peacekeepers; one hopes that those can be expanded in the future. A central command will not necessarily guarantee the success of the mission, but it will help retain strong international control over the operation and prevent embarrassing incidents that might lead the protagonists to question the impartiality of the peacekeeping troops.

Finally, peacekeeping operations can help guarantee neutrality by continuing to draw most of their personnel from nonaligned and disinterested states in the absence of a permanent force composed of international civil servants. This will be a key element in affecting the perceptions of the force by the disputants. The end of the Cold War should now broaden the pool of possible contributing states for any given conflict. This recommendation is in line with traditional peacekeeping practice.

There may be circumstances that justify some exceptions to a fully nonaligned composition of a peacekeeping force. If one or more of the protagonists insists that a major power act as a guarantor for the operation, it may be necessary to incorporate troops and administrative personnel from that state. The MFO was created under these circumstances, as the United States assumed the leading role in the operation and continues to supply a large portion of the troops. As long as all parties acquiesce in this requirement, it is probably worth the risk of bias in order to permit the peacekeeping operation to be deployed.

These four guidelines will not guarantee that a peacekeeping mission will operate smoothly, but they will enhance the probability of success significantly. Various other guidelines for peacekeeping operations might include ideas for stable financing, clear mandates, better coordination, and the like. Although such ideas may make the operation more efficient and are therefore desirable, they will have little impact on the ultimate success of the operation. Furthermore, these operational components are described in detail elsewhere.[4]

In looking at potential contemporary applications of traditional peacekeeping forces, two categories of disputes will form the bulk of future threats to international peace and security: interstate border or territorial disputes and nationalist conflicts. The former seem well suited to the application of the peacekeeping strategy. Peacekeeping troops might be placed at a disputed border or throughout the territory in question until sovereignty over the area is settled. The geographic configuration and the limited number of actors in these interstate disputes make results more promising than under other peacekeeping scenarios.

According to Day et al., there are approximately sixty-seven interstate border or territorial disputes in the world.[5] Not all require a peacekeeping force; indeed, most are latent disputes with only a slight prospect for war in the near future. Nevertheless, war in the Persian Gulf might have been avoided if a peacekeeping force had been deployed to the disputed oil fields on the border of Kuwait and Iraq, especially at the time of rising tensions in July 1990. Peacekeeping troops might also be sent to replace observers in the disputed Kashmir region between India and Pakistan, which has been the scene of heightened tensions in the past few years. Peacekeeping forces could also calm hostilities along the border of Burma and Bangladesh, or China and some of her neighbors, such as Vietnam or India.

The outlook for the use of peacekeeping troops in nationalist struggles is less promising. The end of the Cold War has permitted the rekindling the nationalist passions of many peoples around the globe. On all the major continents, ethnic and racial groups are seeking greater autonomy or independence from their central governments. These are primarily civil conflicts, in which peacekeeping troops have had difficulty, and one must be cautious about sending in peacekeeping forces. Nationalist conflicts best suited to peacekeeping operations would be those that have seen an agreement among warring parties to solve the dispute; the peacekeeping force is then charged with assisting in the implementation of that agreement by supervising an election or monitoring a cease-fire in the transition or subsequent period.

Short of such an agreement, peacekeeping forces should perhaps only be used when (1) the primary protagonists request a peacekeeping force, (2) the area of deployment and the population of the areas controlled by the respective parties do not include a large number of citizens of the opposite national group, and (3) there is an easily identifiable line of demarcation between the warring parties.

In the fall of 1992, U.N. peacekeeping troops, the U.N. Protection Force (UNPROFOR) were stationed in Sarajevo (in Yugoslavia or Bosnia) attempting, with limited success, to carry out humanitarian functions. No cease-fire had lasted long, and there was significant opposition among Serbians to the U.N. presence. The United Nations also faced the problem that it would most likely have to deploy troops before an agreement resolved the issues in dispute and would have to do so in areas in which the population was of mixed ethnic character, even though the borders between the Yugoslav republics are relatively clear. Prospects for a fully deployed operation and therefore success would improve when all the main protagonists agreed to cooperate with the peacekeeping mission. Other possibilities for peacekeeping troops in nationalist struggles in 1992 included some protection of the Kurds in Iraq or separation of the Tamil Tigers and government forces in Sri Lanka; nevertheless, in those cases, there was no sign that the host governments would request or support a peacekeeping operation.

The weakening of central governments internally and the rise of semi-autonomous and powerful subnational groups will likely make nationalist struggles an increasing problem in the future.[6] Unfortunately, peacekeeping operations cannot play a central role in all those challenges; they may best be utilized as an implementing mechanism when conflict resolution is attained.

Conflict Resolution

Analysis suggests that peacekeeping operations have been largely ineffective in promoting conflict resolution. There are several possible explanations for this failure, but the most comprehensive and credible is that peacekeeping operations are developed and organized to supervise ceasefires and limit armed conflict, not achieve diplomatic successes.

Even if peacekeeping operations cannot bring about meaningful negotiations or a peace settlement, they can stop fighting, save many lives, and bring some stability to troubled areas of the world. These are notable achievements and should provide sufficient justification, in the absence of more effective alternatives, for the deployment of peacekeeping troops. Nevertheless, the substitution of peacekeeping for collective security has left a large void—what to do after the fighting stops. Despite the problems that peacekeeping has with peacemaking, some guidelines might be followed.

The most desirable situation would have peacekeeping troops deployed *following* a settlement of the dispute, either by informal agreement between the parties or as a specific provision of a peace treaty. The MFO in the Sinai is an example of this kind of operation. Furthermore, the new roles for peacekeeping troops that have the most promise, such as election supervision, arms control verification, share this characteristic. When peacekeeping forces act as an implementing agency of a peace agreement, they encounter fewer difficulties. Having peacekeeping after peacemaking provides an escape from peacekeeping's inability to promote conflict resolution.

More often than not, however, a resolution of serious conflict is not possible. Peacekeeping troops may be introduced to stop the fighting, with other efforts at conflict resolution to follow. In that event, negotiations may not necessarily lead to peace, but steps can be taken to encourage progress and minimize complications that might be caused by the presence of peace-keeping troops. First, the peacekeeping operation should be separated from any efforts at negotiation or mediation; of course, this does not include efforts to resolve disputes over the conduct of the peacekeeping operation or cease-fire violations. Whether peacemaking and peacekeeping were connected or not seemed irrelevant in charting progress toward a peace agreement. Yet peacekeeping is more effective in limiting armed conflict when its functions are limited. Peacekeeping operations will also not be jeopardized by a breakdown in negotiations.

Although separating peacekeeping duties from mediation efforts may allow the former to be more successful, there still remains the problem of resolving the conflict. The failure to reach a settlement is likely to end in renewed warfare at worst or an indefinite stationing of peacekeeping troops in the area at best. It is not the focus of this book to analyze the best means by which a dispute might be peacefully settled, and this will vary according to the dispute. Some efforts must be made, however, as a follow-up to the deployment of peacekeeping troops. Because most peacekeeping operations have been and will likely continue to be conducted under the auspices of an international organization, that organization, together with other relevant parties, must initiate diplomatic activities to help resolve the conflict.

Whatever the chosen mechanisms for peacemaking, they should not be intertwined with the peacekeeping operation. This requirement involves more than separate authorizations for the peacekeeping operation and for any diplomatic initiatives. It also includes different personnel under separate commands, continuance of the peacekeeping mission irrespective of the existence or success of the peacemaking initiatives, and efforts to shield the peacekeeping operation from the political dealings of the diplomatic process. It might be wise to set up a commission or liaison office between the disputants to deal with any controversies arising from the peacekeeping troops. In this way, problems with the peacekeeping force do not contaminate or interrupt efforts at peacemaking. The result may not be lasting peace—indeed, stalemate may occur despite these precautions—but failure to act in this manner heightens the chances for renewed bloodshed and makes the prospects for lasting peace more elusive.

Peacekeeping will not lead to true peace unless it is supplemented by other diplomatic efforts. It can provide the opportunity for negotiation, but other means must offset the lack of time pressure when hostilities have diminished. Without that pressure, peaceful change is unlikely. Nevertheless, as long as stopping war is better than the alternative, traditional peacekeeping operations will provide a valuable service to the international community, even if peacemaking is not the end product.

Beyond Traditional Peacekeeping

If the guidelines suggested for peacekeeping operations are followed, one might expect the number of traditional missions to remain relatively small (although perhaps more than the average in previous decades), in the absence of any tremendous increase in serious conflict incidents. Yet the number of peacekeeping operations could increase if the form or roles of those operations change or expand.

Institutional Alternatives

The marginal advantages of a permanent peacekeeping force over the traditional ad hoc U.N. operation appear insubstantial, suggesting that the creation of such a force should not be a high priority. Nevertheless, a permanent peacekeeping force has some desirable features, and, in principle, one should be created. Ideally, this force would resemble the most far-reaching of the proposals discussed in chapter 5, although even earmarking troops or having standby forces would be preferable to the current arrangements. Thus, at some point in the future, the United Nations should move toward the creation of a permanent peacekeeping force.

Several considerations, however, should guide the adoption of this admittedly low-priority item. The United Nations must be on sounder financial footing before it can accommodate the costs of a permanent peacekeeping force. As noted earlier, the United Nations is already running a deficit for its current peacekeeping operations, which leaves some doubts as to whether the membership of the organization would pay for this new venture. In addition, the United Nations is experiencing fiscal constraints, and new initiatives at this time do not have a good chance of being funded. Finally, the cost of new, unconventional peacekeeping operations may further stretch the organization's resources and the membership's desire to put more money into peacekeeping infrastructure. It is disconcerting to recall that financial considerations led to a reduction in the size of the UNTAG force, below levels thought to be adequate for the mission.

There is also the question of how large the permanent force should be.

If the number of peacekeeping operations does increase, then one might presume that the size of the permanent force must increase in a commensurate fashion; of course, the costs would also rise significantly. Most likely, the permanent peacekeeping force will not be able to accommodate all the new peacekeeping operations, and some ad hoc arrangements will have to be made. If this is the case, one wonders whether pursuing a permanent force is worth its few advantages.

More probable than a permanent force in the future are peacekeeping operations led by institutions other than the United Nations. Analysis indicated that regional and multinational peacekeeping operations have some advantages over U.N. missions, but not enough to make the critical difference between the success or failure of peacekeeping operations. Furthermore, significant disadvantages, such as problems with neutrality, attended both regional and multinational operations that might jeopardize their effectiveness. It appears that regional and multinational peacekeeping operations succeed and fail for many or most of the same reasons as U.N. operations. Given the choice, however, a U.N. operation would seem preferable in most circumstances. The United Nations has more experience with peacekeeping and is therefore more likely to run an efficient operation with few serious problems. The other institutional options did not have major advantages that outweigh the potential disadvantages that come with moving away from the U.N. mode.

Despite the preference for U.N. operations, circumstances might favor the use of regional or multinational alternatives. One such scenario occurs when the disputants favor an arrangement other than a U.N.-sponsored operation, perhaps placing greater trust in a regional organization. One could conceive of an OAU-based instead of a U.N. operation intervening in civil conflict in Africa, much as the ECOWAS force did in Liberia. Similarly, the disputants may ask a major power to guarantee the operation, and therefore the peacekeeping operation may be a multinational one with a significant contingent from that major power. The MNF and MFO operations fit this profile. Multinational groupings might also be called upon to implement a peace settlement in the Middle East, perhaps even in the context of an autonomous or independent Palestinian territory. South Africa might choose to rely on the United States or Britain in the process of ending apartheid and holding democratic elections.

A second context for increased regional and multinational peacekeeping operations joins those alternate institutional schemes with U.N. apparatus. In this fashion, a peacekeeping operation may be authorized and directed by a regional organization or by a collection of states, yet the United Nations may assist in the financing, logistics, and other aspects of the mission, taking advantage of its expertise and resources. This mixed type of operation may be able to capture the advantages of the regional and multinational structures while retaining the benefits of U.N. experience and assets. Peacekeeping operations on the African continent may be good candidates for this arrangement. The OAU may have the political will to conduct peacekeeping operations, but the ill-fated experiment in Chad indicates that the organization needs external assistance to perform peacekeeping duties.

Third, and in the longer term, regional peacekeeping operations may expand as regional structures develop. The few multipurpose regional organizations that exist today have vague or underdeveloped provisions for dealing with threats to regional peace and security. Much like the United Nations, none specifically mentions peacekeeping in its charter. A prerequisite for greater regional involvement is the development of structures and procedures in those organizations that can accommodate peacekeeping operations. This will go hand in hand with a greater desire by the organization's members to have the regional grouping play a larger role in security matters. The European Community (EC) and the Conference on Security and Cooperation in Europe (CSCE) appear to be the best candidates to develop in this fashion, at least in the near future. The EC considered deploying peacekeeping troops to Yugoslavia in 1991 and is just now expanding its concerns outside the economic realm to include security matters. An EC or CSCE peacekeeping operation, perhaps even a naval one, in response to a crisis or war between Greece and Turkey is conceivable sometime before the turn of the century. As regional organizations gain more experience with peacekeeping, the number and roles of the operation will also likely increase. Yet this seems decades away, if it happens at all, for most regional groupings.

Functional Alternatives

The prospects for change in traditional modes of peacekeeping seem brightest with respect to innovations in their functions. Among the eight new roles reviewed for peacekeeping troops, most likely to succeed were those that deviated incrementally from traditional operations rather than represented fundamental changes, were deployed following some measure of conflict resolution, and were sent to contexts other than ongoing civil wars. Those new roles that include some or all of these characteristics were election supervision, trip-wire, arms control verification, and naval peacekeeping. Less fruitful roles appeared to be combatting terrorism, humanitarian assistance, drug interdiction, and enforcement. The United Nations is most actively considering the functions of humanitarian assistance, election supervision, and trip-wire; it has largely rejected the idea of drug interdiction.[7] Even for those roles that I do not recommend or that are not under active consideration, the reader is best advised by understanding how those ideas might be implemented.

There are several potential contemporary applications of trip-wire peacekeeping forces. In many instances, they could be placed in locations similar to traditional peacekeepers but deployed before the onset of crises or wars, instead of following them. The replacement of U.N. observers with trip-wire troops at the Iraq-Kuwait border might strengthen the deterrent against another invasion. Peacekeeping troops might replace current unarmed observers in the Kashmir region of India as a buffer against Pakistan and be deployed in northern Chad to form a deterrent to Libyan adventurism. Finally, one might even see peacekeeping troops positioned along China's borders with Vietnam, India, or the former Soviet Union; in each case, the border areas are heavily militarized and have a history of violent confrontations and several wars.

The use of peacekeeping troops in election supervision is already well under way. The stability of Namibia following UNTAG-supervised elections has given rise to a host of proposed similar operations. The United Nations Transnational Authority in Cambodia (UNTAC) has begun to assist in that country's transition to democracy. This peacekeeping operation has the advantage of implementing a peace treaty agreed to by all factions in the civil war as well as by the relevant external actors. Nevertheless, one of those factions, the Khmer Rouge, has refused to disarm itself according to the stipulations of the peace agreement, objecting that the withdrawal of Vietnamese troops from Cambodia can not be fully certified by U.N. officials. This problem may prove to be only a minor glitch on the way to a successful operation or a bad omen.

Proposed agreements to end civil conflict and hold elections in El Salvador, Western Sahara, and Angola also include peacekeeping provisions for election supervision. The large flow of arms over the years into those countries and the tremendous political distrust among factions makes peacekeeping a virtual necessity as part of a peaceful solution to those conflicts. Peacekeeping troops and observers may become a regular part of the election process anywhere on the globe where violence and mistrust otherwise block free elections.

Peacekeeping forces have already performed arms control verification in a limited fashion, supervising troop withdrawals as part of a cease-fire agreement. Using international peacekeepers to aid in verification is applicable to almost any arms agreement in Europe that reduces troops or eliminates a class of weapons—indeed, peacekeeping troops might have been suitable for verifying the 1987 Intermediate-range Nuclear Forces (INF) treaty. Peacekeeping troops might also supervise proposed bans on chemical weapons production or the destruction of nuclear weapons in the former Soviet Union. The use of U.N. arms control inspectors in Iraq following the Persian Gulf war is illustrative of such activities. In those cases, and in dozens of more hypothetical situations, peacekeeping forces could insure that arms accords are executed to the satisfaction of both sides without the accompanying intrusion common to national means of verification.

Naval peacekeeping has a narrower applicability, confined to instances of war proximate to international waters and involving a significant threat to neutral shipping. Nevertheless, a naval peacekeeping patrol and minesweeping operation could prove very useful in the event of another war in the Persian Gulf. Naval peacekeeping might also be an appropriate mechanism in conflicts that threaten neutral shipping through the Suez or Panama canals.

Despite the risks, using peacekeepers for humanitarian assistance might be possible in several areas of the world. The United Nations is currently trying to alleviate the suffering of the residents of Sarajevo in the midst of the Yugoslav civil war. Somalia, in the middle of a civil war in 1992, seems to be urgently in need of this solution.[8] Similarly, peacekeeping forces supervising and protecting humanitarian relief efforts could alleviate problems caused by civil wars in El Salvador and the Philippines. States that are victims of any type of natural disaster, such as an earthquake or volcano eruption, might benefit from rapid and efficient relief efforts by peacekeeping troops. Bangladesh, beset by damaging rains and flooding on a regular basis, would seem to be a logical candidate for such assistance.

The disputes that the United States has had with Cambodia, Peru, and Bolivia over narcotics might be ameliorated if U.N. peacekeeping troops were introduced into the drug war. Those efforts might also be more effective than weak national programs financed by the United States. Similarly, the golden triangle in Asia, crossing several national boundaries, seems a good target for peacekeeping and drug interdiction. Using peacekeeping troops in the war against terrorism is most realistic as an aid to security at airports that have had serious problems with terrorism in the past, such as Beirut International Airport, or at airports with weak security known to be transit points for terrorists, such as the airport in Athens.

Conclusion

At the first convocation of the United Nations, there was great hope for the future of that organization and its role in preserving international peace and security. Over the next forty-five years, many of the most idealistic conceptions of the role of the United Nations faded. At the same time, the peacekeeping strategy was developing as a realistic alternative to the failure of collective security and the inadequacy of peace observation. We are now faced with a "new world order" again, with renewed optimism concerning the important contribution that the United Nations and its members can make to world peace. Peacekeeping operations will likely be an important part, if not the centerpiece, of new initiatives by the United Nations and others.

Peacekeeping operations can be useful but analysis suggests several caveats, lest the current optimism change to cynicism in the face of repeated failures of ill-advised peacekeeping operations. First, peacekeeping operations are not a panacea for all threats to international peace. Decision makers must show more imagination and initiative when faced with serious crises or war. The United Nations will need to rely on its broad repertoire of approaches to peace, not fall into the trap of applying old solutions to new problems. Second, when peacekeeping is an option, its exercise must still be judicious. The conditions under which peacekeeping operations have met with success are limited. This will necessarily result in a relatively small number of traditional peacekeeping operations at a given time, even though the number is likely to increase with the end of the Cold War. Finally, modifications to the traditional peacekeeping mode are unlikely to overcome its limitations to any great extent. The ad hoc U.N. system performs remarkably well in comparison to a variety of institutional alternatives. Room for innovation in peacekeeping is present in the expansion of the roles that the troops perform. Nevertheless, peacekeeping troops are not appropriate for all international functions, and they remain governed by the limitations of the peacekeeping strategy itself.

Peacekeeping operations will assume a prominent role in the next decade and beyond. The extent of their success will vary according to how well decision makers use them, whether decision makers follow their deployment with conflict resolution mechanisms, and the degree to which decision makers can recognize and employ better alternatives.

Chapter **VIII**

Epilogue: Applications to Some Recent Peacekeeping Operations

THE EMERGENCE of a new world order, with the collapse of the Cold War and the superpower rivalry, has raised expectations about the potential for U.N. peacekeeping operations to play a major role in addressing threats to international peace and security. The apparent end of the superpower stalemate in the Security Council and the emerging norm that international intervention is justified, even contrary to traditional conceptions of sovereignty,[1] are powerful evidence that some aspects of international relations have been fundamentally altered. Nevertheless, some elements have remained constant, with the persistence of regional conflict in the Middle East, South Asia, and elsewhere. Other problems of the new world order, primarily ethnic and nationalist conflict, have reemerged after a relatively dormant existence after World War II. These continuing challenges are particularly disturbing because they involve purely civil or internationalized civil conflict, exactly the type of challenge with which the United Nations has had so much difficulty in the past.

In this chapter, I consider the success of U.N. peacekeeping operations in three of the most prominent operations of the early 1990s: the United Nations Transitional Authority in Cambodia (UNTAC), the United Nations Operation in Somalia (UNOSOM I and II), and the United Nations Protection Force (UNPROFOR) in the former Yugoslavia. These three operations represent good tests of the United Nations in the new world order in as much as they reflect different situations and involve a variety of tasks for the peacekeeping forces, including some of the new roles discussed in chapter 6; in that sense, they can be considered "second generation multinational forces."[2] The Cambodian operation occurred following a peace agreement between all relevant parties. In contrast, deployment of peacekeeping forces in the former Yugoslavia took place *during* an internationalized civil war, with only periodic (and often fleeting) cease-fire arrangements. Finally, UNOSOM faced a situation in which no host state government existed, and this case may provide lessons for future U.N. intervention in "failed states."[3] The range of assigned roles also varied, with U.N. personnel in Cambodia taking responsibility for quasi-governmental tasks and election supervision, and the U.N. peacekeepers in Somalia and Bosnia focusing on humanitarian relief operations. Judging by the peacekeeping operations since the end of the Cold War and those in the nascent stage,[4] it appears likely that these tasks (election supervision and humanitarian assistance) will constitute a disproportionate share of new U.N. peacekeeping efforts.

For each of the three new world order peacekeeping operations, I will briefly outline its history and purpose, as well as make some judgments about its success. I recognize that it is difficult to make an assessment of peacekeeping success for these operations because several operations are ongoing at this writing and only of a few years duration—compared to previous, more traditional operations. It is particularly difficult to assess the prospects for conflict resolution given ongoing mediation efforts and the lack of historical hindsight to evaluate any peace agreements that are achieved. Nevertheless, each of the operations has had both problems and achievements and can be evaluated, at least in a preliminary fashion, according to the criteria of conflict abatement and conflict resolution used throughout this book.

With some assessment of each operation, the next step is to examine the factors identified in earlier chapters (e.g., neutrality, geography) that help account for the relative success (or lack thereof) of the mission. The result not only helps us test our ideas in the context of new world order peacekeeping operations but also provides some insights into recent policy successes and tragedies by the United Nations and its leading member states. In that sense, we gain some insights into the limits for U.N. peacekeeping in the post–Cold War era.

U.N. Operations in Somalia

The problems in Somalia extend beyond those normally associated with a civil war. When President Siad Barre fled the country as rebel troops approached the capital of Mogadishu in January 1991, no other group or individual was powerful enough to take his place. The result was that national government ceased to exist and most forms of social and political order broke down. Meanwhile, the civil war between different factions raged on. Further complicating this was widespread famine, especially in the countryside, which threatened a large portion of the Somali population. Thus, Somalia was beset by the twin problems of civil war and mass starvation, and it lacked any effective governmental structure to handle the human disaster that threatened the population.

More than a year after the overthrow of Barre, the United Nations established UNOSOM I. Faction leaders had agreed to a cease-fire in the capital city and to allow the distribution of humanitarian assistance. UNOSOM was supposed to supervise that cease-fire, provide protection for U.N. personnel in the capital, and escort humanitarian relief shipments in the immediate area. Only five hundred U.N. personnel were ultimately deployed for this purpose. In the summer of 1992 the prospects for peace were favorable, as factional leaders signed a declaration laying the groundwork for a political solution to the civil strife, but optimistic hopes were soon dashed as the scope of the humanitarian crisis became apparent. The rural areas were not being properly serviced by the United Nations and other relief agencies. Accordingly, the mandate of UNOSOM was expanded to include areas beyond the immediate outskirts of Mogadishu.

Despite a special emergency program in the early fall of 1992, UNOSOM was largely ineffective in its mission to stabilize the situation and ensure the delivery of relief supplies. Peacekeeping forces regularly came under attack by factional troops and bandits in the rural areas, making the distribution of food very inefficient, if not impossible in some cases. Relief organizations had to resort to bribery and other techniques to ensure that some portion of the humanitarian assistance got through. Even in the capital city, warehouses storing supplies were looted, and food was diverted to the black market. The lull in the fighting following the initial agreement ended; it should be noted, however, that despite repeated cease-fire violations, full-scale war has not recurred following the U.N.-sponsored agreement. The first phase of UNOSOM might be judged a failure because significant violence occurred during its deployment and humanitarian relief operations experienced severe problems despite the presence of U.N. peacekeepers. Of course, one must not forget that there was some lessening of violence for a period of time, and some aid was delivered to starving peoples; yet the mission fell far short of its goals.

With the worsening of the situation, the United States agreed to send military troops to protect humanitarian relief shipments, and in December 1992 the Security Council authorized (Resolution 794) states to use "all means necessary" to provide a safe environment for the relief operation.

Twenty-eight thousand U.S. troops, supplemented by those from several other countries, were deployed. The military operation was generally successful in halting the fighting and increasing the amount of humanitarian assistance that reached populations in areas distant from the capital city. Within five months the U.S.-led operation had made enough progress to turn over the mission to the United Nations, and UNOSOM II was created. UNOSOM was given an expanded mandate, which included enforcement actions and provided for the disarming of Somali militias. Disarming them would take away much of the power of the warlords, and not surprisingly they resisted efforts to force them to relinquish their weapons. In June 1993, Pakistani peacekeepers were ambushed and twenty-five of them killed. Sniper attacks increased, and it was often difficult for the peacekeepers to fire back without jeopardizing the lives of innocent civilians. In response, the Security Council called for an investigation into the attacks and the arrest of those responsible; evidence pointed to General Aideed and his followers.

The manhunt for Aideed commenced the most difficult phase of the UNOSOM mission. U.N. troops led a number of raids against suspected Aideed hideouts and strongholds, but without ultimate success, although some of Aideed's associates were captured. This effort was not without casualties on either side. Aideed's followers suffered some losses in the raids, as did U.S. forces, most notably the loss of eighteen Americans during an October 1993 raid. Journalists were also attacked by angry mobs of Aideed's followers, and the body of a U.S. serviceman was paraded through the streets of Mogadishu. Aideed's followers accused the United Nations of imposing its will on the country and called for retaliation against the troops. Support among member states for the operation also declined, and the United States pulled out its troops at the end of March 1994. The United Nations abandoned efforts to capture General Aideed and redoubled its efforts to find a permanent peace solution. Negotiations persist, without resolution at this writing, but the food crisis has been ameliorated.

Overall, UNOSOM has had mixed success at best in moderating the armed conflict and safeguarding humanitarian assistance. It has also made little progress in finding a resolution to the civil war. Several factors account for these problems in what was supposed to be a benchmark operation for nation-building in the post–Cold War era.

The successes and failures of the Somali mission are clearly tied to the circumstances that the peacekeepers faced and also to some unfortunate choices made by the United Nations and the leading states in the peacekeeping operation. First, the logistics of delivering humanitarian assistance proved difficult for the peacekeepers. Working with U.N. and private relief agencies, the peacekeepers had to ensure that the food and other aid was transported from the capital city Mogadishu to outlying refugees camps and other areas of greatest need. This was problematic. The small peacekeeping force was not well-suited to guarding the warehouses where the supplies were kept, and they were frequently stolen by armed groups and even by those indigenous personnel working for the United Nations. Transporting the supplies left the peacekeepers in vulnerable positions at the port and on the trek through the countryside, so it was not surprising that the peacekeepers were frequently attacked or highjacked by bandits seeking food for the black market. As noted in chapter 6, humanitarian assistance is difficult to achieve over a broad area, and the initial deployment of a few hundred personnel in UNOSOM I was woefully inadequate to the task, even with the assistance of nongovernmental organizations.

A second difficulty was the lack of cooperation by subnational actors. Although various factions and faction leaders expressed their support for the humanitarian operation, there were built-in incentives for various groups to disrupt the shipments. Beyond the desire to prevent food and supplies from going to enemies or those of another ethnic group, there was a powerful profit motive in stealing the supplies. Stealing the provisions would mean not only more food for one's own forces but also that the food could be sold on the black market for enormous profits. Furthermore, many of the armed groups operating in chaotic Somalia were no more than informal gangs who were not under the control of any faction or organization. The condition of anarchy makes promises of cooperation by identifiable subnational actors insufficient in practice. A peacekeeping force is ill-equipped to establish the law and order necessary when full cooperation from all relevant actors can be assured only by deterrence or coercion.

This brings us to our third consideration, the choice of peacekeeping versus enforcement as an appropriate option. In some sense, the UNOSOM operations reflected varying mixes of these strategies at different junctures. The initial small operation was largely carried out under traditional U.N. principles, albeit modified by the new functional role of humanitarian assistance. The U.S. military intervention was primarily an enforcement action, and one cannot really label that a part of the U.N. operation at all. After the withdrawal of many U.S. troops, the operation reverted back to the U.N. peacekeeping forces, although they too undertook some subsequent enforcement responsibilities. Generally, one can conclude that the peacekeeping aspects of the mission have been failures, and the enforcement ones (with a notable exception discussed below) have been more successful in delivering food and other aid.

The peacekeeping strategy seems largely inappropriate to the tasks required in humanitarian assistance. Even given reinforcements, however, a small peacekeeping force of lightly armed troops who could only fire in self-defense could not function effectively under the conditions present in Somalia. The local groups and bandits were certainly not as well armed as the Bosnian Serb army, but they could effectively match or exceed the firepower of the U.N. peacekeepers, and snipers were a persistent source of danger. In contrast, U.S. Marines had greater firepower and the authorization to take whatever means might be necessary to secure areas for food distribution. This is not to say that they had no problems with snipers — but they did have the training and the weaponry to meet most circumstances that they faced. More importantly, in the early stages, their show of force had a deterrent effect on the local population and therefore made the apparent costs of attacking food convoys greater than the perceived benefits. Thus, the military aspect of the food distribution was better handled by military forces than by peacekeeping troops.

UNOSOM II had more success than its predecessor, but perhaps not as much as a pure military operation. A continuing problem was the failure of the U.N. operation to disarm the various factions (this mandate was disputed by several states, which disagreed with the assignment of this task by Secretary-General Boutros-Ghali). That it was not achieved complicated the mission, and it also constitutes an obstacle to the stability of any political settlement. In any case, such a mandate is more suitable for a military force and goes well beyond the arms verification role (in which peacekeepers supervise a consensual agreement by all parties) that U.N. peacekeeping forces might play.

The major problem with UNOSOM II was that it violated the canon of neutrality which has been the centerpiece of the peacekeeping strategy. Admittedly, U.N. forces did come under attack, and the faction led by General Aideed was judged to be responsible. Nevertheless, the shift in U.N. policy, supported by the major powers, to arrest General Aideed and those responsible inherently removed the force from an impartial position. U.N. troops became embroiled in the local conflict as they searched for General Aideed and his lieutenants. Furthermore, those supportive of General Aideed rallied to his aid, conducting demonstrations in the capital city and clashing with U.N. personnel. The number of violent incidents, sniper attacks, and casualties (among both civilians and U.N. personnel) escalated during this period. Those who supported General Aideed regarded the

U.N. force as a tool of the United States or at least as foreign, Western invaders; they were no longer the humanitarian saviors they once were, and nationalist or tribalist appeals resonated within this group.

The U.N. attempt to capture General Aideed was a miserable failure in several respects. Most obviously, the United Nations was unable to capture the factional leader, the goal of the new mandate. Second, the United Nations undermined its credibility as a neutral force in the area and complicated its ability to find a political solution to the chaos. Getting the Aideed faction to cooperate with the United Nations in the future is going to be problematic, and it will be difficult for U.N. actions to be viewed as impartial when implementing any settlement. Third, both loss of life and injuries increased as a result of the manhunt. Finally, and perhaps most importantly, the operation undermined the support of U.N. initiatives by several key U.N. members, including the United States and Italy. U.S. public opinion, in particular, became less supportive of U.S. participation or leadership in U.N. operations after the spectacle of seeing the body of an American dragged through the streets by an angry mob. It was probably no coincidence that the level of violence decreased after the United Nations had abandoned its mandate to capture General Aideed in favor of trying to find a negotiated solution, involving even the Aideed faction.

The final difficulty in the Somali operations was the relatively low priority given to efforts at conflict resolution. Of course, this might be understandable in part because, in the face of thousands of people on the brink of starvation, initial efforts must be aimed at addressing their suffering. Nevertheless, Somalia poses some unique problems for the United Nations in both the short and the long run. The absence of governmental authority not only means that there are no viable structures on which to build a peace settlement, but the actors who participate in negotiations are less defined. Nevertheless, even if the United Nations was able to halt all the fighting in the country and provide for the basic human needs of Somali citizens, then what? Could it continue to play that role indefinitely? Should it assume such a role?[5] Does it even aspire to such a role? The United Nations has successfully convened peace conferences even at the height of fighting, but the various factions have been unable to reach agreement, and there has been criticism of U.N. mediation efforts. The consequences of failure at conflict resolution are much greater here than in traditional peacekeeping operations such as UNFICYP, where a tolerable stalemate is the result. In Somalia, the failure to get a peace agreement means not only that civil war could erupt again but also that the United Nations, in conjunction with private agencies, may have to provide many relief services indefinitely if we see a renewal of widespread starvation. This is both an expensive and a risky circumstance.

UNOSOM I and II were initially met with great optimism by the world community as blueprints for peacekeeping operations in the new world order. Yet, the operations have been handicapped by the inherent constraints imposed by the geographic scope of their duties and incentives present for subnational actors to disrupt the distribution of humanitarian aid. Nevertheless, the U.N. peacekeeping effort was also damaged by its own actions, namely, the use of offensive military actions in contravention to an impartial standard of behavior. The Somali experience further illustrates the difficulty in peacemaking experienced by peacekeeping forces and suggests that some missions may be better performed by traditional military groupings, although it is recognized that the political will of the member states may be lacking for such endeavors.

U.N. Protection Force

The origins of the conflict in Yugoslavia might very well be traced back several hundred years. More immediately, the present troubles stem from the decisions of Croatia and Slovenia to declare their independence in 1991 from the Yugoslav federation. Serbian-dominated Yugoslavia resisted these efforts, and long-standing enmities between ethnic groups were rekindled. The net effect was a bloody civil war, driving many of those in the region to become refugees in neighboring territories (the alternative too often was to be killed).

European states attempted to mediate the conflict by sending their own representative, Lord Owen, but among the key European powers— Germany, France, and Great Britain—consensus on what to do could not be achieved. These peacemaking efforts were joined by special representative Cyrus Vance, appointed by U.N. Secretary-General Perez de Cuellar. Initial diplomatic overtures were responsible for some progress, and a cease-fire was achieved in late 1991. Short-lived, it was the first step in a pattern of repeated cease-fire agreements and broken promises.

Finally, in early 1992, the United Nations authorized (Resolution 743) the United Nations Protection Force (UNPROFOR). The force was initially designed to enter Croatia and set up "United Nations Protected Areas," ensuring the creation of demilitarized zones and the protection of the local population. UNPROFOR's responsibilities expanded when Bosnia and Herzegovina held a referendum on independence, which was approved by an overwhelming majority (although it was boycotted by Bosnian Serbs). Fighting between Bosnian Serbs and Muslims intensified, and the United Nations' focus turned to this part of the former Yugoslavia. The peace-keeping operation's mandate was expanded to include security for the airport at Sarajevo and the delivery of humanitarian assistance to that city and the surrounding areas. Finally, U.N. peacekeepers were sent to Macedonia at the end of 1992 in response to a request by that territory's president to ensure that the war did not spread to new environs (this is similar to what we called the "trip-wire" function in chapter 6).

The U.N. force, especially in Bosnia, ran into difficulties almost from the outset. "Ethnic-cleansing" campaigns, disproportionately carried out by the Bosnian Serbs, led to the slaughter of civilians whose only crime was being of a different ethnic group. Various other human rights violations, including concentration camps, rape, and torture, were frequently used as a part of the war. Despite numerous cease-fire declarations, the fighting was rarely halted for more than one day, and the United Nations seemed powerless to put a halt to the killing. Efforts at humanitarian relief were no more successful. Relief convoys were directed toward Muslim areas, but Serbian military commanders often refused to stop shelling or fighting around Sarajevo and other cities so that supplies could get through. U.N. food convoys often had to detour hundreds of miles over dangerous roads to reach locations (a few miles away) that would have been easily accessible had the disputants cooperated in the operation. Furthermore, Serbian women and children were mobilized to block roads and stop the convoys. An attempted air lift of supplies (with no guarantee of who would get them) proved to be an inadequate substitute.

While Bosnia occupied center stage, things were relatively quiet in the Croatian and Macedonian portions of the operation. Negotiations continued between the various parties with an apparent breakthrough agreement, the Vance-Owen Plan, which was signed by parties to the conflict and endorsed by the Serbian government of the former Yugoslavia. It appeared that the United Nations was on the brink of facilitating the end of the conflict. Yet the agreement legitimized territorial gains made by military force, violating principles of international law long established and reiterated in various U.N. resolutions. Even though the Bosnian Serb leader signed the accord, he could not get his supporters to endorse the pact, and it collapsed. Bosnian Serbs and Croats continued the war to gain more territory and "cleanse" more villages, whereas the Muslims had the poor choice of continuing to fight or accept widespread losses of territory and political rights.

Threats from NATO and the United Nations to carry out air strikes or enforcement actions in order to lift the sieges of Sarajevo and other areas proved to be empty. Ironically, it may have been the placement of peace-keeping troops that, in part, made some states unwilling to support the use of military force. Some European states whose nationals served as UNPROFOR peacekeepers feared that air strikes would prompt Serbian retaliation against those troops, and thus they would not heed the U.S. call for military action. When a bombing in a marketplace in Sarajevo stimulated more U.N. outrage, leaders of the NATO member states did conduct a few air strikes, and shelling stopped around Sarajevo. Later, similar circumstances led to the de facto safe area around Gorazde, which had theoretically been under U.N. protection for some time. Nevertheless, the Bosnian Serb military took every advantage they could and were ultimately coerced only at the last minute to observe U.N. edicts. Still, even as they withdrew from the area around Sarajevo, they intensified their military campaigns elsewhere in Bosnia.

Several years after the introduction of UNPROFOR into the former Yugoslavia, there is little to show for its efforts. It might be argued that the trip-wire troops in Macedonia have kept the war from spreading, but one could question how important their role really has been. It is clear in Bosnia that U.N. efforts at delivering humanitarian assistance and safeguarding populations have been repeatedly stymied. Most successes in achieving cease-fires or safe havens have been fleeting and small in scale relative to the killing that has occurred.

Unlike previous peacekeeping operations, peacemaking efforts have been a high priority for the United Nations, and there has been almost continuous effort directed toward a long-term cease-fire and a lasting agreement resolving major disputes. Yet, other than the aborted Vance-Owen plan, the United Nations has been hampered by some disagreement among its leading states and, more importantly, by the intransigence of the disputants. The incentives for the Serbs, and in some instances the Croats, to keep fighting have been great, and empty threats of retaliation have not changed this equation. Even the Bosnian Muslims hold out some hope that things can improve beyond what they could gain at the bargaining table; in their view, things could not get much worse. Perhaps the only glimmers of hope were the 1994 agreement between Muslims and Croats to form a federation, separate forces, and parcel out territory and a proposed U.N. plan to divide Bosnia almost equally between the Serbs and the Muslims. The reasons for the failure of UNPROFOR share some similarities with those in Somalia, but there are some features that make this case unique and offer important lessons for the conduct of humanitarian operations in the future.

The geographic layout of Bosnia complicated the ability of peacekeepers to complete their missions. The peacekeepers were responsible for supervising large cities and for transporting humanitarian assistance across great distances. With respect to the cities, safe havens could not be guaranteed when military units took positions in the hillsides surrounding Sarajevo and consistently shelled targets there. This also hindered the ability, at various junctures, to assign responsibility for those attacks; thus, the safe havens were not effective in separating the combatants or in aiding with assigning blame once violations were detected. Transporting humanitarian assistance put the peacekeepers at constant risk as they traveled in war zones. Furthermore, U.N. food convoys could easily be stopped by blocking or seizing key roads leading into relief areas. Finally, the weather complicated efforts. Heavy snow sometimes made transportation difficult, and dense cloud cover hampered the ability of NATO planes to monitor (or launch air strikes against) Serbian military positions. It is thus not surprising that U.N. officials repeatedly asked their membership for an increase in manpower—requests that went largely unheeded.

UNPROFOR was deployed without first having a stable cease-fire. The problems this occasioned were more severe than those in Somalia. Somali weaponry lacked sophistication with a typical group being armed with a pickup truck retrofitted with a machine gun. In Bosnia, the Serbs had access to the most sophisticated weaponry of the former Yugoslavia. This dramatically increased the danger of delivering humanitarian assistance for U.N. troops. It also meant that the task of monitoring the actions of the various disputants was very complex. Even after the Serbs had agreed to remove weaponry from around Sarajevo and Gorazde, the United Nations subsequently discovered caches of arms hidden in the exclusion zones. The destructive capability of the weaponry also made every failed cease-fire very costly. Once again, lightly armed peacekeepers were wholly inappropriate for deployment during the war, especially one with the ferocity and destructive power of this one.

UNPROFOR suffered from an incentive structure that led disputants to disrupt humanitarian shipments. The war in Bosnia, and to a lesser extent in Croatia, involved explicit strategies by one ethnic group to kill or drive out members of another ethnic group. Placing a blockade around a city and shelling it were among the tactics employed. For those pursuing such actions, it would be incongruous to allow relief agencies access to those areas so that food and medical supplies could be provided to the besieged population; military commanders also feared that arms might be smuggled in along with the humanitarian aid. In their minds, humanitarian aid only helped prolong the resistance of their enemies. When ethnic cleansing campaigns are legitimized by a given ethnic group, moral appeals for providing food and medical care to the enemy are unlikely to have much impact. The distribution of humanitarian aid can be problematic during any civil war, but it becomes almost impossible when strong incentives exist for local actors to prevent or disrupt such programs.

Beyond some common problems with the UNOSOM operation, UNPROFOR suffered from a series of other difficulties. Perhaps none was more significant than the actions of third party states and subnational actors. The former Yugoslavia, or Serbia, assisted its ethnic comrades in Bosnia through the supply of troops and arms, and that state moved to undermine U.N. efforts at every juncture until the Vance-Owen accord. Serbia endorsed that agreement and, after its failure, announced that it would no longer support the Bosnian Serbs in their further efforts to carry on the war; yet U.N. sanctions against the rump Yugoslavia continued, evidence that it continued to arm Serbian elements in Bosnia. Nevertheless, this is indicative of the key role that Serbia played in instigating the fighting in Bosnia, as well as its impotence in ending the conflict; in effect, the initial support created a Frankenstein that could not be stopped later in the war.

Russia has also not been fully supportive of U.N. actions designed to put pressure on the Serbs. Domestic political considerations in Russia favor the support of their fellow Slavs, the Serbs. Consequently, the Russians have been reluctant to support U.N. efforts to bomb Serbian targets or take any action that would compromise the Serbs' position. This has not only undermined U.N. efforts, but it has lessened the credibility of the U.N. threats, because the Bosnian Serbs can rightly feel that Russia will protect them from the severest punishments of the international community— although Russia did support a NATO ultimatum on lifting the siege of Gorazde. Some political groups in Russia even call for the lifting of sanctions against Serbia, a position at odds with that of other leading states in the global organization. Serbian action has clearly been deleterious to the U.N. peacekeeping force, and Russian actions may have done some damage as well. With respect to Russia, it has probably been the absence of their full cooperation that has harmed the mission. Perhaps more pressure from them on the Serbs might have induced a lessening of the atrocities or facilitated a peace agreement in which Serbian elements would have made concessions. Croatia has also complicated the mission of the United Nations. The Croats are guilty, although perhaps to a lesser extent, of many of the same war crimes attributed to the Serbs. They have been involved in a significant portion of the fighting, alternately supporting Serb or Muslim positions as it suited their own interests.

Beyond third party states, subnational actors have undermined UN-PROFOR efforts. It is obvious that the major parties within Bosnia have worked against the efforts of the peacekeeping force, with even the Muslims, who have borne most of the brunt of the war, being occasionally uncooperative. What may be less apparent is the behavior of the Bosnian Serb military. That military establishment has repeatedly continued the war, despite cease-fire agreements or promises made by the Bosnian Serb political leadership. As an effectively autonomous actor, they appear to have defied the United Nations at almost every step and have backed down only when the consequences of further actions were immediate, severe, and highly likely; U.N. threats have rarely met this standard.

Unlike most of the peacekeeping missions analyzed in this book, UNPROFOR had command and control problems that have seriously hindered its mission. As with most operations, troops in the operation remained under national control. Yet added to this layer of command is NATO, to which some troop-contributing states belong. Beyond this, the United States, within and outside of NATO, has been a key actor. Finally, the special representative of the secretary-general has been given a decision-making role beyond what has been accorded U.N. personnel in the past. Before the United Nations has taken action, even simple actions such as returning fire, approval by the U.N. representative as well as some of the major states or NATO has been required. There has not always been consensus among these actors, and, consequently, the process itself led to delay when quick decisive action was required. The United States and some other NATO members have been especially critical of the special representative's reluctance to authorize military actions even in the face of bold violations of agreements by Serbian forces. The claim that the operation in Bosnia is one in which "everyone is in charge and therefore no one is in charge" has some validity.

The attempts to combine peacekeeping and enforcement actions in Bosnia illustrate the difficulty, if not the incompatibility, of the two options. By choosing to send peacekeeping troops, the United Nations limited its options for enforcement actions; contributing states were reluctant to support coercive actions for fear of retaliation against those troops. The neutrality of U.N. personnel was also called into question when the organization was imposing harsh sanctions on Serbia, threatening air strikes against Serbian military positions, and delivering food and other supplies to Bosnian Muslims; the expectation that U.N. peacekeeping personnel could be perceived as impartial in this context was unreasonable. Combining elements of enforcement and peacekeeping here (admittedly inadequate efforts on both counts) produced no better outcome than in Somalia.

The peacemaking efforts of the United Nations were ambitious in Bosnia, but general failure here may not be attributable to the organization, although its non-neutral stance and the behavior of some of its leading members did not help. Finding a way to resolve the crisis has been difficult because, as noted above, incentives exist for the sides to keep fighting, and it is not clear that agreements made by political leaders will hold on the battlefield. It may also be that ethnic hatred with a pedigree of hundreds of years,[6] and now reinforced by the horrors of this civil war, will make any comprehensive agreement tenuous in the long run. Once again U.N. diplomatic efforts cannot engender peace when the parties involved do not want it or their demands are fundamentally irreconcilable.

The UNPROFOR operation exemplified a peacekeeping force placed in the nearly impossible situation of a brutal civil war with the expectation of performing its mission without the cooperation of the warring parties, subnational actors, and key third party states. It is thus not surprising that the mission encountered so much difficulty. What benefits have been gained from the operation may be negated by the lost opportunities and problems created by its presence.

U.N. Transitional Authority in Cambodia

One legacy of the Vietnam War is that Cambodia suffered through years of civil conflict in which, according to some estimates, one quarter of the population was killed. In 1991, representatives of the major actors in the conflict, namely, the Vietnamese-backed government, Prince Sihanouk and his supporters, and the Khmer Rouge (rulers of Cambodia before their overthrow in a Vietnamese invasion) signed a peace agreement, which provided for an end to the civil war and set up the mechanisms for peaceful democratic transition in the country. The agreement was facilitated by U.N.-sponsored negotiations and represented one in a series of diplomatic triumphs (including the Soviet troop withdrawal from Afghanistan and the 1988 Nobel Peace Prize) for the organization.

The United Nations had an extremely ambitious mandate, of which UNTAC was a central part. The United Nations was charged with supervising the cease-fire and disarming the various factions, repatriating refugees, maintaining law and order, conducting some governmental functions, and most significantly, organizing, conducting, and monitoring democratic elections. UNTAC was not alone in this endeavor. The operation included administrative components whose job was to construct an electoral system, register voters, and conduct the election. There was also a civilian police component, which helped maintain law and order, supervise local police, and investigate human rights violations. In all, UNTAC was supplemented by seven thousand U.N. personnel performing tasks essential to the election and the mandate.

Prior to the actual time of the election, the prognosis for a successful election was probably not good. As Brian Urquhart notes, the United Nations had two notable failures in fulfilling its mandate.[7] It did not do a very good job in performing some of the governmental functions, and there was violence and harassment of the opposition parties during the election campaign. More significantly, UNTAC was not able to disarm 70 percent of the disputants' military forces. The threat of violence was significant, and the Khmer Rouge, in particular, threatened to disrupt the election, especially in the areas it controlled. A series of incidents also indicated that U.N. forces were not operating efficiently. U.N. personnel came under attack at different points, and the Khmer Rouge accused the peacekeepers of supporting the interests of the Vietnamese-backed party of the extant government and of failing to ensure that all Vietnamese troops were withdrawn from the country.

The Khmer Rouge became increasingly hostile toward the U.N. operation. Beyond its refusal to disarm and turn over administrative control to the United Nations, the Khmer Rouge threatened at several points to pull out of the peace process and renew its armed struggle. Just prior to the election this looked likely, and it was unclear what would happen when the voting took place. To the surprise of many, the response of the Cambodian people was overwhelming. Approximately 90 percent of those eligible voted, including those in areas of Khmer Rouge support. That faction may have decided that it could not disrupt a process with such widespread popular support, and so it did not carry through with its threats. The election was judged to be free and fair and a resounding success. A Cambodian government of unity was then formed, based on the election results.

Although the mandate was not fully achieved and there were significant problems with the U.N. operation, the bottom line was that the election went smoothly and there were few allegations of irregularities. In that sense, the UNTAC operation could be considered a success in performing election supervision just as UNTAG was before it.

Of the three operations, UNTAC might be considered the most successful, owing in part to the deployment of peacekeeping forces *following*
a peace agreement between the warring parties. This had a number of
advantages. First, it set out specific tasks for the peacekeeping force to
complete, and it ensured broad, although not universal, acceptance by the
parties involved. Thus, there was less chance that one of the disputants
would object to the U.N. presence, especially given that the disputant
signed the accord authorizing the operation. Second, the peacekeeping
force had legitimacy in conducting operations in the country and would
not necessarily favor the interests of the host government, something that
other peacekeeping operations in civil disputes might be prone to do. Third,
the agreement provided for a set timetable and an endpoint for the operation, preventing UNTAC from lingering in Cambodia for years as other
peacekeeping operations had done in Lebanon and Cyprus.

Another reason for the success of the operation was the unprecedented
support given the agreement by the major powers. The United States,
Russia, and China strongly backed the agreement and pressured their allies
in Cambodia to make peace and abide by the provisions of the pact. Had
the major powers taken the opposite position, it is unlikely that a peace
agreement would even have been signed. Even given agreement, actions
against the election process by those states might have caused one of the
flashpoints that occurred during the operation to escalate, thus sabotaging
the election. It was also important that Vietnam did not take any action
that directly threatened the election. Its behavior was in marked contrast
to the actions of the former Yugoslavia in the UNPROFOR operation and
those of Belgium in ONUC.

Although UNTAC is generally regarded as a success, it was not without
its problems. As with the other operations in civil disputes, geography
hampered its ability to perform monitoring and disarmament duties. The
operation and its personnel were too often confined to the capital city of
Phnom Penh. Sections of the countryside remained under control of the
Khmer Rouge, and, as noted below, they were less than cooperative with
the peacekeeping force. The rural character of Cambodia and the lack of
governmental control limited the United Nations' ability to operate in all
areas, even with the largest peacekeeping force in history and a sizable
contingent of administrative personnel.

The most complicating factor for UNTAC was the opposition of the
Khmer Rouge. Despite its accession to the peace agreement, it was not
surprising that the guerrilla group would continue its opposition. The electoral prospects for the Khmer Rouge were not promising, and even given

the varying estimates of membership, their numbers were small. Their influence in the political process had been a function of their military prowess and the territory they controlled. The peace agreement would disarm them and remove much of their power. The election would probably lead to the end of their domination of certain areas and a relatively minor role in a new government. It is significant, however, that the strong support of the Cambodian people, even in Khmer Rouge areas, led the organization to back down on its threats to disrupt the election, and the Khmer Rouge finally acquiesced at the most critical time in the process, during the actual voting. This illustrates the point made in earlier chapters that opposition by subnational groups can be harmful but is not necessarily fatal to a peacekeeping operation and must be weighed against the group's level of popular support and its capacity for disruption.

Technically, peacemaking was not an issue for UNTAC, because the peacekeepers implemented a peace agreement after, rather than before, conflict resolution had been achieved. Nevertheless, despite the free and fair election and the establishment of a unified Cambodian government, the Khmer Rouge restarted military activity in early 1994, and it seems that the peace agreement and the election have only partially solved the internal conflict of that state. This indicates that even under the best of circumstances, the United Nations and its peacekeeping operations may not be able to facilitate or impose peace in the long run.

Conclusion

Three recent peacekeeping operations (UNOSOM, UNTAC, and UNPROFOR) share the common characteristic of facing civil conflict, which we have identified as the most difficult context in which the United Nations operates. Furthermore, many of the new functional roles (e.g., humanitarian assistance, election supervision) of peacekeeping operations are evident in these recent cases. So, too, are the warnings about nationalistic or ethnic conflicts (see chapter 7), particularly with respect to Bosnia.

The early returns from the post–Cold War peacekeeping operations are not strongly favorable and clearly do not meet the raised expectations of the global community. There are many positive trends, including cooperation among the major powers on many security issues and a wave of democratization sweeping certain regions of the world. Yet, at the same time, the new challenges faced by the United Nations include a broader geographic range of conflicts (with the end of superpower spheres of influence) and many long-standing rivalries that have been rekindled. Only

UNTAC can be considered a success among the three cases here, and this might primarily be owing to its deployment *following* a peace agreement and its assumption of a new role (election supervision) most conducive to the peacekeeping strategy. The remaining two operations performed a task (humanitarian assistance) that may be inappropriate for lightly armed peacekeepers, and they did so under the most difficult conditions of an ongoing war. Furthermore, geographic considerations and the behavior of third parties caused problems for all the operations.

Although these three cases may not be indicative of peacekeeping in the twenty-first century, they do suggest that peacekeeping operations will not necessarily be more effective in the post–Cold War era than they were during the previous forty-five years, even though the number and scope of those operations may be greatly increased (subject, of course, to looming financial constraints). Peacekeeping operations are also not a suitable substitute for fully developed enforcement operations. They may be politically substitutable, given the reluctance of U.N. members to authorize enforcement actions, but practically they cannot achieve the same goals. The peacekeeping strategy will still be viable in many contexts, but the early failures of the post–Cold War era suggest that the United Nations must construct new mechanisms to meet its challenges, much as the peacekeeping strategy was born in response to new challenges and realities in the face of the superpower rivalry.

Notes

Chapter I. Concepts and Development of International Peacekeeping

Epigraph: K. Venata Raman, "United Nations Peacekeeping and the Future of World Order," in Henry Wiseman, ed., *Peacekeeping: Appraisals and Proposals* (New York: Pergamon, 1983), 372.

1. J. David Singer and Michael Wallace, "Inter-Governmental Organization and the Preservation of Peace, 1816–1965: Some Bivariate Relationships," *International Organization* 24 (1970): 520–47.

2. Ernst Haas, *The United Nations and Collective Management of International Conflict* (New York: United Nations Institute for Training and Research, 1986).

3. An exception may be John Mackinlay, *The Peacekeepers: An Assessment of Peacekeeping Operations at the Arab-Israeli Interface* (London: Unwin Hyman, 1989).

4. See, for example, Bjorn Skogmo, *UNIFIL: International Peacekeeping in Lebanon, 1978–1988* (Boulder, Colo.: Rienner, 1989).

5. See, for example, Indar Jit Rikhye, *The Theory and Practice of International Peacekeeping* (New York: St. Martin's, 1984), Alan James, *Peacekeeping in International Politics* (London: Macmillan, 1990b), and International Peace Academy, *Peacekeeper's Handbook* (New York: Pergamon, 1984).

6. See, for example, David Wainhouse, *International Peace Observation* (Baltimore: Johns Hopkins University Press, 1966) and *International Peacekeeping at the Crossroads: National Support Experience and Prospects* (Baltimore: Johns Hopkins University Press, 1973).

7. Indar Jit Rikhye, "The Future of Peacekeeping," in Indar Jit Rikhye and Kjell Skjelsbaek, eds., *The United Nations and Peacekeeping: Results, Limitations, and Prospects—The Lessons of 40 Years of Experience* (New York: St. Martin's, 1991), 171–99.

8. See James, 1990b, and Wainhouse, 1966.

9. This definition is quoted in Indar Jit Rikhye, Michael Harbottle, and Bjorn Egge, *The Thin Blue Line: International Peacekeeping and Its Future* (New Haven: Yale University Press, 1974), 11.

10. The basic principles of peacekeeping, as outlined by Dag Hammarskjold, can be found in Masaki Sato, *Concepts and Principles of Dag Hammarskjold's Peacekeeping Operations* (Master's thesis, University of Georgia, 1986). A more general treatment is given in Mircea Malitza, "The Improvement of Effectiveness of United Nations Peacekeeping Operations," in United Nations Institute for Training and Research, *The United Nations and the Maintenance of International Peace and Security* (Dordrecht: Martinus Nijhoff, 1987), 237–51.

11. A discussion of the differences between traditional military training and training for peacekeeping operations appears in Mackinlay, 1989.

12. A partial exception was the Congo peacekeeping operation (ONUC), which was placed in the middle of an ongoing civil conflict and actually participated in the fighting.

13. Nathan Pelcovits, "UN Peacekeeping and the 1973 Arab-Israeli Conflict,"

Orbis 19 (1975): 146–65, and Odd Bull, *War and Peace in the Middle East: The Experiences and Views of a U.N. Observer* (Boulder, Colo.: Westview, 1973).

14. For a good discussion of the theoretical underpinnings and practical requirements for collective security, see chapter 12 of Inis Claude, *Swords into Plowshares: The Problems and Progress of International Organization,* 4th ed. (New York: Random House, 1971).

15. On this point, see John Holmes, "The Political and Philosophical Aspects of U.N. Security," *International Journal* 19 (1964): 292–307.

16. Jack Garvey, "United Nations Peacekeeping and Host State Consent," *American Journal of International Law* 64 (1970): 241–69. Legal consent is technically only required of the state on whose territory the troops are stationed, yet it would be foolish to deploy a peacekeeping operation along a border with a protagonist that does not acquiesce, even if legal consent is not required; this is especially dangerous if that state does not support the cease-fire. Nevertheless, observer missions have been sent with only the cooperation of one party. For example, an observation force was sent to monitor an Albanian-Yugoslavian border dispute despite the noncooperation of Yugoslavia.

17. The breakdown of functions here is similar to Thomas Weiss and Jarat Chopra, *United Nations Peacekeeping: An ACUNS Teaching Text* (Academic Council of the United Nations System, 1992).

18. Alan James, *The Politics of Peacekeeping* (New York: Praeger, 1969).

19. A guide to all the operational details of a typical peacekeeping mission can be found in International Peace Academy, 1984.

20. See, for example, Claude, 1971.

21. Gabriella Rosner, "The International Military Force Idea: A Look at Modern History," in Joel Larus, ed., *From Collective Security to Preventive Diplomacy* (New York: Wiley, 1965), 445–56.

22. Ibid.

23. Leland Goodrich, "Efforts to Establish International Peace Force down to 1950," in William Frye, *A United States Nations Police Force* (New York: Oceana, 1957), 172–94.

24. See W. W. Willoughby, *The Sino-Japanese Controversy and the League of Nations* (Westport, Conn.: Greenwood, 1969).

25. See George Baer, *Test Case: Italy, Ethiopia, and the League of Nations* (Stanford, Calif: Hoover Institution Press, 1976).

26. For a full analysis of reasons for the League's failure, see F. S. Northedge, *The League of Nations: Its Life and Times, 1920–1946* (New York: Holmes and Meier, 1986); and Elmer Bendinger, *A Time for Angels: The Tragicomic History of the League of Nations* (New York: Knopf, 1975).

27. There were some inter-American regional peace observation efforts prior to World War II, but these were limited and had little impact on the development of the peacekeeping strategy. For details on these cases, see Wainhouse, 1966, and James, 1990b.

28. See James Barros, *The Aaland Islands Question: Its Settlement by the League of Nations* (New Haven: Yale University Press, 1968).

29. James, *Peacekeeping in International Politics.*

30. James Barros, *The League of Nations and the Great Powers: The Greek-Bulgarian Incident* (Oxford: Oxford University Press, 1970).

31. James, 1990b.

32. See Sarah Wambaugh, *The Saar Plebiscite* (Cambridge: Harvard University Press, 1970).

33. Technically, this was not a fully international force in that General Brind gave orders to national commanders which they then implemented. This is not quite an international chain of command.

34. Reprinted in Wainhouse, 1966, 27–28.

35. See also ibid., 83–85, which is the proposed "Convention to Improve the Means of Preventing War, 1931"; this was an attempt to make changes based on ten years of League experience.

36. Leland Goodrich, "From League of Nations to United Nations," *International Organization* 1 (1947): 3–21.

37. Two qualifications deserve mention. First, the Security Council was originally composed of 11 members; it has since expanded to 15. Second, according to custom, an abstention (or absence) is not regarded as a negative vote; thus Security Council action cannot be blocked by the absence of one of the permanent members, but only by an explicit negative vote.

38. A good discussion of the flaws in the enforcement procedures of the U.N. Charter is found in Alan James, "The Enforcement of the United Nations Charter," in United Nations Institute for Training and Research, *The United Nations and the Maintenance of International Peace and Security* (Dordecht: Martinus Nijhoff, 1987), 213–35.

39. Action could still have been taken against the People's Republic of China, however, because Taiwan occupied the permanent Chinese seat in the Security Council until 1972.

40. The Soviet Union tried to revive the Military Staff Committee following the Iraqi invasion of Kuwait, but this idea was rejected by the United States.

41. The United Nations has adopted a definition of aggression, although it is not a legally binding statement and Western members of that organization strongly object to some of its provisions. Nevertheless, according to the definition, Israel would be labeled the aggressor because it used military force first; no right of anticipatory self-defense is recognized. See *Department of State Bulletin* 72 (February 3, 1975), 155–62 for the next of the U.N. declaration and a statement of U.S. objections.

42. A/1775.

43. For a detailed discussion of the General Assembly's powers with respect to peace and security, see N. D. White, *The United Nations and the Maintenance of International Peace and Security* (Manchester, N.H.: Manchester University Press, 1990).

44. Resolution 678 (1900); see also Resolutions 660 (1990) and 661 (1990).

45. For a good review of peacekeeping and observation missions in the post–World War II era, see Henry Wiseman, "The United Nations and International Peacekeeping: A Comparative Analysis," in United Nations Institute for Training and Research, *The United Nations and the Maintenance of International Peace and Security* (Dordrecht: Martinus Nijhoff, 1987), 263–333.

46. See John Campbell, "The Greek Civil War," in Evan Luard, ed., *The International Regulation of Civil Wars* (London: Thames and Hudson, 1972), 37–64.

47. See Alastair Taylor, *Indonesian Independence and the United Nations* (London: Stevens, 1960).

48. See Larry Leonard, "The United Nations and Palestine," *International Conciliation* 454 (1949): 607–786.

49. See Wainhouse, 1966.

50. See Sylvain Lourie, "United Nations Military Observation Group in India and Pakistan," *International Organization* 9 (1955): 19–31.

51. Quoted in Brian Urquhart, *Hammarskjold* (New York: Knopf, 1972), 138.

52. See Gabriella Rosner, *The United Nations Emergency Force* (New York: Columbia University Press, 1963).

53. S/3671.

54. S/3710, see also S/3713/Rev. 1.

55. A/3256.

56. Resolution 998 (ES-I) (1956).

57. William Frye, *A United Nations Peace Force* (New York: Oceana, 1957).

Chapter II. Cases of International Peacekeeping

1. This may be changed somewhat in the future if the roles of peacekeeping operations are expanded or modified; see chapter 6.

2. Among other analysts mentioning this criterion are Henry Wiseman, "Peacekeeping in the International Political Context: Historical Analysis and Future Directions," in Indar Jit Rikhye and Kjell Skjelsbaek, eds., *The United Nations and Peacekeeping: Results, Limitations, and Prospects—The Lessons of 40 Years of Experience* (New York: St. Martin's, 1991), 32–51, and Kjell Skjelsbaek, "UN Peacekeeping: Expectations, Limitations, and Results," in ibid, 52–67.

3. Melvin Small and J. David Singer, *Resort to Arms* (Beverly Hills: Sage, 1982).

4. Definition is taken from, and more details can be found in, Charles Gochman and Zeev Maoz, "Militarized Interstate Disputes, 1816–1976: Procedures, Patterns, and Insights," *Journal of Conflict Resolution* 28 (1984): 585–616. All data on militarized disputes are taken from the most recently available files of the Correlates of War Project.

5. Among analysts mentioning this criterion is Emmanuel Erskine, *Mission with UNIFIL: An African Soldier's Reflections* (London: Hurst, 1989).

6. See Robert Axelrod, *The Evolution of Cooperation* (New York: Basic Books, 1984).

7. See Alan James, *The Politics of Peacekeeping* (New York: Praeger, 1969).

8. Gary Goertz and Paul Diehl, *Territorial Changes and International Conflict* (London: Routledge, 1992).

9. Karl Deutsch, J. David Singer, and Keith Smith, "The Organizing Efficiency of Theories," *American Behavioral Scientist* 9 (1965): 30–33.

10. Arend Lijphart, "Comparative Politics and the Comparative Method," *American Political Science Review* 65 (1971): 682–93.

11. The U.N. observer missions and their beginning dates are: U.N. Truce Supervisory Organization (UNTSO), 1948; U.N. Military Observer Group in India and Pakistan (UNMOGIP), 1949; U.N. Observer Group in Lebanon (UNOGIL), 1958; U.N. Yemen Observation Mission (UNYOM), 1963; Mission of the Representative of the Secretary-General in the Dominican Republic (DOMREP), 1965; U.N. India-Pakistan Observation Mission (UNIPOM), 1965; U.N. Good Offices Mission in Afghanistan and Pakistan (UNGOMAP), 1988; U.N. Iran-Iraq Military Observer Group (UNIIMOG), 1988; U.N. Angola Verification Mission (UNAVEM), 1989; U.N. Observer Group in Central America (ONUCA), 1989; and U.N. Iraq Kuwait Observation Mission (UNIKOM), 1991. Source: United Nations, *United Nations Peace-Keeping* (New York: U.N. Department of Public Information, 1990), and New Zealand Ministry of External Relations and Trade, *United Nations Handbook 1991* (Auckland: New House, 1991).

12. This position contrasts with most other studies of peacekeeping, which do not distinguish between peacekeeping operations and peace observation missions.

13. For discussion of the comparative case study method, see Lijphart, 1971, Alexander George, "Case Studies and Theory Development: The Method of Struc-

tured Focused Comparison," in Paul Lauren, ed., *Diplomacy: New Approaches in History, Theory, and Policy* (New York: Free Press, 1979), 43–68, and Adam Przeworski and Henry Teune, *The Logic of Comparative Social Inquiry* (New York: Wiley, 1970).

14. For a history of the UNEF I operation, see William Frye, *A United Nations Police Force* (New York: Oceana, 1957), Gabriella Rosner, *The United Nations Emergency Force* (New York: Columbia University Press, 1963), and Brian Urquhart, *Hammarskjold* (New York: Knopf, 1972).

15. See Chaim Herzog, *The Arab-Israeli Wars: War and Peace in the Middle East* (New York: Random House, 1982).

16. David Wainhouse, *International Peace Observation* (Baltimore: Johns Hopkins University Press, 1966).

17. See Herzog, 1982.

18. Resolution 340 (1973).

19. S/11198. The procedures were actually based on the secretary-general's report of the previous October.

20. For background on the Congo conflict, see Alan Merriam, *Congo: Background of Conflict* (Evanston, Ill.: Northwestern University Press, 1961).

21. S/4387, see also S/4389.

22. S/4426.

23. For more details on the ONUC operation, see Ernest Lefever, *Uncertain Mandate: Politics of the U.N. Congo Operation* (Baltimore: Johns Hopkins University Press, 1967), George Abi-Saab, *The United Nations Operation in the Congo* (London: Oxford University Press, 1978), and Arthur House, *The U.N. in the Congo* (Washington, D.C.: University Press of America, 1978).

24. S/4741 (the Soviet Union and France abstained).

25. S/5002.

26. Indar Jit Rikhye, *The Theory and Practice of International Peacekeeping* (New York: St. Martin's, 1984).

27. This meets the operational definition of civil war in Small and Singer, 1982.

28. Ibid., Roslyn Higgins, *United Nations Peacekeeping, 1946–1967: Documents and Commentary* (Oxford: Oxford University Press, 1980).

29. Lefever, 1967.

30. Background to the Cyprus independence problem can be found in Nancy Crawshaw, *The Cyprus Revolt* (London: Unwin Hyman, 1978).

31. Resolution 186 (1964).

32. For more information on UNFICYP, see James Stegenga, *The United Nations Force in Cyprus* (Columbus: Ohio State University Press, 1968), and Alan James, "The UN Force in Cyprus," *International Affairs* 66 (1989): 481–500.

33. See Mehmet Ertekun, *The Cyprus Dispute and the Birth of the Turkish Republic of North Cyprus* (Nicosia: K. Rustem, 1984).

34. Resolution 355 (1974).

35. United Nations, 1990.

36. Resolutions 425 and 426 (1978).

37. For more information on UNIFIL, see Bjorn Skogmo, *UNIFIL: International Peacekeeping in Lebanon, 1978–1988* (Boulder, Colo.: Rienner, 1989) and Ramesh Thakur, *International Peacekeeping in Lebanon: United Nations Authority and Multinational Force* (Boulder, Colo.: Westview, 1987).

38. Rikhye, 1984.

39. United Nations, 1990.

40. Typical of this view is Marianne Heiberg, "Peacekeepers and the Local Population: Some Comments on UNIFIL," in Rikhye and Skjelsbaek, 1991, 147–169.

41. There was an agreement between Israel and Lebanon after the 1982 Israeli invasion that normalized relations between the two countries. This agreement was subsequently cancelled by the Lebanese during the MNF deployment and negotiations between various Lebanese factions (see chapter 4 for more details).

42. For more information on the MNF, see Richard Nelson, "Multinational Peacekeeping in the Middle East and the United Nations Model," *International Affairs* 61 (1984–85): 67–89, and Anthony McDermott and Kjell Skjelsbaek, eds., *The Multinational Force in Beirut, 1982–1984* (Miami: Florida International University Press, 1991).

43. U.S. Congress, House, *Report on the Situation in Lebanon.* Communication from the President of the United States, House Document 170, 98th Cong., 2d sess., 1984, 7.

Chapter III. Peacekeeping and the Limitation of Armed Conflict

1. Alan James, "Painful Peacekeeping: The United Nations in Lebanon, 1978–1982," *International Journal* 38 (1983): 613–34.

2. Brian Urquhart, "Beyond the 'Sheriff's Posse,'" *Survival* 32 (1990): 196–205, and Richard Nelson, "Multinational Peacekeeping in the Middle East and the United Nations Model," *International Affairs* 61 (1984–85): 67–89.

3. In his study of different U.N. and multinational peacekeeping and observation missions in the Middle East, Mackinlay argues that a non-U.N. operation, and by implication one composed of non-neutral troops, can be successful; in particular, he points to the MFO operation in the Sinai. See John Mackinlay, *The Peacekeepers: An Assessment of Peacekeeping Operations at the Arab-Israeli Interface* (London: Unwin Hyman, 1989).

4. Geoffrey Carnall, *To Keep the Peace: The United Nations Peace Force* (London: Peace News, 1965).

5. Charles Moskos, *Peace Soldiers: The Sociology of a United Nations Military Force* (Chicago: University of Chicago Press, 1976).

6. Emmanuel Erskine, *Mission with UNIFIL: An African Soldier's Reflections* (London: Hurst, 1989). F. T. Liu, *United Nations Peacekeeping: Management and Operations,* International Peace Academy Occasional Paper No. 4 (New York: International Peace Academy, 1990), James Jonah, "The Management of UN Peacekeeping," in Indar Jit Rikhye and Kjell Skjelsbaek, eds., *The United Nations and Peacekeeping: Results, Limitations and Prospects — The Lessons of 40 Years of Experience* (New York: St. Martin's, 1991), 75–90, Mackinlay, 1989, Nathan Pelcovits, "What Went Wrong" in Anthony McDermott and Kjell Skjelsbaek, eds., *The Multinational Force in Beirut, 1982–1984* (Miami: Florida International University, 1991), 37–79, and Brian Urquhart, "United Nations Peacekeeping Operations and How Their Role Might Be Enhanced," in United Nations Institute for Training and Research, *The United Nations and the Maintenance of International Peace and Security* (Dordrecht: Martinus Nijhoff, 1987), 253–61. A list of potential logistics problems is given in J. D. Murray, "Military Aspects of Peacekeeping: Problems and Recommendations," in Henry Wiseman, ed., *Peacekeeping: Appraisals and Proposals* (New York: Pergamon, 1983), 175–202.

7. Liu, 1990.

8. Mackinlay, 1989.

9. Liu, 1990.

10. An elaboration of ONUC's problem in this regard is given by Lincoln Bloomfield, "Political Control of International Forces in Dealing with Problems of Local Stability," in Arthur Waskow, *Quis Custodiet? Controlling the Police in a Disarmed World* (Washington, D.C.: Peace Research Institute, 1963), appendix E. See also Ernest

Lefever, *Uncertain Mandate* (Baltimore: Johns Hopkins University Press, 1967), which argues that although ONUC's command system was formally centralized in some respects, it was very inefficient.

11. An excellent operations manual detailing the mechanics of setting up and conducting a peacekeeping operation is International Peace Academy, *Peacekeeper's Handbook* (New York: Pergamon, 1984).

12. Kjell Skjelsbaek, "UN Peacekeeping: Expectations, Limitations and Results - Forty Years of Mixed Experience" in Rikhye and Skjelsbaek, 1991, 52–67.

13. Naval peacekeeping forces were suggested by the Soviet Union for duty during the Iran-Iraq War. Such forces would have been responsible for escorting oil tankers through the Persian Gulf safely. The United States rejected this idea, and national navies handled the escorting duties under their own flags. For more the idea of naval peacekeeping, see Indar Jit Rikhye, "The Future of Peacekeeping," in Rikhye and Skjelsbaek, 1991, 171–99 and chapter 6.

14. Skjelsbaek, 1991.

15. Mackinlay, 1990.

16. On clarity, see Nelson, 1984–85, and Naomi Weinberger, "Peacekeeping Options in Lebanon," *Middle East Journal* 37 (1983): 341–69. On specificity, see Mackinlay, 1990.

17. U.S. President, *Public Papers of the President of the United States: Ronald Reagan* (Washington, D.C.: U.S. Government Printing Office, 1983), 2: 1202. See also Zeev Schiff, "Israeli Expectations and Conclusions" in McDermott and Skjelsbaek, 1991, 199–208.

18. Lefever, 1967.

19. Mackinlay, 1990.

20. The mandate for the UNFICYP was not changed after the 1974 invasion and became largely anachronistic thereafter. See Alan James, "The UN Force in Cyprus," *International Affairs* 66 (1989): 481–500.

21. William Frye, *A United Nations Peace Force* (New York: Oceana, 1957).

22. Arguing for the influence of funding and shortfalls on operations is Ralph Bunche, "The United Nations Operation in the Congo," in Andrew Cordier and Wilder Foote, eds., *The Quest for Peace: The Dag Hammarskjold Memorial Lectures* (New York: Columbia University Press, 1965), 119–38. On financing methods, see Alan James, "The Security Council: Paying for Peacekeeping," in David Forsythe, ed., *The United Nations in the World Political Economy* (New York: St. Martin's, 1989), 13–35, and Susan Mills, "The Financing of UN Peacekeeping Operations: The Need for a Sound Financial Basis," in Rikhye and Skjelsbaek, 1991, 91–100.

23. International Court of Justice, *Certain Expenses of the United Nations* (1962).

24. The United States had sought to suspend Soviet membership for being in financial arrears to the United Nations. The prospect of the Soviets withdrawing from the organization and the reluctance of some states to use article 19 (for fear it might be used against them later) led the United States to drop the action. Since that time, article 19 has remained in the charter, but has not seriously been considered, even in the face of a large U.S. debt to the organization in the 1980s.

25. The classic analysis of this problem is given in Mancur Olson, *The Logic of Collective Action* (Cambridge: Harvard University Press, 1965). NATO has historically experienced similar free-rider problems, as many of the smaller members have not met established standards of contributions to the common defense. See John Oneal, "Collective Burden Sharing in NATO," *International Organization* 34 (1990): 426–48.

26. December 1990 figures quoted in United Nations, *Blue Helmets*, 2d ed. (New York: United Nations, 1991).

27. There is some disagreement on whether financial problems affected the duration of the ONUC operation. Arguing that they did is David Wainhouse, *International Peace Observation* (Baltimore: Johns Hopkins University Press, 1966). Taking the opposite position is Lefever, 1967.

28. Azinna Nwafor, *United Nations Use of Armed Force in Internal War Conditions for the Maintenance of International Stability* (Ann Arbor, Mich.: University Microfilms, 1970), 47. See also Augustus Richard Norton and Thomas Weiss, "Rethinking Peacekeeping," in Rikhye and Skjelsbaek, 1991, 22–31.

29. Paul Diehl, "What Are They Fighting For? The Importance of Issues in International Conflict Research," *Journal of Peace Research* 29 (1992): 333–44.

30. Over three-fourths of militarized interstate disputes involve only two parties. See Charles Gochman and Zeev Maoz, "Militarized Interstate Disputes, 1816–1976: Procedures, Patterns, and Insights," *Journal of Conflict Resolution* 28 (1984): 585–616.

31. Kenneth Arrow, *Social Choice and Individual Values* (New York: Wiley, 1951).

32. Wainhouse, 1966, 557. See also Alan James, "Peacekeeping and the Parties," in Rikhye and Skjelsbaek, 1991, 125–46.

33. Weinberger, 1983, argues that a weak host state is a poor context for peacekeeping operations.

34. Brian Urquhart, "Peacekeeping: A View from the Operational Center," in Wiseman, 1983c, 161–74, and Alan James, "International Peacekeeping: The Disputants' View," *Political Studies* 38 (1990): 215–30.

35. Geoffrey Kemp, "The American Peacekeeping Role in Lebanon," in McDermott and Skjelsbaek, 1991, 131–42.

36. Skjelsbaek, 1991, and Augustus Richard Norton, "The Shiites and the MNF," in McDermott and Skjelsbaek, 1991, 226–36.

37. James Rosenau, *Turbulence in World Politics* (Princeton: Princeton University Press, 1990).

38. For a review of superpower behavior during some peacekeeping operations, see John Stoessinger, *The United Nations and the Superpowers: China, Russia, and America,* 4th ed. (New York: Random House, 1977).

39. Nathan Pelcovits and Kevin Kramer, "Local Conflict and U.N. Peacekeeping: The Uses of Computerized Data," *International Studies Quarterly* 20 (1976): 533–52.

40. Urquhart, 1990.

41. Augustus Richard Norton and Thomas Weiss, "Superpowers and Peace-Keepers," *Survival* 32 (1990): 212–20.

Chapter IV. When Peacekeeping Does Not Lead to Peace: Peacekeeping and Conflict Resolution

1. H. Hanning, "Report on Workshop," in H. Hanning, ed., *Peacekeeping and Technology—Concepts for the Future,* International Peace Academy Report No. 17 (New York: International Peace Academy, 1983).

2. The history of diplomatic attempts to solve the Arab-Israeli conflict after 1973 is detailed in Saadia Touval, *The Peace Brokers: Mediators in the Arab-Israeli Conflict, 1948–1979* (Princeton: Princeton University Press, 1982), and Howard Sacher, *Egypt and Israel* (New York: Marek, 1981).

3. The Camp David peace process is nicely described and analyzed in William Quandt, *Camp David: Peacemaking and Politics* (Washington, D.C.: Brookings Institution, 1986).

4. Indar Jit Rikhye, "Peacekeeping and Peacemaking," in Henry Wiseman, ed., *Peacekeeping: Appraisals and Proposals* (New York: Pergamon, 1983), 5–18, calls UNEF II an important ingredient for the Camp David accords.

5. See Indar Jit Rikhye, Michael Harbottle, and Bjorn Egge, *The Thin Blue Line: International Peacekeeping and Its Future* (New Haven: Yale University Press, 1974), and Touval, 1982.

6. Noted in Roslyn Higgins, *United Nations Peacekeeping, 1946–1967: Documents and Commentary* (New York: Oxford University Press, 1981) and Mehmet Ertekun, *The Cyprus Dispute and the Birth of the Turkish Republic of North Cyprus* (Oxford: K. Rustem, 1984).

7. Ernest Lefever, *Crisis in the Congo: A United Nations Force in Action* (Washington, D.C.: Brookings Institution, 1965).

8. David Wainhouse, *International Peace Observation* (Baltimore: Johns Hopkins University Press, 1966). On leaving conciliation to others or to chance, see Ernest Lefever, *Uncertain Mandate* (Baltimore: Johns Hopkins University Press, 1967), George Abi-Saab, *The United Nations Operation in the Congo* (London: Oxford University Press, 1978), Arthur House, *The U.N. in the Congo* (Washington, D.C.: University Press of America, 1978), Ram Chandra Pradhan, *The United Nations and the Congo Crisis* (New Delhi: MANAS, 1975), and Mugur Valahu, *The Katanga Circus: A Detailed Account of Three UN Wars* (New York: Speller, 1964).

9. The impossibility of reconciling the divergent preferences of three or more individual or groups was demonstrated by Kenneth Arrow, *Social Choice and Individual Values* (New York: Wiley, 1951).

10. Lefever, 1967, and House, 1978.

11. Van Coufoudakis, "United Nations Peacekeeping, Peacemaking, and the Cyprus Question," *Western Political Quarterly* 29 (1976): 457–73, argues that peacekeeping and peacemaking are interrelated and that failure in the latter will jeopardize success in the former.

12. The conventional argument is that peacekeeping buys time for negotiations and allows a cooling-off period. An example of this argument is Augustus Richard Norton and Thomas Weiss, "Rethinking Peacekeeping," in Indar Jit Rikhye and Kjell Skjelsbaek, eds., *The United Nations and Peacekeeping: Results, Limitations, and Prospects—The Lessons of 40 Years of Experience* (New York: St. Martin's, 1991), 22–31.

13. Samuel Komorita and Marc Barnes, "Effects of Pressures to Reach Agreement in Bargaining," *Journal of Personality and Social Psychology* 13 (1969): 245–52, Dean Pruitt and Douglas Johnson, "Mediation as an Aid to Face Saving in Negotiation," *Journal of Personality and Social Psychology* 14 (1970): 239–46, and David Brookmore and Frank Sistrunk, "The Effects of Perceived Ability and Impartiality of Mediators and Time Pressure on Negotiation," *Journal of Conflict Resolution* 24 (1980): 311–27.

14. A contrary opinion is contained in Alan James, *The Politics of Peacekeeping* (New York: Praeger, 1969).

15. The risk of hardening bargaining positions is particularly great the longer the peacekeeping force is deployed; this suggests the need for quick diplomatic action after the peacekeeping operation is in place. See Nathan Pelcovits, "UN Peacekeeping and the 1973 Arab-Israeli Conflict," *Orbis* 19 (1975): 146–65.

16. These are suggested by Brian Urquhart, "United Nations Peacekeeping Operations and How Their Role Might Be Enhanced," in United Nations Institute for Training and Research, *The United Nations and the Maintenance of International Peace and Security* (Dordrecht: Martinus Nijhoff, 1987), 253–61.

17. See Donald Wittman, "How a War Ends: A Rational Model Approach," *Journal of Conflict Resolution* 23 (1979): 743–63.

18. Paul Martin, "Peacekeeping and the United Nations—A Broader View," *International Affairs* 20 (1964): 191–204, and Nathan Pelcovits, "What Went Wrong," in Anthony McDermott and Kjell Skjelsbaek, eds., *The Multinational Force in Beirut,*

1982–1984 (Miami: Florida International University Press, 1991), 37–79.

19. International Peace Academy, *Peacekeeper's Handbook* (New York: Pergamon Press, 1984).

Chapter V. Institutional Alternatives to Traditional U.N. Peacekeeping Operations

1. Despite their ad hoc character, draft guidelines of operations do exist for U.N. peacekeeping operations. See "Draft Formulae for Articles of Agreed Guidelines for United Nations Peace-Keeping Operations (1977) - Report of the Special Committee on Peace-Keeping Operations, Eleventh Report of the Working Group," A/32/394 Annex II Appendix I of 2 December 1977).

2. An excellent description of the various official proposals through the 1960s for a permanent peacekeeping force is given in Larry Fabian, *Soldiers without Enemies: Preparing the United Nations for Peacekeeping* (Washington, D.C.: Brookings Institution, 1971), 73ff.

3. Ibid., 139.

4. General Assembly Resolution 2006 (1965).

5. Some efforts in international nongovernmental organizations (INGO) were even attempted. The World Veterans Federation worked to improve the technical aspects of peacekeeping operations, but their efforts were short-lived. See Fabian, 1971.

6. The various proposals in this section are taken from official proposals noted above and from a variety of other sources including William Frye, *A United Nations Peace Force* (New York: Oceana, 1957), Indar Jit Rikhye, *The Theory and Practice of Peacekeeping* (New York: St. Martin's Press, 1984), Fabian, 1971, Lincoln Bloomfield, ed., *International Military Forces: The Questions of Peacekeeping in an Armed and Disarming World* (Boston: Little, Brown, 1964), Grenville Clark and Louis Sohn, *World Peace through World Law* (Cambridge: Harvard University Press, 1958), David Steele, *The Reform of the United Nations* (London: Croom Helm, 1987), David Wainhouse, *International Peace Observation* (Baltimore: Johns Hopkins University Press, 1966), Ann Florini and Nina Tannenwald, *On the Front Lines: The United Nations' Role in Preventing and Containing Conflict* (New York: United Nations Association of the United States of America, 1984), Indar Jit Rikhye, Michael Harbottle, and Bjorn Egge, *The Thin Blue Line: International Peacekeeping and Its Future* (New Haven: Yale University Press, 1978), and D. W. Bowett, *United Nations Forces: A Legal Study* (New York: Praeger, 1964).

7. See Richard Swift, "United Nations Military Training for Peace," *International Organization* 28 (1974): 267–80.

8. Rikhye, 1984. As noted in the previous chapter, however, peacekeeping experience can substitute for, or be superior to, previous training in peacekeeping tactics. See Charles Moskos, *Peace Soldiers: The Sociology of a United Nations Military Force* (Chicago: University of Chicago Press, 1976).

9. International Peace Academy, *Peacekeeper's Handbook* (New York: Pergamon Press, 1984), 37.

10. For a series of related arguments, see Frye, 1957.

11. John Mackinlay, *The Peacekeepers: An Assessment of Peacekeeping Operations at the Arab-Israeli Interface* (London: Unwin Hyman, 1989).

12. Basic problems with logistics in a peacekeeping operation are detailed in Edward Bowman and James Fanning, "Logistics: Experience and Requirements," in Bloomfield, 1964, 145–71.

13. James Boyd, *United Nations Peacekeeping Operations: A Military and Political Appraisal* (New York: Praeger, 1971).

14. International Peace Academy, 1984, 37.

15. Kjell Skjelsbaek, "UN Peacekeeping: Expectations, Limitations, and Results: Forty Years of Mixed Experience" in Indar Jit Rikhye and Kjell Skjelsbaek, eds., *The United Nations and Peacekeeping: Results, Limitations, and Prospects—The Lessons of 40 Years of Experience* (New York: St. Martin's, 1991), 52–67.

16. Hans Morgenthau, "Political Conditions for a Force," in Bloomfield, 1964.

17. Mircea Malitza, "The Improvement of Effectiveness of United Nations Peacekeeping Operations," in United Nations Institute for Training and Research, *The United Nations and the Maintenance of International Peace and Security* (Dordrecht: Martinus Nijhoff, 1987), 237–51.

18. There may need to be even more dramatic changes in the global system before a permanent peacekeeping force becomes an effective reality. See Brian Urquhart, "Peacekeeping: A View from the Operational Center," in Henry Wiseman, ed., *Peacekeeping: Appraisals and Proposals* (New York: Pergamon, 1983), 161–74.

19. Robert Butterworth, *Moderation from Management: International Organizations and Peace* (Pittsburgh: University Center for International Studies, 1978), and Ernst Haas, *The United Nations and Collective Management of International Conflict* (New York: United Nations Institute for Training and Research, 1986), and Butterworth, 1978.

20. The classification of international organizations according to purpose and scope of membership is taken from Harold Jacobson, *Networks of Interdependence: International Organizations and the Global Political System*, 2d ed. (New York: Knopf, 1984).

21. See Vaidyanathan Shiv Kumar, *U.S. Intervention in Latin America: Dominican Crisis and the OAS* (New Delhi: Radiant, 1987), and Bruce Palmer, *Intervention in the Caribbean: The Dominican Crisis of 1965* (Lexington: University of Kentucky Press, 1989).

22. See Amadu Sesay, "The Limits of Peace-Keeping by Regional Organization: The OAU Peace-Keeping Force in Chad," *Conflict Quarterly* 11 (1991): 7–26.

23. See Naomi Weinberger, *Syrian Intervention in Lebanon: The 1975–76 Civil War* (New York: Oxford University Press, 1986), and Adeed Dawisha, *Syria and the Lebanese Crisis* (New York: St. Martin's, 1980).

24. See Terry Mays, "Nigeria and ECOWAS Peacekeeping in Liberia" (Paper presented at the annual meeting of the International Studies Association, Atlanta, 1992), and George Klay Kieh, "The Economic Community of West African States and Conflict Resolution in Africa" (Paper presented at the annual meeting of the International Studies Association, Atlanta, 1992).

25. A. Leroy Bennett, *International Organizations: Principles and Issues*, 5th ed. (Englewood Cliffs, N.J.: Prentice-Hall, 1991).

26. See Roger Kanet and Edward Kolodziej, eds., *The Cold War as Cooperation* (Baltimore: Johns Hopkins University Press, 1991).

27. Wainhouse, 1966.

28. Gino Naldi, *The Organization of African Unity: An Analysis of Its Rule* (London: Mansell, 1989), and Henry Wiseman, "The OAU: Peacekeeping and Conflict Resolution," in Yassin El-Ayouty and William Zartman, eds., *The OAU after Twenty Years* (New York: Praeger, 1984), 123–54.

29. Naldi, 1989, Wiseman, 1984, and Nathan Pelcovits, "Peacekeeping: The African Experience" in Wiseman, 1983c, 256–97.

30. Wiseman, 1984.

31. See James Jose, *An Inter-American Peace Force within the Framework of the Organization of American States* (Metuchen, N.J.: Scarecrow, 1970).

32. Bennett, 1991.

33. Ibid., Jose, 1970, and Jessica Byron, "Regional Security in Latin American and Africa: The OAS and the OAU in Light of Contemporary Security Issues," PSIS Occasional Papers, 1/84 (Geneva: Graduate Institute of International Studies, 1984).

34. James, 1983b. Mackinlay, 1989, and Nathan Pelcovits, *Peacekeeping on the Arab-Israeli Fronts: Lessons from the Sinai and Lebanon* (Boulder, Colo.: Westview, 1984).

35. Paul Diehl, "Avoiding Another Beirut Disaster: Strategies for the Deployment of U.S. Troops in Peacekeeping Roles," *Conflict* 8 (1988): 261–70, and Ghassan Tueni, "A Tragic Experiment in the Diplomacy of Misunderstandings," in Anthony McDermott and Kjell Skjelsbaek, eds., *The Multinational Force in Beirut, 1982–1984* (Miami: Florida International University Press, 1991), 184–92.

36. Pelcovits, 1984, and Mala Tabory, *The Multinational Force and Observers in the Sinai: Organization, Structure, and Function* (Boulder, Colo.: Westview Press, 1986).

37. Ibid.

38. Pelcovits, 1984.

39. H. Hanning, "Report on Workshop," in H. Hanning, ed., *Peacekeeping and Technology—Concepts for the Future*, International Peace Academy Report No. 17 (New York: International Peace Academy, 1983).

40. Frank Gregory, *The Multinational Force: Aid or Obstacle to Conflict Resolution?* (London: Institute for the Study of Conflict, 1984).

41. Tabory, 1986.

42. Geoffrey Kemp, "The American Peacekeeping Role in Lebanon," in McDermott and Skjelsbaek, 1991, 131–42.

43. Alan James, "Symbol in the Sinai: The Multinational Force and Observers," *Millenium* 14 (1985): 255–71.

44. Gregory, 1984.

Chapter VI. Functional Alternatives to Traditional U.N. Peacekeeping Operations

1. Indar Jit Rikhye, "The Future of Peacekeeping," in Indar Jit Rikhye and Kjell Skjelsbaek, eds., *The United Nations and Peacekeeping: Results, Limitations, and Prospects—The Lessons of 40 Years of Experience* (New York: St. Martin's, 1991), 171–99; see also Paul Diehl and Chetan Kumar, "Mutual Benefits from International Intervention: New Roles for United Nations Peacekeeping Forces," *Bulletin of Peace Proposals* 22 (1991): 369–75, and Brian Urquhart, "Beyond the Sheriff's Posse," *Survival* 32 (1990): 196–205.

2. Rikhye, 1991.

3. For an elaboration on peacekeeping forces as deterrents, see Bruce Russett and James Sutterlin, "The U.N. in a New World Order," *Foreign Affairs* 70 (1991): 69–83.

4. Rikhye, 1991.

5. Gwyn Prins, "The United Nations and Peace-Keeping in the Post-Cold-War World: The Case of Naval Power," *Bulletin of Peace Proposals* 22 (1991): 135–55.

6. Ibid.

7. Michael Krepon and Jeffrey Tracey, " 'Open Skies' and UN Peacekeeping," *Survival* 32 (1990): 251–63. See also Brian Mandell, *The Sinai Experience: Lessons in Multimethod Arms Control Verification and Risk Management* (Ottawa: Department of External Affairs, 1987).

8. William Stokes, "Technology and the Future of Peacekeeping," in Henry

Wiseman, ed., *Peacekeeping: Appraisals and Proposals* (New York: Pergamon, 1983), 218–30.

9. For a discussion of a possible U.N. satellite agency, see John Tirman, "International Monitoring for Peace," *Issues in Science and Technology* 4 (1988): 53–58.

10. Rikhye, 1991, and Leon Gordenker and Thomas Weiss, eds., *Soldiers, Peacekeepers, and Disasters* (New York: St. Martin's, 1991). For scenarios of peacekeeping operations and humanitarian assistance, see Frederick Cuny, "Dilemmas of Military Involvement in Humanitarian Relief," in ibid. 52–81.

11. John Mackinlay, "The Role of Military Forces in a Humanitarian Crisis," in ibid., 13–32.

12. For a review of past efforts, see F. T. Liu, "Peacekeeping and Humanitarian Assistance," in ibid., 33–51.

13. Rikhye, 1991.

14. Ibid.

15. Yves Beigbeder, "Another Role for the United Nations: The Supervision of Democratic Elections" (Paper presented at the annual meeting of the International Studies Association, Atlanta, 1992), provides details on this and other cases of U.N. involvement in election supervision.

16. On Namibia, see Robert Jaster, *The 1988 Peace Accords and the Future of South-Western Africa*, Adelphi Papers, vol. 253 (London: Brassey's, 1990), and Chester Crocker, "Southern African Peace-Making," *Survival* 32 (1990): 221–32.

17. Several of these insights are taken from Paul Diehl and Sonia Jurado, "United Nations Election Supervision in South Africa? Lessons from the Namibian Peacekeeping Experience," *Studies in Conflict and Terrorism* (forthcoming).

18. Alun Roberts, "Namibia: What They Did Not Tell Us," *Africa Report* 34 (1989): 62.

19. "UN Council Agrees to Cut Namibian Peace Force," *New York Times*, January 17, 1989, 19.

20. Russett and Sutterlin, 1991, and John Mackinlay, "Powerful Peace-Keepers," *Survival* 32 (1990): 241–50.

21. Alan James, "Peacekeeping and Keeping the Peace," *Review of International Studies* 15 (1989): 371–78.

Chapter VII. The Prospects for International Peacekeeping

1. Thomas Weiss and Meryl Kessler, "Moscow's UN Policy," *Foreign Policy* 79 (1990): 94–112.

2. See Alan James, "The United Nations," *Diplomacy and Statecraft* 1 (1990): 182–95.

3. These options and more are listed in article 33 and chapter 7 of the U.N. Charter and detailed in Inis Claude, *Swords into Plowshares*, 4th ed. (New York: Random House, 1971).

4. International Peace Academy, *Peacekeeper's Handbook* (New York: Pergamon, 1984).

5. The basic information is contained in Alan Day, ed., *Border and Territorial Disputes*, 2d ed. (Essex: Longman, 1987). Classification of the interstate disputes and a list of those disputes is given in Gary Goertz and Paul Diehl, *Territorial Changes and International Conflict* (London: Routledge, 1992).

6. James Rosenau, *Turbulence in World Politics* (Princeton: Princeton University Press, 1990).

7. I would like to thank Juergen Dedring of the United Nations for this information.

8. A international humanitarian relief effort already exists in Sudan—Operation Lifeline Sudan. See Larry Minear and Thomas Weiss, "Humanitarian Politics in the Sudan," in Leon Gordenker and Thomas Weiss, eds., *Soldiers, Peacekeepers, and Disasters* (New York: St. Martin's, 1991), 97–114.

Epilogue: Applications to Some Recent Peacekeeping Operations

1. Michael Barnett, "The New U.N. Politics of Peace: From Juridical Sovereignty to Empirical Sovereignty," *Global Governance* 1 (forthcoming).

2. John Mackinlay and Jarat Chopra, "Second Generation Multinational Operations," *Washington Quarterly* 15 (1992): 113–34.

3. Gerald Helman and Steven Ratner, "Saving Failed States," *Foreign Policy* 89 (1992): 3–20.

4. See United Nations, *United Nations Peace-Keeping* (New York: United Nations, 1993).

5. See Helman and Ratner.

6. Some argue that this history of hatred is overstated because the people of Yugoslavia had managed to live together in peace for more than forty years after World War II, and the calls for ethnic nationalism have been self-interested and politically motivated ones made by chauvinistic leaders.

7. Brian Urquhart, "Who Can Police the World?" *New York Review,* Mary 12, 1994, 29–33.

Bibliography

Abi-Saab, George. 1978. *The United Nations Operation in the Congo.* London: Oxford University Press.

Arrow, Kenneth. 1951. *Social Choice and Individual Values.* New York: Wiley.

Axelrod, Robert. 1984. *The Evolution of Cooperation.* New York: Basic Books.

Baer, George. 1976. *Test Case: Italy, Ethiopia, and the League of Nations.* Stanford, Calif.: Hoover Institution Press.

Barros, James. 1970. *The League of Nations and the Great Powers: The Greek-Bulgarian Incident.* Oxford: Oxford University Press.

———. 1968. *The Aaland Islands Question: Its Settlement by the League of Nations.* New Haven: Yale University Press.

Beattie, Clayton. 1983. "The International Peace Academy and the Development of Training for Peacekeeping." In Wiseman, *Peacekeeping: Appraisals and Proposals,* 203–17.

Beigbeder, Yves. 1992. "Another Role for the United Nations: The Supervision of Democratic Elections." Paper presented at the Annual Meeting of the International Studies Association, Atlanta.

Bendinger, Elmer. 1975. *A Time for Angels: The Tragicomic History of the League of Nations.* New York: Knopf.

Bennett, A. Leroy. 1991. *International Organizations: Principles and Issues.* 5th ed. Englewood Cliffs, N.J.: Prentice-Hall.

Bloomfield, Lincoln (ed.). 1964. *International Military Forces: The Question of Peacekeeping in an Armed and Disarming World.* Boston: Little, Brown.

———. 1963. "Political Control of International Forces in Dealing with Problems of Local Stability." In Waskow, appendix E.

Boulden, Jane. 1991. "The UN Charter, Article 43, and the Military Staff Committee: From San Francisco to the Collective Measures Committee." In Cox, 9–29.

Bowett, D. W. 1964. *United Nations Forces: A Legal Study.* New York: Praeger.

Bowman, Edward, and James Fanning. 1964. "Logistics: Experience and Requirements." In Bloomfield, 145–71.

Boyd, James. 1971. *United Nations Peacekeeping Operations: A Military and Political Appraisal.* New York: Praeger.

Brookmire, David, and Frank Sistrunk. 1980. "The Effects of Perceived Ability and Impartiality of Mediators and Time Pressure on Negotiation." *Journal of Conflict Resolution* 24:311–27.

Bull, Odd. 1973. *War and Peace in the Middle East: The Experiences and Views of a U.N. Observer.* Boulder, Colo.: Westview.

Bunche, Ralph. 1965. "The United Nations Operation in the Congo." In Cordier and Foote, 119–38.

Butterworth, Robert. 1978. *Moderation from Management: International Organization and Peace.* Pittsburgh: University Center for International Studies.

Byron, Jessica. 1984. "Regional Security in Latin America and Africa: The OAS and the OAU in Light of Contemporary Security Issues." PSIS Occasional Papers, 1/84. Geneva: Graduate Institute of International Studies.

Campbell, John. 1972. "The Greek Civil War." In Evan Luard (ed.), *The International Regulation of Civil Wars*, 37–64. London: Thames Hudson.

Carnall, Geoffrey. 1965. *To Keep the Peace: The United Nations Peace Force.* London: Peace News.

Cassesse, Antonio (ed.). 1978. *United Nations Peacekeeping: Legal Essays.* Alphen aan den Rijn, The Netherlands: Sijthoff and Noordhoff.

Clark, Grenville, and Louis Sohn. 1958. *World Peace through World Law.* Cambridge, Mass.: Harvard University Press.

Claude, Inis. 1971. *Swords into Plowshares: The Problems and Progress of International Organization.* 4th ed. New York: Random House.

Cordier, Andrew, and Wilder Foote, eds. *The Quest for Peace: The Dag Hammarskjold Memorial Lectures.* New York: Columbia University Press.

Coufoudakis, Van. 1976. "United Nations Peacekeeping, Peacemaking, and the Cyprus Question." *Western Political Quarterly* 29:457–73.

Cox, Arthur. 1967. *Prospects for Peacekeeping.* Washington, D.C.: Brookings Institution.

Cox, David, ed. 1991. *The Use of Force by the Security Council for Enforcement and Deterrent Purposes: A Conference Report.* Ottawa: Arms Control Centre.

Crawshaw, Nancy. 1978. *The Cyprus Revolt.* London: Unwin Hyman.

Crocker, Chester. 1990. "Southern African Peace-Making." *Survival* 32:221–32.

Cuny, Frederick. 1991. "Dilemmas of Military Involvement in Humanitarian Relief." In Gordenker and Weiss, 52–81.

Dawisha, Adeed. 1980. *Syria and the Lebanon Crisis.* New York: St. Martin's.

Day, Alan, ed. 1987. *Border and Territorial Disputes.* 2d ed. Essex: Longman.

Deutsch, Karl, J. David Singer, and Keith Smith. 1965. "The Organizing Efficiency of Theories." *American Behavioral Scientist* 9:30–33.

Di Blase, Antonietta. 1978. "The Role of the Host State's Consent with Regard to Non-Coercive Actions by the United Nations." In Cassese, 55–94.

Diehl, Paul. 1993. "Institutional Alternatives to Traditional U.N. Peacekeeping: An Assessment of Regional and Multinational Options." *Armed Forces and Society* 19:209–30.

———. 1992. "What Are They Fighting For? The Importance of Issues in International Conflict Research." *Journal of Peace Research* 29:333–44.

———. 1989. "A Permanent U.N. Peacekeeping Force: An Evaluation." *Bulletin of Peace Proposals* 20:27–36.

———. 1988a. "Avoiding Another Beirut Disaster: Strategies for the Deployment of U.S. Troops in Peacekeeping Roles." *Conflict* 8:261–70.

———1988b. "Peacekeeping Operations and the Quest for Peace." *Political Science Quarterly* 103:485–507.

Diehl, Paul, and Chetan Kumar. 1991. "Mutual Benefits from International

Intervention: New Roles for United Nations Peacekeeping Forces." *Bulletin of Peace Proposals* 22:135–55.

Diehl, Paul, and Sonia Jurado. Forthcoming. "United Nations Election Supervision in South Africa? Lessons from the Namibian Peacekeeping Experience." *Studies in Conflict and Terrorism.*

Erskine, Emmanuel. 1989. *Mission with UNIFIL: An African Soldier's Reflections.* London: Hurst.

Ertekun, Mehmet. 1984. *The Cyprus Dispute and the Birth of the Turkish Republic of North Cyprus.* Nicosia: K. Rustem.

Fabian, Larry. 1971. *Soldiers without Enemies: Preparing the United Nations for Peacekeeping.* Washington, D.C.: Brookings Institution.

Florini, Ann, and Nina Tannenwald. 1984. *On the Front Lines: The United Nations' Role in Preventing and Containing Conflict.* New York: United Nations Association of the United States of America.

Forsythe, David. 1972. "UN Peacekeeping and Domestic Instability." *Orbis* 15:1064–84.

Frye, William. 1957. *A United Nations Peace Force.* New York: Oceana.

Gagnon, Mona Harrington. 1967. "Peace Forces and the Veto: The Relevance of Consent." *International Organization* 21:812–36.

Garvey, Jack. 1970. "United Nations Peacekeeping and Host State Consent." *American Journal of International Law* 64:241–69.

George, Alexander. 1979. "Case Studies and Theory Development: The Method of Structured Focused Comparison." In Paul Lauren, ed., *Diplomacy: New Approaches in History, Theory, and Policy,* 43–68. New York: Free Press.

Gochman, Charles, and Zeev Maoz. 1984. "Militarized Interstate Disputes, 1816–1976: Procedures, Patterns, and Insights." *Journal of Conflict Resolution* 28:585–616.

Goertz, Gary, and Paul Diehl. 1992. *Territorial Changes and International Conflict.* London: Routledge.

Goodrich, Leland. 1957. "Efforts to Establish International Police Force down to 1950." In Frye, 172–94.

———. 1947. "From League of Nations to United Nations." *International Organization* 1:3–21.

Gordenker, Leon, and Thomas Weiss, eds. 1992. *Soldiers, Peacekeepers, and Disasters.* New York: St. Martin's.

Gregory, Frank. 1984. *The Multinational Force: Aid or Obstacle to Conflict Resolution?* London: Institute for the Study of Conflict.

Greindl, Gunther. 1991. "Peacekeeping and Peacemaking." In Rikhye and Skjelsbaek, 68–74.

Haas, Ernst. 1986. *The United Nations and the Collective Management of International Conflict.* New York: United Nations Institute for Training and Research.

Hagglund, Gustav. 1990. "Peace-Keeping in a Modern War Zone." *Survival* 32:233–40.

Hanning, H. 1983. "Report on Workshop." In H. Hanning, ed., *Peacekeeping and Technology—Concepts for the Future.* International Peace Academy Report No. 17. New York: International Peace Academy.

Heiberg, Marianne. 1991. "Peacekeepers and the Local Population: Some Comments on UNIFIL." In Rikhye and Skjelsbaek, 147–69.

Herzog, Chaim. 1982. *The Arab-Israeli Wars: War and Peace in the Middle East.* New York: Random House.

Higgins, Roslyn. 1980. *United Nations Peacekeeping, 1946–1967: Documents and Commentary.* Oxford: Oxford University Press.

Holmes, John. 1964. "The Political and Philosophical Aspects of U.N. Security." *International Journal* 19:292–307.

Holst, Johan. 1990. "Enhancing Peace-Keeping Operations." *Survival* 32:264–75.

House, Arthur. 1978. *The U.N. in the Congo.* Washington, D.C.: University Press of America.

International Peace Academy. 1984. *Peacekeeper's Handbook.* New York: Pergamon.

Jacobson, Harold. 1984. *Networks of Interdependence: International Organizations and the Global Political System.* 2d ed. New York: Knopf.

James, Alan. 1991. "Peacekeeping and the Parties." In Rikhye and Skjelsbaek, 125–46.

———. 1990a. "International Peacekeeping: The Disputants' View." *Political Studies* 38:215–30.

———. 1990b. *Peacekeeping in International Politics.* London: Macmillan.

———. 1990c. "The United Nations." *Diplomacy and Statecraft* 1:182–95.

———. 1989a. "Peacekeeping and Keeping the Peace." *Review of International Studies* 15:371–78.

———. 1989b. "The Security Council: Paying for Peacekeeping." In David Forsythe, ed., *The United Nations in the World Political Economy,* 13–35. New York: St. Martin's.

———. 1989c. "The UN Force in Cyprus." *International Affairs* 66:481–500.

———. 1987. "The Enforcement Provisions of the United Nations Charter." In United Nations Institute for Training and Research, *The United Nations and the Maintenance of International Peace and Security,* 213–35. Dordrecht: Martinus Nijhoff.

———. 1985. "Symbol in the Sinai: The Multinational Force and Observers." *Millenium* 14:255–71.

———. 1983a. "Painful Peacekeeping: The United Nations in Lebanon, 1978–1982." *International Journal* 38:613–34.

———. 1983b. "The Politics of Peacekeeping in the 1980s." In H. Hanning, ed., *Peacekeeping and Technology: Concepts for the Future.* International Peace Academy Report No. 17. New York: International Peace Academy.

———. 1969. *The Politics of Peacekeeping.* New York: Praeger.

Jaster, Robert. 1990. *The 1988 Peace Accords and the Future of South-Western Africa.* Adelphi Papers, vol. 253. London: Brassey's.

Jonah, James. 1991a. "Developing a United Nations Capacity for Humanitarian Support Operations." In Gordenker and Weiss, 82–96.

———. 1991b. "The Management of UN Peacekeeping." In Rikhye and Skjelsbaek, 75–90.

Jose, James. 1970. *An Inter-American Peace Force within the Framework of the Organization of American States.* Metuchen, N.J.: Scarecrow.

Kanet, Roger, and Edward Kolodziej, ed. 1991. *The Cold War as Cooperation.* Batltimore: Johns Hopkins University Press.

Kemp, Geoffrey. 1991. "The American Peacekeeping Role in Lebanon." In McDermott and Skjelsbaek, 131–42.

Kieh, George Klay. 1992. "The Economic Community of West African States and Conflict Resolution in Africa." Paper presented at the annual meeting of the International Studies Association, Atlanta.

Komorita, Samuel, and Marc Barnes. 1969. "Effects of Pressures to Reach Agreement in Bargaining." *Journal of Personality and Social Psychology* 13:245–52.

Kotani, Midejiro. 1964. "Peacekeeping: Problems for Smaller Countries." *International Journal* 19:308–25.

Krasulin, Boris. 1991. "Current Organizational and Military Requirements for Effective Action by the Security Council: A Soviet View." In Cox, 49–53.

Krepon, Michael, and Jeffrey Tracey. 1990. " 'Open Skies' and UN Peacekeeping." *Survival* 32:251–63.

Kumar, Vaidyanathan Shiv. 1987. *U.S. Intervention in Latin America: Dominican Crisis and the OAS.* New Delhi: Radiant.

Lefever, Ernest. 1967. *Uncertain Mandate: Politics of the U.N. Congo Operation.* Baltimore: Johns Hopkins University Press.

———. 1965. *Crisis in the Congo: A United Nations Force in Action.* Washington, D.C.: Brookings Institution.

Leonard, Larry. 1949. "The United Nations and Palestine." *International Conciliation* 454:607–786.

Lijphart, Arend. 1971. "Comparative Politics and the Comparative Method." *American Political Science Review* 65:682–93.

Liu, F. T. 1991. "Peacekeeping and Humanitarian Assistance." In Gordenker and Weiss, 33–51.

———. 1990. *United Nations Peacekeeping: Management and Operations.* International Peace Academy Occasional Paper No. 4. New York: International Peace Academy.

Lourie, Sylvain. 1955. "United Nations Military Observation Group in India and Pakistan." *International Organization* 9:19–31.

McDermott, Anthony, and Kjell Skjelsbaek, eds. 1991. *The Multinational Force in Beirut, 1982–1984.* Miami: Florida International University Press.

Mackinlay, John. 1991a. "The Role of Military Forces in a Humanitarian Crisis." In Gordenker and Weiss, 13–32.

———. 1991b. "A Summary of the International Workshop." In McDermott and Skjelsbaek, 251–63.

———. 1990. "Powerful Peace-Keepers." *Survival* 32:241–50.

———. 1989. *The Peacekeepers: An Assessment of Peacekeeping Operations at the Arab-Israeli Interface.* London: Unwin Hyman.

Malitza, Mircea. 1987. "The Improvement of Effectiveness of United Nations Peacekeeping Operations." In United Nations Institute for Training and Research, *The United Nations and the Maintenance of International Peace and Security,* 237–51. Dordrecht: Martinus Nijhoff.

Mandell, Brian. 1987. *The Sinai Experience: Lessons in Multimethod Arms Control Verification and Risk Management.* Ottawa: Department of External Affairs.

Martin, Paul. 1964. "Peacekeeping and the United Nations—A Broader View." *International Affairs* 20:191–204.

Mays, Terry. 1992. "Nigeria and ECOWAS Peacekeeping in Liberia." Paper presented at the annual meeting of the International Studies Association, Atlanta.

Merriam, Alan. 1961. *Congo: Background of Conflict.* Evanston, Ill.: Northwestern University Press.

Mills, Susan. 1991. "The Financing of UN Peacekeeping Operations: The Need for a Sound Financial Basis." In Rikhye and Skjelsbaek, 91–110.

Minear, Larry, and Thomas Weiss. 1991. "Humanitarian Politics in the Sudan." In Gordenker and Weiss, 97–114.

Morgenthau, Hans. 1964. "Political Conditions for a Force." In Bloomfield, 175–86.

Moskos, Charles. 1976. *Peace Soldiers: The Sociology of a United Nations Military Force.* Chicago: University of Chicago Press.

Murray, J. D. 1983. "Military Aspects of Peacekeeping: Problems and Recommendations." In Wiseman, *Peacekeeping: Appraisals and Proposals,* 175–202.

Naldi, Gino. 1989. *The Organization of African Unity: An Analysis of Its Rule.* London: Mansell.

Nelson, Richard. 1991. "The Multinational Force in Beirut." In McDermott and Skjelsbaek, 95–100.

———. 1984–85. "Multinational Peacekeeping in the Middle East and the United Nations Model." *International Affairs* 61:67–89.

New Zealand Ministry of External Relations and Trade. 1991. *United Nations Handbook 1991.* Auckland: New House.

Northedge, F. S. 1986. *The League of Nations: Its Life and Times, 1920–1946.* New York: Holmes and Meier.

Norton, Augustus Richard. 1991a. "The Demise of the MNF." In McDermott and Skjelsbaek, 80–94.

———. 1991b. "The Shiites and the MNF." In McDermott and Skjelsbaek, 226–36.

Norton, Augustus, and Thomas Weiss. 1991. "Rethinking Peacekeeping." In Rikhye and Skjelsbaek, 22–31.

———. 1990. "Superpowers and Peace-Keepers." *Survival* 32:212–20.

Nwafor, Azinna. 1970. *United Nations Use of Armed Force in Internal War Conditions for the Maintenance of International Stability.* Ann Arbor, Mich.: University Microfilms.

Olson, Mancur. 1965. *The Logic of Collective Action.* Cambridge: Harvard University Press.

Oneal, John. 1990. "Collective Burden Sharing in NATO." *International Organization* 34:426–48.

Palmer, Bruce. 1989. *Intervention in the Caribbean: The Dominican Crisis of 1965.* Lexington: University of Kentucky Press.

Paz-Barnica, Edgardo. 1983. "Peacekeeping within the Inter-American System." In Wiseman, *Peacekeeping: Appraisals and Proposals,* 237–55.

Pearson, Lester. 1965. "Keeping the Peace." In Cordier and Foote, 99–119.

Pelcovits, Nathan. 1991. "What Went Wrong." In McDermott and Skjelsbaek, 37–79.

———. 1984. *Peacekeeping on the Arab-Israeli Fronts: Lessons from the Sinai and Lebanon.* Boulder, Colo.: Westview.

———. 1983. "Peacekeeping: The African Experience." In Wiseman, *Peacekeeping: Appraisals and Proposals,* 256–97.

———. 1975. "UN Peacekeeping and the 1973 Arab-Israeli Conflict." *Orbis,* 19:146–65.

Pelcovits, Nathan, and Kevin Kramer. 1976. "Local Conflict and U.N. Peacekeeping: The Uses of Computerized Data." *International Studies Quarterly* 20:533–52.

Pradhan, Ram Chandra. 1975. *The United Nations and the Congo Crisis.* New Delhi: MANAS.

Prins, Gwyn. 1991. "The United Nations and Peace-Keeping in the Post-Cold-War World: The Case of Naval Power." *Bulletin of Peace Proposals* 22:135–55.

Pruitt, Dean, and Douglas Johnson. 1970. "Mediation as an Aid to Face Saving in Negotiation." *Journal of Personality and Social Psychology* 14:239–46.

Przeworski, Adam, and Henry Teune. 1970. *The Logic of Comparative Social Inquiry.* New York: Wiley.

Quandt, William. 1986. *Camp David: Peacemaking and Politics.* Washington, D.C.: Brookings Institution.

Raman, K. Venata. 1983. "United Nations Peacekeeping and the Future of World Order." In Wiseman, *Peacekeeping: Appraisals and Proposals,* 371–401.

Rikhye, Indar Jit. 1991. "The Future of Peacekeeping." In Rikhye and Skjelsbaek, 171–99.

———. 1984. *The Theory and Practice of International Peacekeeping.* New York: St. Martin's.

———. 1983. "Peacekeeping and Peacemaking." In Wiseman, *Peacekeeping: Appraisals and Proposals,* 5–18.

Rikhye, Indar Jit, Michael Harbottle, and Bjorn Egge. 1974. *The Thin Blue Line: International Peacekeeping and Its Future.* New Haven: Yale University Press.

Rikhye, Indar Jit, and Kjell Skjeslbaek, eds. 1991. *The United Nations and Peacekeeping: Results, Limitations, and Prospects—The Lessons of 40 Years of Experience.* New York: St. Martin's.

Rosenau, James. 1990. *Turbulence in World Politics.* Princeton: Princeton University Press.

Rosner, Gabriella. 1965. "The International Military Force Idea: A Look at Modern History." In Joel Larus, ed., *From Collective Security to Preventive Diplomacy,* 445–56. New York: Wiley.

———. 1963. *The United Nations Emergency Force.* New York: Columbia University Press.

Russett, Bruce, and James Sutterlin. 1991. "The U.N. in a New World Order." *Foreign Affairs* 70:69–83.

Sacher, Howard. 1981. *Egypt and Israel.* New York: Marek.

Saksena, K. P. 1977. "Not By Design: Evolution of UN Peacekeeping Operations and Its Implications for the Future." *International Studies* 16:459–81.

Sato, Masaki. 1986. *Concepts and Principles of Dag Hammarskjold's Peacekeeping Operations.* Master's thesis, University of Georgia.

Schiff, Zeev. 1991. "Israeli Expectations and Conclusions." In McDermott and Skjelsbaek, 199–208.

Sesay, Amadu. 1991. "The Limits of Peace-Keeping by a Regional Organization: The OAU Peace-Keeping Force in Chad." *Conflict Quarterly* 11:7–26.

Siekmann, Robert. 1991. *National Contingents in United Nations Peace-Keeping Forces.* Dordrecht: Martinus Nijhoff.

———. 1985. *Basic Documents on United Nations and Related Peace-Keeping Forces.* Dordrecht: Martinus Nijhoff.

Singer, J. David, and Michael Wallace. 1970. "Inter-Governmental Organization and the Preservation of Peace, 1816–1965: Some Bivariate Relationships." *International Organization* 24 (1970): 520–47.

Skjelsbaek, Kjell. 1991. "UN Peacekeeping: Expectations, Limitations, and Results—Forty Years of Mixed Experiences." In Rikhye and Skjelsbaek, 52–67.

Skogmo, Bjorn. 1989. *UNIFIL: International Peacekeeping in Lebanon, 1978–1988.* Boulder, Colo.: Lynne Rienner.

Small, Melvin, and J. David Singer. 1982. *Resort to Arms.* Beverly Hills: Sage.

Steele, David. 1987. *The Reform of the United Nations.* London: Croom Helm.

Stegenga, James. 1968. *The United Nations Force in Cyprus.* Columbus: Ohio State University Press.

Stevenson, Adlai. 1965. "From Containment to Cease-Fire and Peaceful Change." In Cordier and Foote, 51–66.

Stoessinger, John. 1977. *The United Nations and the Superpowers: China, Russia, and America.* 4th ed. New York: Random House.

Stokes, William. 1983. "Technology and the Future of Peacekeeping." In Wiseman, *Peacekeeping: Appraisals and Proposals,* 218–30.

Swift, Richard. 1974. "United Nations Military Training for Peace." *International Organization* 28:267–80.

Tabory, Mala. 1986. *The Multinational Force and Observers in the Sinai: Organization, Structure, and Function.* Boulder, Colo.: Westview.

Taylor, Alastair. 1960. *Indonesian Independence and the United Nations.* London: Stevens.

Thakur, Ramesh. 1991. "UN Authority and U.S. Power." In McDermott and Skjelsbaek, 101–28.

———. 1987. *International Peacekeeping in Lebanon: United Nations Authority and Multinational Force.* Boulder, Colo.: Westview.

Tirman, John. 1988. "International Monitoring for Peace." *Issues in Science and Technology* 4:53–58.

Touval, Saadia. 1982. *The Peace Brokers: Mediators in the Arab-Israeli Conflict, 1948–1979.* Princeton: Princeton University Press.

Tueni, Ghassan. 1991. "A Tragic Experiment in the Diplomacy of Misunderstandings." In McDermott and Skjelsbaek, 184–92.

Underdal, Arild. 1983. "Causes of Negotiation Failure." *European Journal of Political Research* 11:183–95.

United Nations. 1991. *Blue Helmets*. 2d ed. New York: United Nations.

———. 1990. *United Nations Peace-Keeping*. New York: U.N. Department of Public Information. Brochure.

United States Congress, House of Representatives. 1984. *Report on the Situation in Lebanon*. Communication from the President of the United States, House Document 170. 98th Cong., 2d sess., 7.

United States President. 1983. *Public Papers of the President of the United States: Ronald Reagan*. Book 2. Washington, D.C.: U.S. Government Printing Office.

Urquhart, Brian. 1990. "Beyond the 'Sheriff's Posse,'" *Survival* 32:196–205.

———. 1987. "United Nations Peacekeeping Operations and How Their Role Might Be Enhanced." In United Nations Institute for Training and Research, *The United Nations and the Maintenance of International Peace and Security*, 253–61. Dordrecht: Martinus Nijhoff.

———. 1983. "Peacekeeping: A View from the Operational Center." In Wiseman, *Peacekeeping: Appraisals and Proposals*, 161–74.

———. 1972. *Hammarskjold*. New York: Knopf.

Valahu, Mugur. 1964. *The Katanga Circus: A Detailed Account of Three UN Wars*. New York: Speller.

Van Slyck, Philip. 1963. *Peace: The Control of National Power*. Boston: Beacon.

Wainhouse, David. 1973. *International Peacekeeping at the Crossroads: National Support Experience and Prospects*. Baltimore: Johns Hopkins University Press.

———. 1966. *International Peace Observation*. Baltimore: Johns Hopkins University Press.

Wambaugh, Sarah. 1970. *The Saar Plebiscite*. Cambridge: Harvard University Press.

Waskow, Arthur. 1963. *Quis Custodiet? Controlling the Police in a Disarmed World*. Washington, D.C.: Peace Research Institute.

Weinberger, Naomi. 1986. *Syrian Intervention in Lebanon: The 1975–76 Civil War*. New York: Oxford University Press.

———. 1983. "Peacekeeping Options in Lebanon." *Middle East Journal* 37:341–69.

Weiss, Thomas, and Jarat Chopra. 1992. *United Nations Peacekeeping: An ACUNS Teaching Text*. Academic Council of the United Nations System.

Weiss, Thomas, and Kurt Campbell. 1991. "Military Humanitarianism." In *Humanitarianism and War: Learning the Lessons from Recent Armed Conflicts*, 50–71. Occasional Number 8. Providence, R.I.: Watson Institute for International Studies.

Weiss, Thomas, and Meryl Kessler. 1990. "Moscow's U.N. Policy." *Foreign Policy* 79:94–112.

White, N. D. 1990. *The United Nations and the Maintenance of International Peace and Security*. Manchester, N.H.: Manchester University Press.

Willoughby, W. W. 1969. *The Sino-Japanese Controversy and the League of Nations*. Westport, Conn.: Greenwood.

Wiseman, Henry. 1991. "Peacekeeping in the International Political Context: Historical Analysis and Future Directions." In Rikhye and Skjelsbaek, 32–51.

———. 1987. "The United Nations and International Peacekeeping: A Comparative Analysis." In United Nations Institute for Training and Research, *The United Nations and the Maintenance of International Peace and Security*, 263–333. Dordrecht: Martinus Nijhoff.

———. 1984. "The OAU: Peacekeeping and Conflict Resolution." In Yassin El-Ayouty and William Zartman, eds., *The OAU after Twenty Years*, 123–54. New York: Praeger.

———. 1983a. "Peacekeeping: The Dynamics of Future Development." In Wiseman, *Peacekeeping: Appraisals and Proposals*, 341–70.

———. 1983b. "United Nations Peacekeeping: An Historical Overview." In Wiseman, *Peacekeeping: Appraisals and Proposals*, 19–63.

———, ed. 1983c. *Peacekeeping: Appraisals and Proposals*. New York: Pergamon.

Wittman, Donald. 1979. "How a War Ends: A Rational Model Approach." *Journal of Conflict Resolution* 23:743–63.

Index